Leaving Little Havana

A Memoir of Miami's Cuban Ghetto

Cecilia M. Fernandez

Published 2013 by Beating Windward Press LLC

For contact information, please visit:
www.BeatingWindward.com

First Edition
ISBN: 978-1-940761-04-6

About the Cover Artist
Victor Bokas grew up on Florida's Gulf Coast against a backdrop
of sunbathing tourists, palm trees, fish and other tropical images.
A graduate of The University of Florida, Victor is Senior Designer
for Tupperware and full-time painter. His work appears in several
Permanent Collections, including Tupperware, Darden, Maitland
Art Center, Orlando City Hall, Walt Disney Production and the
Orlando International Airport. "Florida Vacation" became part of
Orlando International Airport Public Art Project in 2000. Victor's
painting was turned into an 88' x 15' mosaic masterpiece welcoming
visitors to Orlando.

Always, for my mother.

Advance Praise

Cecilia Fernandez gives us a coming of age story told with wide open eyes and vivid details of growing up in Little Havana. Broken-hearted more times than she can count, she gradually finds a path to new beginnings and the infinite promises of the American Dream. A poignant and important chronicle of the Miami Cuban immigrant journey.

— Ruth Behar, author of *Traveling Heavy: A Memoir in Between Journeys*

Every so often along comes a book that seizes you by the collar and arrests you on the spot. From page one, Leaving Little Havana *is a brilliant, voice-driven book that will make your heart skip a few beats. My experience reading this book was similar to the first time I read* The House on Mango Street *by Sandra Cisneros when you instantly know you are reading a classic, a story so achingly beautiful and unforgettable you relish every last word as if it were the buzzing of a hummingbird at your lips feeding you honey. This book is about family, about what happens to family in exile, about how people come into a great world of struggle and manage to get by and survive. The author has a great gift for capturing that world-known enclave of Miami we love and call Little Havana. This might be the book that puts it on the literary map for good and forever.*

— Virgil Suárez, author of *Latin Jazz, The Cutter,*
and *90 Miles: Selected and New Poems*

Leaving Little Havana *is the compelling story of a Cuban girl seeking a new life in the U.S. with her family as the Cuban revolution unfolds in the early sixties. "Cecilita's" personal account, and sexual awakening, is transparent, sad, and triumphant, sprinkled with anecdotes of an emerging Cuban-American landscape. In short, this book is a colorful reminiscence of historical scenes on both sides of the Straits of Florida, providing closure to a Cuban American journalist coming to terms with her turbulent past.*

— Guarione M. Diaz, President Emeritus,
Cuban American National Council

Leaving Little Havana *is a candid, touching, and engaging memoir of a young Cuban exile's coming of age. Cecilia Fernandez writes with passion and intensity, both of her missteps and her triumphs, casting fresh light on the American experience in the process.*

— Les Standiford, author of *Havana Run and Bringing Adam Home*

Cecilia Fernandez's memoir of growing up Cuban in Miami is not only fascinating reading, it tells more about the story of Cubans in this U.S. than a truckload of sociology textbooks - and is a thousand times more entertaining!

— Dan Wakefield, author of *New York in the Fifties* and *Going All The Way*

In Leaving Little Havana, *Cecilia Fernandez treats the reader to a pungent, vivid story of growing up in exile Miami in the 60s and 70s. We watch Fernandez transform from a perceptive child, shadowed by the lost past and trapped in the wreckage of her family, into a feisty, honest, adventurous young woman, as she seeks the means to redefine departure on her own terms.*

— Lynne Barrett, author of *Magpies*

Cecilia Fernandez's writing is just the right amount of flowery and just the right amount of raw. It's hard not to fall little bit in love with the rebellious and independent Cuban girl who's trying her damnedest to make it in a Miami that is going through a time of historical transformation. Read this if you love memoirs, if you love South Florida and Cuba, or simply if you love a good story.

— Melanie Neale, author of *Boat Girl* and *Boat Kid*

One is not in bondage to the past,
to race, inheritance, and background.
—Anais Nin

THUNDER IN LA HABANA

*Memory is the tattooing by which
the weak, the betrayed, the exiled,
believe they have armed themselves.*
— Rene Crevel

1.

Let this tale, created from memories, artifacts, photographs, letters, history books and street maps, begin with my mother. She wanted so badly for me to live that she stayed in bed nine months, ensuring a narrative of my own. When she walked, pale as the underside of an oyster shell, into a neighborhood clinic that January morning, she didn't know our story would take its place in the huge, sprawling neighbor to the north, the United States. I say "our" because this is the story of the Cuban middle class families of the island's first migration when Fidel Castro took power in 1959. Those of my generation are the children of the earliest "exiles," unprepared for life on the other side of the Florida Straits, and unwittingly paving the way for a vast exodus of nearly a million.

As my mother breathed in the head-clearing smell of antiseptic drying on the freshly waxed floors of the Centro Medico and braced herself for another wave of nausea, our departure from the island could not be imagined. In 1954 she was 29, and, after ten years of marriage, praying that her baby would be born alive. "I hope this one makes it," she whispered, holding my father's hand. She thought of the first child, the one my father scraped from her uterus, saying he had to finish medical school before he could become a parent. She thought of the second child, the stillborn, who died when she fell climbing on the bus to go to work. She had not known he was dead. After she labored for hours, the baby slipped out of her, a gray dried-up bundle. Through a mist of sedatives and painkillers, she saw it was a boy and named him Rafael.

A strong contraction interrupted the guilt and regret that had not eased in the last decade. Now the contractions were stronger, more regular, pressing into her so tightly she felt paralyzed. My father, who had been working at another clinic when she called him, guided her to the birthing chair, keeping up a lively banter with the doctors and nurses attending to other patients.

Just six months before, members of the left-wing *Ortodoxo* party, some aligned with the Communist Youth, attacked two military barracks on the east end of the island. Some had been murdered, others tortured, still others imprisoned, including the newly recognized hero, Fidel Castro. Several months later, Castro had appeared at a highly publicized trial after, the rumor went, an attempt was made to poison him.

"And that's the end of Fidel," said a doctor scrubbing at a sink. "He was sentenced to 15 years. His revolution is many years away."

"That doesn't mean anything," my father declared. "This is the beginning of civil war and the end of The Republic of Cuba." The island, under Spanish rule since Christopher Columbus came ashore, had gained formal independence in 1902. "Don't be silly," the doctor answered.

A liquid lighter and clearer than water ran down my mother's legs. Pain twisted her features.

"You'll see I'm right," my father called out, hoisting my mother's legs up onto the metal stirrups.

When my mother shifted her body into place, she thought about her dead mother. If only she were here to comfort, to encourage; it hurt so much. To the nurse holding her hand, she screamed, "I can't stand it!" Then, her moans stretched into shrieks for twenty-four hours.

At last, with the obstetrician ordering, "Push! Push now!" and with one final convulsion, she expelled my body into the glaring lights of the surgical suite. It was eight in the morning. The obstetrician examined me while my father watched from a corner, dressed in green scrubs. I weighed nearly ten pounds, my mother's third and last conception and only surviving child.

"She looks like a daisy, *una margarita*," my father said. "Let's name her Cecilia Margarita."

I was born on a fertile, mountainous, tropical island encircled by loops of sandy beaches the color and texture of fine sawdust and locked in the embrace of the sea. It was during a time historians refer to as "pre-revolutionary Cuba," the heyday of the island, evoking images of Mafia gangster Meyer Lansky, the Las Vegas-style Tropicana Nightclub, and foreign conglomerates like the United Fruit Company just before the U.S. embargo, the food shortages and the Soviet missiles transformed its landscape. When I traveled throughout the United States in the seventies and eighties, this accident, the place and time of my birth, was the cause of constant comment from people I met: most knew little about Cuba and wondered about its geographical location. One expressed outrage that my parents had taken me forcefully from my homeland at an age when I couldn't possibly make a decision for myself. She was angry they had not given Fidel – an idol in some circles at that time – an opportunity to right the wrongs of Fulgencio Batista, the dictator who had wrested control of the island in a military coup in 1952. This viewpoint shocked me, unheard of in Miami's Little Havana, the Cuban enclave from which I wanted so desperately to escape.

Because I shared a birthday—the 28th of January-- with the writer and hero, Jose Marti, who died on a horse fighting for Cuban independence from Spain in 1897, the day was celebrated not only in my family but also remarked upon throughout the island each year. Later, I playfully told friends and colleagues that I had inherited not only Marti's literary talents and uncompromising love of *patria,* nation, but also his inclination toward engaging in numerous, tempestuous love affairs.

When my mother came home from the clinic, embracing a wriggling pink blanket, our housekeeper and my future nanny, Ana Maria, greeted her with cries of reproach. "Why didn't you sign up for the *canastilla?*" Ana Maria shook her head and took me in her arms to stare disbelieving into my red-rimmed eyes. "You could have won, imagine that!" she exclaimed.

That year, CMQ radio had sponsored a contest for mothers whose children were born on Marti's birthday. The lucky families received a free bassinette, a matching set of crib sheets, towels, and baby clothes that usually cost hundreds of dollars.

"That's right, we could have won," my mother agreed, with mock dismay. My *canastilla* had been ready for weeks. When my parents and Ana Maria entered my bedroom, my bassinette stood prominently in the center, covered with lace and trussed with pink and white satin bows on every corner. A finely textured mosquito net formed a protective cloud over its length. My parents' numerous female relatives had embroidered stacks of linen sheets and cotton coverlets with my initials and piled them on a bureau. An armoire with opened doors showcased pink and white outfits decorated with ribbons. Drawers bulged with silk cuffed socks and white booties. But the focal point was the étagère where a porcelain china doll, whose hand is meant to be hidden until she grants a wish, stood elegantly next to a smirking Pierrot. A set of glass animals propped up books of European fairy tales.

"I guess we didn't need the *canastilla,*" my father said, already suspecting that in six years, the remnants of my sheets and pillowcases, along with the china doll--her hand taped securely to her side-- would be stuffed in crates and suitcases and shipped to a warehouse in Miami.

2.

My uncle Cesar Perez, a businessman born and raised in Galicia, Spain, built his wife a house on a chicken farm surrounded by the sea and named it after her. Villa America welcomed visitors with its spacious veranda and varnished wooden rockers next to the sandy shores of Playa Baracoa, a thirty minute drive from La Habana -- as the island's capital is known in Cuba -- and the former home of the Taino and Ciboney Indians centuries ago. In 1955, the villa sported a glossy tile floor, gleaming white paint and a freshly manicured inner garden. When my parents and I visited, I listened for two sounds: the lonely lowing of the cows in the field and the sorrowful wails of the guitar in the *canciones guajiras*, country ballads, that Tio Cesar's housekeepers kept tuned on the radio. Clean and sharp, the air smelled of salt.

Cesar, a tall, trim, muscular man with a high forehead, tanned but creased face and thick strands of gray hair falling into his eyes, greeted us at the door. He wore a stiffly ironed white *guayabera*, a boxy shirt with pleats in the front. His wife, America Castellanos, my maternal grandmother's sister and my mother's and my godmother, stood apart, clad in a simple gray dress, holding their son's hand. A chemistry professor at a teacher's college, America never tired of planning lessons for Cesarito, their twenty-year-old son afflicted with Down's Syndrome. When he saw me, Cesarito forced out joyful grunts, like a walrus, and rushed to hold me in his arms.

The ocean breezes whipped up around us to a full wind, different from that of a summer's day, and a rumble of thunder could be heard far off in the distance. My mother, Cesarito and I leaned against the veranda railing while my father, Tio Cesar, America and the housekeeper, Mercedes, who was a member of the family, sat in rockers. Two cooks banged pots in the kitchen, preparing a feast of *lechon asado*, roast pork, rice, beans and *tostones*, fried green plaintains.

"The best way to cook *flan* is through a method called *baño Maria*," America said. This entailed steaming the dish of custard in the middle of a pot of boiling water. Mercedes agreed. Then Tio Cesar told a story about leaving Spain for Cuba in 1937, during the Civil War under Generalisimo Francisco

Franco. Every word that had the "s" sound turned into a "z" sound on Cesar's tongue in the Spanish way of enunciating. My father listed Franco's attributes, proclaiming him the best leader Spain had ever had.

"That's what we should have here in Cuba, someone like Franco," he said. "Fidel and his brother would have been shot by now."

In May, Fidel and Raul Castro, along with 18 followers involved in an attack on a military barracks two years before, left the Isle of Pines prison under a Cuban amnesty law, their 15-year prison sentence revoked. My father said Batista should have executed the brothers: within weeks the Castros departed for Mexico and began to form a trained group that would provide the backbone of a guerrilla troop to overthrow Batista. Fidel, the leader of the revolutionary organization known as the 26 of July Movement, had delivered a speech entitled *History Will Absolve Me*, which, the summer before, had appeared in a pamphlet and circulated throughout the island. In the pamphlet, Fidel called for a 15-point program of reforms, including the distribution of land like Tio's among peasant families, and nationalization of public services, education and industry.

"There is no doubt Fidel is a communist," my father said.

"Negotiations with Batista are still possible," Cesar countered. "It's the only way out of this mess. There's a tourism and building boom going on right now. Cuba has the highest standard of living compared to any other Latin American nation. Communism can't come in here."

"Fidel will never forget his defeat at the Moncada barracks. He's going to come back from Mexico and try to overthrow Batista. If he does, he will confiscate all private property, including mine." A few years earlier my father had invested in oceanfront property, a move he now regretted.

"Cesarito, let's go to the water," my mother said, tiring of the conversation, "*vamos.*" She took his hand and held me up in the crook of her other arm. Cesarito, tall and trim like his father, had tar black hair that, like Cesar's, slid into his eyes. He sported a neat, sparse mustache as if each hair were implanted and stood on its own. His walk was lumbering, heavy, uncoordinated, but his arms bulged with muscles. He placed his hand on my mother's waist as she walked toward the shore.

The unrelenting winds ruffled the ocean, transparent as water in a glass, and, carrying just a trace of the smell of rain, tickled our skin like a dozen feather dusters. When I didn't live there anymore, it was difficult to stop longing for the breezes that relieved the heat's monotony and for that fine sand to caress my toes. It was even more challenging to lie awake in a California apartment listening to a monotonous rainstorm that did not bring ripping thunder or lightning spears across the sky as it so often did in La Habana.

My mother sat back on a narrow bench built into a small gazebo suspended over the villa's beach and stared at the sea, while Cesarito and I watched seaweed flutter in the ripple of the waves. I focused on small round black marine animals called *erizos* or sea urchins, covered with quills as long and sharp as a porcupine's. I wanted to touch them, but Cesarito grunted and shook his head, forcing distorted sounds from his throat. Dozens of these creatures clung to coral rocks along the water's edge. I had no idea that the central portion of the animal served as a tasty appetizer. I leaned under the railing of the gazebo, flat on my stomach, and plunged my hand in the water. Cesarito's grunts heightened into screams and my mother, with a look of being deep into thoughts that can't be shared, leaned down and pulled me up.

"*Ya esta todo*," the cook yelled from the kitchen window that dinner was ready. The singer on the radio screeched a raw protest to the twang of the guitar. With me safely in her arms, my mother walked with Cesarito through the chicken coops on the way back to the house. We entered the gate, and a dozen chickens clucked around my mother's heels. A rooster waved his floppy, fleshy comb. "*Ay, que bonitos*," my mother crooned as she knelt, and we both stroked the quivering bundle of feathers. Mercedes waded into the tide of chickens and led us out to the dining room where the rest of the family, clustered around the table, still squabbled about Fidel.

It was the first time my father and Tio Cesar yelled at each other over the dinner table, marking the beginning of an ideological battle that ultimately destroyed my family. When Fidel rolled into La Habana, Tio Cesar – like many of my other relatives -- hoped for a better Cuba and decided to stay put. As the years slipped away, a disbelieving Tio and Mercedes, who had become his wife after the death of America, watched the beauty of the villa melt under the ravages of sun, wind and rain.

3.

We slid past wooden shanties and headed out on the main highway of La Habana in my father's stylish new Buick. The Cuban countryside rose up in bright green around us. Nothing is as cool as the shade of a mountain or as resplendent as a valley going off in all directions. Up and down, the undulating land reached out to the edges of the sea.

It was three in the afternoon, lunchtime on Sunday just before Christmas 1956. A heavy meal at this time of day meant no dinner, only a *café con leche* with toast before bed. My father turned onto a bumpy unpaved road with thick trees on both sides. At the end, a clearing leaped out from the heavy brush, showcasing Rancho Luna, Moon Ranch, my favorite restaurant with its thatched roof, open walls, and earthen floors. Rough logs held up the ceiling. The owners bragged that 324,000 chickens had been eaten here in the last three years.

The structure resembled rural houses called *bohios*, the simple homes of the farmers who lived scattered throughout the island's vast farmlands. These *guajiros* harvested the sugar and tobacco crops that made the island rich and became Cuba's folk heroes, the ones Fidel Castro promised to emancipate. The restaurant, a replica of their homes, paid tribute to their lives.

Earlier that month, Fidel had come back from Mexico on a boat called the Granma and bunkered down in a wooded mountain range, La Sierra Maestra, in the eastern province of Oriente. He shared the space with *bohios* scattered over its length and width.

My father scowled when telling my mother about the communist infiltration of the island. Castro's 26 of July Movement planned to strike during the holidays. Already, bombs were exploding in several towns in Oriente. Batista, on alert, threatened reprisals, including hanging the rebels.

My mother, like Tio Cesar, was skeptical. "*El Diario de La Marina* has just called us the Las Vegas of Latin America," she said. "How bad can things be? Sugar prices are high thanks to the crisis in the Suez Canal."

"It's only a $36 flight to Miami," he said.

"What does that mean?"

"We could leave any time we want."

Beyond our table, several men gathered around a sandy pit. We could see them through the open walls of the restaurant. Two men held roosters with leashes around their necks. They walked to opposite sides of the pit and released the birds into the battle arena. The men's shouts increased as spurts of blood spilled from the necks, eyes, and feet of the angry, suicidal birds attacking each other.

"Don't look," my mother said, pivoting my seat around to block the spectacle.

"It's nothing," my father said.

Fortunately, the food arrived just in time to offer distraction. On the rough wooden lunch table, the waiter set down platters of *arroz con pollo,* chicken with yellow rice, and *platanos maduros*, ripe fried bananas. My father savored each bite, reached over, tore off a piece of flaky bread from a basket and used it to push the rice onto his fork. My mother sampled small morsels from her fork and left half of the food on her plate. I ate a little of everything, just beginning to develop my taste for Cuban food.

"Taste my beer," my father said, tilting his glass toward me, sitting in a high chair between my parents.

I raised the glass to my lips. The foam came up to my nose, and the golden liquid burned my throat. The bitterness repulsed me. My father laughed, and I felt happy because I had made him laugh. I drank water to dissolve the acrid taste.

"Rafael," my mother said, a tense edge to her voice. "Don't give her that again."

"Ay, Cecilia, what's wrong with it?" he asked my mother. (In most Latin American countries, mothers name their daughters after themselves.)

"*Tiene todo de malo.* Everything is wrong with it. Like you. How can I go on living with you after this?" Suddenly, as if the beer tasting had been the last straw, she ripped a letter from her wicker purse gaping open at her feet. She slapped the offending correspondence on the table. My father picked up the missive and withdrew a sheet of onion skin paper.

"*Señora Cecilia, les queremos informar que su esposo, el Dr. Rafael Fernandez Rivas...*" My father read aloud: "Mrs. Cecilia, we want to inform you that your husband, Dr. Rafael Fernandez Rivas..." He stopped, peering at the letter as if what he was seeing was too terrible to voice. He passed his hand over his eyes and through his hair.

My mother pushed her plate away and gripped the table with her hands.

"Don't tell me you are going to believe this," my father choked.

"I don't know what I'm going to do," she whispered. "Don't you love me?"

"I was not unfaithful," he said. "Whoever wrote that letter is lying. There is no other woman." My mother walked out to the car, opened the door and threw herself into the seat. My father took a few more bites, lifted me off the high-chair and paid the bill.

"*Las mujeres son malas*, Cecilita," he said, mumbling about the evils of women. From that time on, my mother became obsessed with my father's mistress. She constantly spoke about it to her relatives. She went through his drawers. She stood silently in the hall listening to his telephone conversations. My father, for his part, began staying away from home. And so began an irreversible game of hide and seek between my parents, a game that – after their divorce -- I continued to play with him throughout his life.

4.

My maternal grandparents' graves lay so close to the street that we could park our car on the curb and walk a few feet to pray for their souls and honor their memory. My mother, dressed in black and wearing a pillbox hat with a short veil that canopied over her eyes, knelt on the grass.

"*Padre nuestro.*" She whispered *The Lord's Prayer* and arranged fresh roses in the vase she had brought with her last Sunday. She placed the old withered flowers in a plastic bag to discard later.

In 1957, when I was three, El Cementerio de Colon became a playground where I ran in and out of tall tombstones. The pointed grass blades, wet from the previous night's storm, held tightly to the raindrops. Flowers in vases scattered about the graveyard drooped from the weight of the moisture. Black mud streaked the green grass. Puddles floated in crevices along the rough flat gray tombstones of the poor on one side of the cemetery, while the tall, white marble mausoleums of the rich reflected spears of light a short distance away. The water trapped on the roofs of these tombs the size of rooms evaporated into steam as the mid-day heat gained momentum. The graves of my grandparents, marked with neatly inscribed white stone, signified the middle class.

My father, despite the asphyxiating warmth, wore a white linen suit with a blue silk handkerchief in his pocket and a blue silk tie. He never failed to display his class status, often boasting that his Spanish grandparents had been wealthy tobacco exporters with ties to the King. I could see his mounting impatience as he watched my mother sob and wipe her nose with a tissue she later tucked between her breasts.

"*Vamos*, China," he called out his pet name for her from the sidewalk. He had the same expression on his face when my mother browsed through a rack of dresses in El Encanto, a department store filled with European fashions.

I stood there for a moment and then ran off to relieve the tension, skipping from one tombstone to another, leaning on the walls of the mausoleums to avoid sinking the tips of my patent leather shoes into the mud. The crinoline under my skirt made the shiny fabric balloon out from my hips like the Dresden dolls on the dining room buffet. Sweat mingled with the steam, dripping into my mouth.

My father shifted his weight from one foot to the other. He took a few steps up and down the sidewalk and climbed into the driver's seat of the car. "We have to go and collect the rents," he called out. My mother owned several houses in a working class neighborhood in the province of Matanzas east of La Habana. Collecting the rent was an important item on our Sunday itinerary and an opportunity for me, an only child, to play with the dozens of children on those blocks. Although they ran around barefooted, I was not allowed to take off my shoes.

Anxious to play, I ran to the car and urged my mother to get up from her knees. Finally, we drove off slowly through the narrow, winding roads of the cemetery. The sleek Buick with long extended fins, leather seats, and cool air blowing out of two small grills on the dashboard moved out into the chaos of a city rebuilding itself into one of the most vibrant cities in Latin America and the Caribbean.

From the back seat window, I could see the dust of bull-dozers rolling over nineteenth-century homes in the Vedado suburb of La Habana. In their place, construction crews built skyscrapers, such as the FOCSA apartment building and the luxury hotels Havana Hilton, Capri and Habana Riviera – the Capri with a swimming pool on its roof on the twenty-fifth floor. More construction could be seen toward the south, inland side of La Habana at La Plaza de la Republica, the new site for government ministries being moved from the old colonial section of the city. Further on, crews worked on a motorway linking the recently completed Via Blanca that led to the resort town of Varadero with the Central Highway.

It took almost 30 minutes to leave La Habana and begin the smooth cruise out to Matanzas. The name of this province translates into "killings," commemorating the slaughter of Indians there by the Spanish conquerors. Stretches of farmland and sloping hills alternated with clusters of rundown shacks with punched-out holes for windows. Finally, we turned into one of the streets; chickens scooted out of the way, and dogs ran barking around the car. Our tires rolled into potholes and uncertainly struggled back out. Groups of children surrounded the moving vehicle. My father maneuvered to a stop in front of a row of small wooden houses with raised porches, the ones where dogs and cats and rats scuttle under when it rains. Rocking chairs with torn seats and backs lined up neatly near the door.

"Ceci!" a woman ran out of the first house, drying her hands on her skirt, and hugged my mother. The woman's husband, Cuco, stood on the porch smiling, and four children of varying ages gathered around, prying open the car door before I had a chance to move. This was the Fierro family. They had lived here for 20 years.

The houses had belonged to my great-grandmother. An immigrant from Barcelona also named Cecilia, she built up with her husband a small plantation back in the mid-1800s and bought the houses with the profits. An economic slump swallowed the plantation, but this first ever Cecilia hung on to the row of houses and passed them on to my grandmother Cecilia, who came out here back then to collect the rent. Now, my mother was the landlord.

"Do you want some coffee?" Reina, Cuco's wife, asked.

My father, charismatic and with an easy social manner, accepted heartily and gripped Cuco's hand in a gesture of friendship.

"*Oye*," my father said, "I want to go fishing next weekend. Do you think you can make it?"

In his linen suit, with neatly combed hair and splash of cologne, my father made quite a contrast to the farm laborer who was his host. Cuco wore neat but stained cotton pants and a checkered shirt rolled up to his elbows to hide several rips in the sleeves. My father loved to speak with the country folk and hire them to pilot his boat, take care of his daughter, wash his car, and oil his rifles. An extrovert with a keen interest in people – and despite his obsession with social status -- he developed strong friendships with the tenants, often inviting himself over for dinner at their houses. The tenants knew that he wouldn't come empty-handed. He always brought the food – his favorite was a pork and vegetable stew called *ajiaco* -- in huge pots from restaurants and then offered to treat their ailments for free.

Joseito, a neighborhood boy with a mouthful of crooked teeth and slightly crossed eyes, ran to my father. "Doctor, doctor," he cried, "my bump is gone."

My father felt the boy's glands. He had operated on Joseito a few months ago, extracting a large tumor from his neck.

"*Que bueno*, Joseito," my father laughed and patted his head.

While he and Cuco planned their fishing expedition on the porch, my mother went into the kitchen with Reina. I sprawled on the floor to play jacks with Reina's daughter, and my mother wrote out a receipt for the rent from a big ledger she kept in a worn leather pouch that belonged to my grandmother. Reina handed her the money. My mother placed the bills in the pouch. Then, with a fork missing a prong, Reina beat a froth of freshly brewed, dark brown espresso with three tablespoons of sugar in a metal container, pouring it back into the rest of the coffee in the pot. This procedure was the secret to the popular Cuban refreshment, *el cafecito*. When she poured the boiling liquid into small cups, the coffee became a thick shot of sugar and caffeine that made hearts beat a quick rhythm. The coffee, seductive and strengthening, reached the farthest taste bud.

"I need this," my mother said, savoring the liquid. "I just came from the cemetery, and I feel very depressed. I have no energy. All I want to do is lay in bed. And my husband….Rafael is never home. He's always so busy."

Reina opened up a can of papaya chunks dripping with syrup and snuggled them against slices of cream cheese on small plates. My father had brought the family canned fruit preserve last month. Reina handed a plate to my mother and took two to the men on the porch. Then she tore large bread chunks from long loaves, crispy on the outside, soft on the inside, soaked them with olive oil and sprinkled them with salt for the children.

"Ceci, we're not doing too well either," Reina answered. "The rain is seeping into the kitchen and the bathroom sink is plugged up."

My mother frowned. She wasn't as generous as my father with her tenants and always maintained distance with those she considered not her equals.

"Rafael," she called out the front door in an exasperated tone. "Where's the phone number of the workman we use in this town?"

My father retrieved it from a small phonebook in the inner pocket of his suit coat. He wrote the name and phone number of every person he knew in this book.

"Here," my mother told Reina, "is the number. Call him and I'll pay for it. He can also fix the roof."

My mother closed her ledger; it was time to go to the next house.

"I'm looking forward to catching a big sailfish next Saturday," my father spoke excitedly to Cuco. "We'll meet at the marina at 4 a.m."

"Don't forget the beer," Cuco answered. "And listen," he added as an afterthought. "Do you think there will be more trouble with the government?"

"Without a doubt."

All over the island, there were reports of arbitrary police executions and arrests leading to permanent disappearances. A few months earlier, Fidel, ensconced with his guerilla army in La Sierra Maestra, called his mountain stronghold "Territorio Libre" and delivered broadcasts to the people on short wave radio, coaxing them to join him. Bombs and Molotov cocktails erupted in schools, buses, stores, streets.

Many professionals in La Habana were apathetic, desensitized to the incessant political skirmishes that, from the time of Columbus, characterized island life. They trusted that Batista, in the midst of one of the greatest economic expansions in the history of Cuba, with millions of dollars in American capital at stake, would call for elections and appease the Castro opposition. But just last week, in a move that took my father by surprise, the Cuban Medical Association issued a letter of protest against Batista. I heard my father say that the doctors had tired of Batista's heavy handed methods; the dictator often sent the G-2, his dreaded political police, to break up the association's gatherings.

"The G-2 will pale in comparison to what Fidel has in mind," my father said. "These doctors are communist or they don't understand Fidel."

"Don't you think Fidel will help the poor like us?" Cuco looked eagerly at my father.

With a spurt of anger, he faced Cuco. "Fidel will enslave the poor, as well as the rich," he declared. "Things are bad, my friend. Our country is in a state of civil war. *El Presidente Eisenhower* y *los Americanos* say they will not intervene in Cuba. One day, we may have to flee for our lives."

"Maybe not," Cuco answered.

5.

While my grandmother was alive, whenever any of the aunts, uncles or cousins spoke about Elsie Lopez, he or she inevitably added the word *solterona*, spinster, as if the forty-something family friend suffered from leprosy. Indeed, at her age in Cuban middle-class society, Elsie was beyond the possibility of getting a husband. But then, a year after my grandmother died in 1943, she shocked the relatives and married my grandfather, Francisco Vargas, the son of immigrants from the Canary Islands and a pharmacist and chemistry professor at the University of La Habana. When she became a wife, a role I never thought quite suited her, the family gossip turned in another direction. Now she was a seductress, with *fuego uterino*, literally having her uterus on fire, a nymphomaniac.

"How could he marry her?" my mother asked. "Your grandmother was so beautiful. And Elsie is so ugly." She was jealous that my grandfather had married Elsie so quickly after her mother's death. My grandmother, Cecilia Castellanos, a graduate of La Escuela del Hogar, a school for girls intent on learning the tasks of wife and mother, died of a brain aneurism when my mother was 18.

"It was a terrible sight to see," my father said the afternoon his mother-in-law died. "When they called me to the house, Cecilia's head was swollen out of all proportion. She had no chance to survive."

My mother, an only child, refused to speak to Elsie for a year after the wedding, insisting her new step-mother was unworthy of her father, so the couple stayed out of everyone's way as if there were some illegitimacy surrounding their union.

"Your mother was so lazy," my father argued back. "She used to lie in bed all day. I think your father needed someone on his level."

Elsie was an English teacher, tall, slender, with small but compassionate black eyes that gazed into yours with intelligence and understanding. She rolled her prematurely white hair into a tight bun at the nape of her neck. When she became a presence in my life, I noticed she wore mainly black, flowing clothes, in mourning for my cigar-smoking grandfather who died of a heart attack nine months after I was born.

"How could such a smart man not know that his indigestion was a sign of heart trouble?" my father asked everyone. My quiet and gentle grandfather had been his role model. "The happiest time of my life was when I lived with my father-in-law," my father said at the funeral.

I soon realized that Elsie, who, like many middle class Cubans of her generation, had been educated in the United States, was a match not only for my grandfather but also for my father when her politics began to veer left. She articulated her arguments succinctly to anyone within hearing distance despite my father's vociferous opposition. She sympathized with the poor and decried the corruption in Batista's government.

In 1958, she thought Fidel, openly broadcasting his leftist views from Radio Rebelde – a station set up by the Argentine Marxist Che Guevara in La Sierra Maestra -- was a good alternative. That year, Batista stepped up his election plans, but strikes, an arms embargo against him, and calls from the Cuban bishop for peace kept excitement and tension in the air. Murders, bombings and disappearances from both sides of the conflict headlined the papers every day.

One afternoon, on one of our now frequent visits to Elsie, who had finally won over my proud mother, I overheard a muffled phone call in the kitchen.

"*Si*, take the provisions to the place in Oriente," Elsie said into the phone. "There will be someone waiting there." Later, I realized that Elsie, like many other Cuban professionals, had been delivering food and supplies to Fidel's guerrilla army in the mountains.

When Elsie came back to the living room, my mother spoke to her rapidly in English, the language she loved and had learned at the Escuela Normal Para Maestros, a college for teachers. It was their private language, the one that held all my mother's secrets and kept them away from me, something I resented then. The staccato sounds hit my ears like pebbles thrown against a wall. The harsh sounds jumbled up into a massive outpouring of blows in the air. I found out later the secret words were about my father's infidelities. When I went to the bathroom, she switched to Spanish.

"I got another letter today," my mother said, staring out the window of Elsie's small apartment. "It must be directly from his mistress this time. She says there's a baby. A baby boy. Could this be possible? Could this woman have borne him a son?" My mother never brought this up again, and we never learned the truth. But, during one of many teenage arguments with my father, I asked how he could be so unjust to his only child. His face changed. He opened his mouth and then shut it; a thought flashed in my mind, "I'm not his only child." I figured he considered the information too much of a blow even for his headstrong daughter.

Back on the couch, I heard despair in my mother's voice but ignored it by shuffling a pack of cards for a game of Old Maid. My mother's tragic face frowned into the emptiness outside. At the time, I had no idea what all this talk could be about.

Elsie, an avid reader of philosophy, literature and history, stopped unpacking a box of books that she was stacking on a long shelf under the window. I saw that it looked like an encyclopedia. The name "Lenin" was on each volume, but it didn't mean anything to me then. My mother was oblivious to the books and tightly crossed her arms in front of her with a shudder as if shielding herself against a cold wind.

"He denies it," my mother said. "But I know it is the truth."

"Ceci, maybe there is nothing to these letters," Elsie said. "Maybe it's someone who wants to do a lot of damage."

I placed the cards on the coffee table and flipped through my grandfather's chemistry textbook, the one he wrote with his colleague Daniel Carrera. Then I found the scrapbook. I turned each thick page slowly, taking in the smell of paper and glue. Each week, Elsie cut out a comic strip of a stray but intrepid mixed-breed dog named Scamp from the newspaper *El Diario de la Marina*. She pasted the week's installment in the scrapbook, and when I visited we went through Scamp's new adventures.

"Cecilita," she said to me, walking away from her pile of books now scattered on the floor. "Let's look at what has happened to Scamp since you were here last! Look. He is standing on top of a doghouse and looking down at the children. What do you suppose he could have done now?"

At that moment, a large but slim book decorated in gold ornate lettering caught my eye, and, without answering Elsie, I opened it, losing myself in "The Little Match Girl" by Hans Christian Anderson. "She's poor," Elsie said, pointing to a black and white ink drawing of the girl shivering in the cold. "Like so many people here in Cuba. It is unjust."

"Why are they poor?"

"No one cares about them," she replied. "So the government must."

The fervor in Elsie's voice communicated urgency. I stared into her troubled face. The soft folds of her black dress, the warmth of her body next to mine, the smell of cinnamon and chocolate in the air created a cocoon of security that I understood the match girl would never experience. It was my first lesson in the dynamics of social class. At that moment, Elsie had planted the seed of compassion and, decades later, I would remember the conversation as the beginning of my own political consciousness.

My mother, immobile by the window and lost in a secret world, did not join the conversation. Throughout my childhood, she embodied both presence and absence, symptoms -- I later learned – of the ravaging mental illness schizophrenia that had already taken hold of her. When the light made her eyes shine, I ran toward her, in need of attention; however, just as I made it to her side, the light flickered out and her eyes turned into opaque black slits, leaving me bewildered and sad on the lap of a silent, withdrawn woman. It was a ritual without end.

Elsie earned her living by tutoring students in English at the dining room table. No one in our family knew the small Vedado apartment − equipped with a tiny sofa and a coffee table piled with books − served as the hub for neighborhood anti-Batista activities. A photograph of me decorated one wall. My mother turned away from the window and straightened the frame, which was tilted to one side.

"Let's play Old Maid, Elsie. I love Old Maid," I cried, tiring of the book. The rules of the game were simple. Players matched up the doubles and chose a card from the other's hand in order to make pairs. Whoever did not have the Old Maid at the end of the game won.

I always lost.

"Elsie, why do you know where my Old Maid is?" I complained.

"*Mi hijita,*" she leaned closer to whisper. "Don't be so predictable. You always put your Old Maid on the right side. I know exactly where she is, so I avoid her."

I looked aghast at my new hand. Yes, there was the Old Maid, on the right side. Disappointment darkened my eyes. To brighten the mood, Elsie jumped up, offered my mother a glass of freshly-squeezed limeade and took a small box from a cabinet.

"Let's see what this is," she said, handing the box to me.

I lifted out a pair of long, red, dangling earrings. Red beads and white crystals were woven together in delicate ropes, sparkling in the now waning light from the window. I laughed, delighted with the gift. I held the earrings up to my ears and admired myself in the small mirror on the wall.

But my mother didn't share our joy. She blew her nose into a wad of tissue she retrieved from the cuff of her long sleeved sweater. Her eyes, voluminous and dark, adopted the look of passive suffering that she would wear on her face for the rest of her life.

6.

Our front patio jutted out like a pouting lip over the sidewalk below. From its dizzying height in our third floor apartment overlooking the fashionable suburb of Nuevo Vedado, I watched Senor Pablo hurrying home in the evenings to eat *bacalao* prepared by his cook; the delicious odors of the marshmallow-soft codfish submerged in olive oil and garlic floated up to reach us.

In the mornings, before school, I watched yellow-haired Oscarito across the street assemble armies of plastic soldiers on the living room carpet. In the afternoons, I could see Señorita Carmen in the corner house playing the piano while her mother stood by the window singing an aria from the Spanish operetta, *La Gran Via*. Sometimes her voice competed with the whine of lawn mowers as gardeners trimmed the hedges surrounding Colegio Kopi a block away, where I went to kindergarten.

If I stared straight down long enough, the mottled granite of the porch on the first floor began to move like waves. To one side, the edges of two wooden rocking chairs with woven cane seats and backs, where Carlito's grandparents rocked in the dusk, swayed in and out of my field of vision. But my favorite place to view was the front patio of the apartment building right next door. There I could clearly see four-year-old Cristy playing with a pile of toys so big it looked like a barricade. The building was only an arm's length away, and, from our patios, Cristy and I carried on daily conversations.

"Cecilita, do you want to play?" Cristy called out. Above a smooth, complacent face, golden lights sparked from her thick hair, which seemed to be on fire in the sunlight. I, on the other hand, had thin, dull, limp, brown hair, but people thought my eyes shone with life and emotion and my face reflected a variety of feelings, mainly curiosity, mischief and joy. It was December of 1958, a month from my fifth birthday, and I overflowed with energy.

"Do you have your dolls with you?"

Playing with Cristy really meant talking back and forth from our front and back patios on spacious flats that took up an entire floor. But my apartment was special because it also had a side patio. Hers didn't. What is it about our first homes that hold us hostage to the past?

Full blown civil war finally had erupted in Cuba. Radio Rebelde transmitted daily broadcasts from Fidel up in the mountains, asking for support. As I played on the front patio with Cristy on her patio, I could hear the radio and, beyond that, arguments between my parents. That day I lined up chairs and created a classroom. I wanted to be a teacher like my mother. Cristy did the same on her patio, and we took turns teaching the dolls.

"Stop arguing," I called out to my parents, holding a book of fairy tales from which I was reading to the dolls seated on rows of chairs.

"We're not arguing," they answered. I could hear the murmurs about infidelity, a few jealous exclamations, and tense words about Fidel.

"*Sigo repitiendo, eso es comunismo*," my father said of Castro's rumored coup against Batista. The island's communist party now openly backed Fidel.

Before going to bed that evening, my father told my mother that her stepmother, my beloved Elsie, had admitted she supported Castro. "We should not talk to Elsie ever again," my father cried. The words bounced hard against the wall of my bedroom next to his. "And we have to leave Cuba."

Lying down, I moved the mosquito net aside to let in more air. Despite my father's adamant opposition to the "communist" Elsie, I continued to correspond with her to the day of her death.

7.

When Ana Maria was 15, my grandmother hired her to keep house and later help care for her child, my mother. Ana Maria, who lived in Matanzas on a small farm, jumped on a milk truck early every Monday morning to go to work in La Habana and stayed at my grandmother's until Saturday evening when she went back home on the same milk truck. Now, this old country woman with her hair tucked in a pompadour all around her head and her eyes aglow with love was my caretaker.

"*Por favor*, Ceci," Ana Maria begged my mother. "Take Cecilita with you to school. It's her birthday. She'll behave better tomorrow; she promised."

A descendant of poor Spaniards who went bankrupt in Cuba, Ana Maria wore flowing flowered dresses and a pair of tiny pearl earrings my grandmother had given her as a gift years ago.

"Impossible," my mother cried. "I am going to punish her." My mother, beautiful, stylish, and in her thirties, wore her hair in a cloud around a face so white and smooth that she resembled my father's nickname, "La China." She worked as a teacher of English at the Centro de Ingles Numero Ocho from six to nine in the evenings. I loved to sit in her class, so this was maximum punishment. I stayed silent, knowing it would do no good to protest.

Amparo, a tall black woman my mother hired to help Ana Maria look after me, tried her influence. Her family came to the island long ago in a slave ship, in chains, to work as field labor in the sugar plantations. She lived in a nearby *solar*, or slum, that at night resonated with the African drum rolls of *santeria* rites.

"*Señora*, it wasn't the girl's fault," she said. Running through the living room, I had bumped into the buffet and caused a crystal vase to crash to the floor.

"Don't interfere," my mother said.

Amparo, who wore a blue, checkered uniform with a short, white apron tied around her waist, rolled her eyes. Both she and Ana Maria, in their 50s, took the bus from their homes each morning to my house to take care of me while my mother graded papers, visited family and friends, or went shopping. Then they took the bus back home when my mother went to work, leaving me in the care of three maids who lived with us.

And now, because my mother did not relent, my fate was to spend the night with this unfriendly trio, a cook, a washer woman responsible only for laundry, and a cleaning woman. These three were sisters, whose names I can't remember, in their early twenties, slender, and with caramel colored skin. All had frizzy hair pulled back into tight buns covered with nets and hard, black eyes. They lived in the "maid's quarters" in the side patio that opened out from the kitchen.

Large steel wash basins lined the walls. In the center, a wrought iron table with several chairs wobbled on the chipped, uneven tile, unlike the smooth floors of my front or back patios. Suspended from above, a long white clothesline sagged with the wet weight of my father's pants, shirts and *camisetas* or undershirts. Our apartment had no air conditioning, so the kitchen door was always open to catch the breeze, making the patio impossible to ignore.

That night, eating dinner, two of the maids dressed up in my mother's fancy house-robes while the third cleaned up the kitchen. One had on a rich, red velvet robe with a high collar. The other wore a soft midnight blue satin with a gold sash. The two had let their hair free from the habitual nets. The black fuzz around their heads jerked up and down as they paraded in front of me, making strange whistling sounds and twisting their arms over their heads as in a Flamenco dance. This was the first time I had seen them do this. Now, I understand their rebellious, bold acts stemmed from Fidel's words about liberating the oppressed. They, like many in Cuba's lower classes, resented the wealthy people who hired them.

"What are you doing?" I asked, confused. They ignored me, continuing with their bizarre shuffling steps.

"*No hay nadie ahí,*" the third maid said, holding a mop. "There's nobody there. It's your imagination." I looked steadily at the two women. Maybe I was imagining them, as I often imagined people sitting with me on my front and back patios. I reached out to touch the sleeve of one of them. They were real.

I stopped eating, a floating feeling filled my stomach. Fear and anger propelled me from my chair. I was angry they were wearing my mother's clothes and fearful of the trickery in their voices. I ran out to the side patio, rushed into the maids' room and locked the door behind me. I lay on the narrow cot, looking out the window that opened to the empty field beyond. The pane was frosted, and I couldn't see anything.

The maids ran after me, laughing. They pounded on the door. One made a low moaning sound and, leaning out the patio wall, she reached over to the window and waved a white cloth in front of it, making the rag dance like a tired ghost. The heat closed in. With the door and window shut, I sweated and felt feverish. I knew it would be a long time before my mother came home, but here in this room they couldn't get to me.

"Cecilita, come out," one of them called. "You have to go to bed now."

"Forget about her," another said. "Let's just do it before *la senora* comes home."

"Chango!" the third shouted. "Obatala!"

They called forth Yoruban gods that in the Afro-Cuban religion of *santeria* coincide with Roman Catholic saints and asked the deities to intercede on their behalf to almighty God, a ritual I knew nothing about at the time. They chanted in a strange language, but I recognized the sounds. I had heard them many times before falling asleep, and I realized now this was a nightly occurrence, just louder tonight since my parents weren't home. Laughing, shrieking, they beat on the now overturned wash basins, their tortured voices swirling in the darkness outside. Trapped in their world of the invisible, I listened as these descendants of African slaves communed with their ancestors.

"*Llevame.* Take me," one of them cried out.

A wave of tobacco smoke sneaked under the door. Then a pungent burning spice followed. I sneezed, but did not move from the bed. I turned my face into the pillow, breathed in the smell of and unwashed hair and closed my eyes. I sang in a low voice as was my custom before going to sleep to stave off loneliness:

El patio de mi casa no es particular
Si llueve, se moja como los demas.
(The patio of my house isn't special
If it rains, it gets wet like all the rest.)

I dozed, dreaming I was inside my house, but the ceiling was filled with holes. When I looked up, raindrops pelted my face. I climbed a ladder to patch the holes with tissue paper. But the flimsy material absorbed the water and the wads fell out.

8.

Early on the morning of the first day of 1959, I woke up with a sore throat.

"Rafael, *la niña* gets a cold every week," my mother spat the words at my father.

"She has to go again for aerosol treatments," my father offered as a solution. These treatments were part of Saturday morning errands. I went to a clinic and sat in what looked to be a dentist's chair, breathing through a tube. The warm steam from a mentholated liquid filled my lungs with the mist my father said could cure my frequent upper respiratory infections.

My nose was running. The fever made my movements appear as in slow motion. Sounds traveled to my ears as if forced through a tunnel of echoes. I felt dizzy, but my mission was to escape into the cool breeze of my back patio that reached out over a field and touched the edge of the sky. The entire floor, suspended in air, offered a haven from the tension of my household. My mother, furious about yet another anonymous letter she had received outlining an affair between a nurse and my father, yelled at my father and banged drawers inside. My father, meanwhile, cursed the stand-off between Castro, who stressed government reforms, and Batista, who promised elections soon. Here in my magical back patio, their howls dissolved into whispers.

I peered through the wire fence my father had attached along the top of the wall to keep our Boston terrier, Negrito, from jumping out into the field three floors below. Instead, our dog jumped against the fence as if to catch a glimpse of the field and bounced back. He did this constantly every time he was in the patio, and now the fence curled over like a hunchback. To me, the field, a grassy expanse with clumps of bushes scattered in careless patterns, provided a sketchbook. On its emptiness I painted stories about my family and friends, set in the streets of La Habana Vieja, the colonial section overshadowed by cathedral spires in the center of a cobblestoned plaza. I held the images out there on the field to look at for a long time. In this patio, I created images in silence, and every day I came out onto the chalky-red Mexican tile to dream.

I imagined scenarios about poor children and hungry mothers begging on street corners as I had read in "The Little Match Girl" and "The Red Shoes" in Elsie's book of fairy tales. I realized later that Elsie, who hated the injustices in Cuba's class structure, highlighted these narratives in rebellion against my father's aristocratic stance. Elsie's comic strip dog Scamp became the hero in several stories where he took food and provisions to people stuck in snowdrifts. Soldiers in olive green uniforms with muskets at their sides figured prominently in several plots since I had recently seen them line up on street corners. My father said they were thieves and murderers. Their faces looked haggard, but set in rigid cruel expressions, a vivid image that contributed to my fear of communism and counter balanced Elsie's social teachings. The irreconcilable views impressed upon me by my father and Elsie never stopped their battle for prominence in my mind as I later read Karl Marx and Adam Smith, trying to figure out what system worked best for a country in trouble.

This first morning of the year, I cranked the hand gear on the sturdy *Tio Vivo*. This contraption resembled a merry-go-round with two seats at opposite ends somewhat like a seesaw that my paternal grandparents had assembled in the middle of the patio. I whizzed around in a circle, leapt out of the seat and skipped inside the wooden playhouse that Elsie had brought me for Christmas.

Inside was a little girl's paradise: a small steel stove and refrigerator, a round table with four chairs, a crib with a baby doll, a high chair and shelves lined with stuffed animals. But my books held center stage, scattered everywhere: on the refrigerator, the table, and inside the crib. Here, as in the front patio, I set up dolls in the chairs to resemble a classroom. Piles of papers, colored pencils, and notebooks cluttered one corner. Instead of mixing a meal on the stove for the dolls, I sat them there for lessons.

I imagined a girl who lived on the next block seated at the table with the dolls. She needed a lesson this morning because her family couldn't pay for the school in the neighborhood. In the mornings as I passed her house with Ana Maria on the way to school, she ran out barefooted to stare with serious tar-black eyes, wearing dresses resembling potato sacks. One time, I looked inside her open door.

"*Niña*," Ana Maria warned, "don't be so curious. It's rude."

I saw two rocking chairs with the woven cane seats ripped in several places. A mattress with a rumpled, stained coverlet hugged one wall. Three other children gazed blankly from the window. Their uncombed hair lay in tangled, greasy clumps. One child had a red scarf tied around his head. Another wore a long necklace of gold plastic beads. No parents were in sight.

"They're gypsies," Ana Maria whispered. "Your mother wouldn't like it. They are not the same as you."

But the gypsy girl attracted me so much that I insisted on visiting her several times a week. One time, I dressed in one of my mother's wide skirts, strapped a belt around my waist and stepped into her high-heeled shoes. We walked down the block to her house, Ana Maria peeking out from the parasol she used against the sun. The girl and I talked together happily, and I showed off my long skirt.

Even at that early hour of the first day of the year, as my imagination called forth a multitude of images and I kept up a steady coughing, the new black and white television set in the living room exploded with chanting that intruded into my daydreams.

Fidel had ousted Batista.

"*Cuba si, Yankees no. Cuba si, Yankees no.*" the chanters screamed. The news anchor delivered sharp words I couldn't make out. I ran out of the playhouse and went inside, making my way carefully past the mahogany buffet filled with gold-edged plates and cups, imported from England by my maternal grandmother years ago when she was a bride. My father, unshaven, sat in front of the TV holding his head in his hands, rocking back and forth. I looked at the screen and saw people waving their arms in a plaza, what came to be known as La Plaza de la Revolucion. Ana Maria and Amparo, my caregivers, sat with my mother next to the television. The three maids stared at the images on the screen from the hallway shadows.

"The peasants are our heroes," Fidel Castro told the crowd as he and his group of revolutionaries marched down from their outpost in La Sierra Maestra and into Santiago to begin an eight-day march to La Habana. The men who had holed up in the mountains with Fidel during those long months waved to supporters who eagerly flanked their slow moving vehicles. Bearded and dressed in olive green fatigues, the men made stops at Channel 2, at radio station CMQ, and the newspaper *Revolucion* and announced their victory over the deposed Batista who, after a New Year's Eve party the night before, fled from La Habana to exile in Miami.

"What are we going to do?" my mother asked my father.

My father looked at the maids shifting their weight from one foot to another in the hallway. "Nothing right now," he mumbled. "Tell them to hurry with the dinner preparations. Our guests arrive at 4 o'clock."

That afternoon, my uncle Cesar, my paternal grandparents Amalia and Rafael Fernandez, doctor friends of my father's and several of my mother's cousins and aunts sat down to dinner with us. But by then, my sore throat forced me into bed, and all I could hear until I fell asleep was the clanking of crystal and the swish of hushed tones.

9.

My father and I watched Fidel on television as *el comandante* divided large privately-owned farms into tracts for state control. Then he parceled out land owned by the deposed Batista to the peasants as he spoke about his new agricultural initiative. My father groaned and placed both hands on the sides of his head.

Fidel smiled, signed documents, promised elections. His face showed patches of skin where his curly beard refused to grow. His olive green headgear, like a baseball cap forced into the shape of a box, stood firmly up like a crown. The tips of his ears extended over the edges of the cap like large mussels. His deep set eyes gazed at the camera at an angle.

"That's how communism starts," my father said, frowning, shaking his head. "The rich lose their property first, then the middle class. Soon we'll all be cutting cane out in the fields."

For weeks since the New Year, looters ransacked the streets of La Habana. Screams and gunshots mingled in the hot air. Men filled with revolutionary fervor invaded the casinos. Others smashed the Shell Petroleum headquarters. Fidel called for a general strike to mark the end of the old regime, and Batista's officials – those who had not managed to escape with the deposed president in the night -- were rounded up, jailed or killed. The bearded men of Fidel, the *barbudos,* had taken over La Habana, running up and down the steps of the Presidential Palace and crowding into all the public places.

The news ended, and a cooking show started. My father turned off the television set. We sat in silence for a while, a rare occasion for us to be alone. But when we were, he conversed with me as if I had the understanding of an adult, speaking of politics as easily as of literature and women.

"The owners of Bacardi Rum and Hatuey Beer," he said, "have offered to pay their taxes in advance to show support for those *barbudos.* They don't know yet they'll be boarding planes out of this country anytime now. If they escape with their lives." He talked about the economy, ruined now, he said, and the kidnappings and hijackings of the past months.

"Let's watch the cooking show," he turned on the set again, but it had been replaced by more news. We watched the rebroadcast of Fidel's arrival in La Habana, on the eighth day of January. Signs inscribed with *Gracias, Fidel* met him and his men as they drove slowly in jeeps and tanks. Fidel held a rifle with a telescopic lens at his side.

My father frowned again. He wore his black hair slicked back with grease. His long lashes formed a canopy over caramel-colored eyes streaked with yellow lights. His gaze, open, inquiring, was unlike the impenetrable black of my mother's, which looked as if a curtain had dropped on stage after a performance. His nose looped out like a hawk's beak, his skin color -- always a matter of concern to Cubans vigilant about the mixture of black and European blood -- the shade of light toast. Once he complained, "people don't know if I'm an Arab, a Jew or a Spaniard! But I'm a Spaniard from both sides of the family." That morning, he wore a crisp white shirt and smelled of cologne.

"Life as we know it," he said, "is over forever."

My father went everywhere with a book in his hand. He read Agatha Christie mysteries and histories of the Greek and Roman empires. "I memorized the entire periodic table for a chemistry exam," he bragged. He liked beautiful women like Elizabeth Taylor and Lana Turner, stopping in his tracks if one walked by him on the street. On Sundays, he concocted saltimbocca and crepes Suzette from gourmet cookbooks. As a gynecologist he made a comfortable, but not extravagant, living. Fishing expeditions were his favorite outings.

One morning in the height of summer, shooting across the choppy waves of the ocean in his yacht, I saw him struggle with a marlin which, as in Ernest Hemingway's *The Old Man and the Sea*, refused to give up. In his excitement, my father tripped over buckets of sardines he used as bait and kicked them aside. He let the line run and then reeled it in. Several other men, including Cuco, yelled encouragement and gesticulated wildly with their arms. I cowered against my mother in a corner, watching and listening to their loud curses. Finally, with one superhuman heave my father hauled his prey on board. The fish spanned more than five feet in length. When it slammed against the floor, I screamed and covered my face with my hands. The fish gasped for air, thrashing about with his tail. My father, face red-hot not only from the sun but from the pleasure of triumph, took out a small revolver from the waistband of his pants and pumped several bullets into the writhing fish. That was my father in the prime of life. That was my father up to the moment of his death.

"No more fishing for a while," he said as he turned off the television for the last time.

Ten months after that, in November 1959, my father was gone. I never saw him pack a suitcase. He never said good-by. Although his absences were nothing new to me during my early years, this absence felt different. Now, it was quiet in my parent's bedroom and throughout the apartment. The three maids walked out forever, and Ana and Amparo came to help with cooking and washing once a week.

I asked few questions, involved with my own life of books and toys. I assembled a family of dolls to keep me company: a ceramic one with a carefully painted face that Elsie had given me, a boy doll I named Rafaelito after my father, and a dancing doll exactly my size whose feet I wrapped around my ankles with ribbons so I could waltz with her around the room.

But when I finally did ask, "Where's my father?" my mother had an answer.

"He went to Mexico to get an American visa for us," she said. "We're going to leave the country soon." But the day of departure was still too far away to worry about. My days continued their leisurely rhythm; my mother remained silent as always, while my father, I later found out, filled out paperwork in Mexico City, and slept on a pallet on the floor in the house of Cuban friends who also opposed Fidel.

"I had to carry a knife everywhere I went," I overheard him say years later. "Mexico City is a savage city, a barbaric, dirty city filled with disease and thieves. Women making tortillas sit on the sidewalk and slap mosquitoes right into the batter."

On the same day that he took a plane to Mexico, the police came to the door of the clinic where he worked. My father claimed Castro had sent them to kill him. When they saw he wasn't there, they smashed cabinets and destroyed lamps and equipment.

"I outsmarted them," he told me. "They had no idea I would be gone. I was against Castro, and I told everybody he was a communist and that our property would be taken away. Someone turned me in. I didn't care who it was because I knew I would leave before anyone came to get me."

But other dissenters weren't as lucky. They didn't leave La Habana in time. Castro's police dragged them out of their homes or offices and shoved them into waiting cars bound for secret places. Why didn't they take my mother or me? My father thought perhaps Elsie, who supported Castro's government, exerted her influence to protect us.

"Elsie hated me," he said, "but she didn't want you or your mother to be hurt."

After his departure, my mother, fired from her teaching job because she refused to join Fidel's literacy campaign, listened more intently to the goings on in the neighborhood. She watched from the front patio, the side patio, the back patio. Shouting in the street made her run to a window. "There might be retribution from the neighbors because your father left," she said. "And we can't leave until he has a job in the United States."

One morning, my nannies, Ana Maria and Amparo, whispered among themselves a shocking piece of news. "*La querida*, his mistress," I overheard them say. "She went with him. Ceci must suspect this. I called the clinic, and they said she had left the country with the doctor."

If my mother suspected that my father had dared to make such a brash move, she accepted it quietly. She, too, wanted to leave. "Communism is intolerable to me," she said. "All the teachers have been forced out to the fields to teach the *guajiros* how to read. It's a miserable existence in the countryside." She hoped, she added, her marriage had a better chance outside of the island, and that sentiment had nothing to do with Castro.

As we waited to get word from my father, everything around us changed rapidly, just as my father had predicted. Contingents of *guajiros* rode their horses to La Habana in support of agrarian reform. A new law empowered the state to take over failing firms, allowing officials to carry out the nationalization of hotels and the companies Bethlehem Steel and International Harvester. Castro's political police were now just as feared in "bourgeois" circles as Batista's had been, arresting anyone on charges of conspiracy. Castro traveled to Washington, DC and shook hands with Vice-President Richard Nixon, denying accusations of imposing a communist regime, while the Russian vice president visited the island to negotiate buying the sugar crop.

One night, an electrician worked for hours on our air conditioning unit and left a gaping hole in the wall of the side patio. He said the new unit my father installed some months before his departure had malfunctioned, and he would try to get a replacement. The electrician took the unit with him, and my mother placed a sheet over the hole to keep out mosquitoes. I sensed her fear about the opening on our side patio wall, making our apartment vulnerable to the discontent evident everywhere. A neighbor whispered that a woman had been found dead in the field in back of our building.

"I hope that because we're on the third floor," she told Ana Maria, "it will be difficult for someone to climb in."

But the hole transformed our already questionable peace into constant anxiety. We watched the opening and waited for the electrician to come back. He never did. Later, someone said that most of the laborers had joined Fidel's militia, probably the fate of our thieving electrician.

10.

During the first six months of 1960 that led up to our departure from La Habana, my nanny Ana Maria continued to walk me to Colegio Kopi, a private neighborhood pre-school just a block away from home. I was now six and excelling in academics. The school took up a two-story house with a wide veranda clinging to the edges like a bib. It had several classrooms, a kitchen, two baths and a fenced-in front yard where we marched around the slide to Philip Sousa's *Stars and Stripes Forever* in a display of patriotic fervor. For Fidel Castro or for Fulgencio Batista, I never knew. But as we marched each morning and afternoon in that enclosed space with the wet grass and mud sticking to our shoes, the island was undergoing a radical transformation that no one had ever dreamed possible.

Fidel organized neighborhood watch committees, precursors to the *Comites de Defensa de la Revolucion,* to quell all dissent. Shouts of "*al paredon,*" to the execution wall, filled the streets. The new government abolished Santa Claus as an imperialist idea and a hated United States import. The Institute for Agrarian Reform took over another 70,000 acres of U.S. owned property. And, while the United States and Fidel haggled over sugar prices, the Soviets increased their presence on the island.

In March, a French freighter, bringing 76 tons of war material to La Habana harbor, exploded, killing and maiming hundreds of Cuban dock workers. Fidel accused the imperialist "Yankees" of sabotage and, on television, frenzied demonstrators screamed "*Cuba si, Yankees no,*" while waiving giant placards of Fidel's likeness. The rumors of invasion by the United States, conspiracy within our own government, and violence against anyone who disagreed with Fidel sharpened our senses to danger.

A year after the Revolution, the students of Colegio Kopi had escaped the curriculum change to Marxist theory because the school had not yet been nationalized. But we watched the news with interest as the *Pioneros*, children committed to the Revolution, wearing red kerchiefs around their necks, saluted *El Comandante* and shook hands with him as he outlined his literacy campaign in an eight-hour speech. My mother did not explain what was going on.

Secretive as usual, she often stopped in mid-sentence when anyone entered the room. I absorbed the metamorphosis of our lives as an unsettling feeling that nothing stays the same. Since my father left Cuba, it felt as if I had emerged from a dark room in a photo lab. Everything reflected a dazzling light. My eyes worked hard to adjust, but the sensation exhilarated me. Something about the anarchy in the air, the shake-up of our social structure, made me feel free -- of what I couldn't name -- and I responded with unruly behavior both at school and at home.

I was particularly cruel to Guillermito, a shy, quiet fellow student who sat in front of me at Colegio Kopi. Whenever anyone spoke to him, he lowered his eyes in shame. He walked lightly, as if fearing his step might make a permanent indentation on the soft mud that circled our school. His eyes, streaked with green and orange, reflected a sadness that should not have been there at his age. His hair, greased flat on his head and parted deeply on the left side, made him look as if he were wearing a shiny helmet like the ones pagan warriors wore, believing they were at the mercy of forces beyond their control. His passive acceptance of fate – the same one I sensed in my mother -- stirred in me a feeling of anger. I wanted to humiliate him. One day, as he sat at his desk with head bent, staring at his folded hands, I did.

"*Maestra*," I said. "Guillermito insulted me. He said bad words." I spoke convincingly.

"Guillermito, is this true?" Señorita Adela, a fashionable young woman with short hair, dressed in a snug, flowered dress and black, patent leather high heels, came up to his desk.

"No," he whispered, still looking down.

"Speak up! Tell me the truth!"

Shame flushed his ears red. He coughed. I could see his profile as his face crumbled before delivering a strenuous sneeze, launching a missile of green and yellow muck thick as applesauce, and, I noted in a flash of recognition, the color of his eyes, right onto his open notebook. I watched in repulsion from my seat behind him as the slime dripped off the desk to the floor. Exasperated, Señorita Adela took Guillermito by the arm and led him to the bathroom in back.

"Wash your mouth," she ordered. "And get some tissue to clean up your desk."

Guillermito, with the most downcast face I have yet to see, slumped forward as he walked with Señorita Adela. He took up a piece of white soap from a holder, opened the faucet, wet the soap and worked up a good lather. He looked out over everyone's head, meeting no one's eyes, and scrubbed his mouth. The students snickered behind their hands. And when he walked back to his desk to wipe up his snot and then laid his head down on his arm to hide his face, I laughed the loudest.

At home, I liked the freedom I felt when my mother went out to run errands.

"*Oye,*" I yelled at the cook, hired for only a few months.

"Go play with your dolls," she urged, busily scrubbing the sink.

"This is my doll," I announced, dragging a lantern that was at least two feet tall. I had dressed it up in my old baby clothes. I lifted the lantern up by the handle as if I were lifting a child by the arms. "This is my baby." I got no response, so I pulled up the cook's wide loose skirt and laughed at her underwear ornamented with rips and worn-out spots. She chased me out of the kitchen. I dragged my "doll" to the telephone and called up randomly, chatting with strangers for hours. I painted my nails bright red in the bathroom and managed to hide them from my mother and Ana Maria. But at school the next day I displayed them proudly.

"*No se permite eso,*" Señorita Rosa declared nail polishing was not permitted in school and handed me a bottle of remover. "When you finish, stand in the corner and face the wall." When she wasn't looking, I grinned and made faces.

Another time, during an after-school activity, I went to the bathroom and discovered no toilet paper. I did not wipe. I took off my underpants and threw them in the trashcan. I went back to the activity and sat on a chair to wait for Ana Maria to take me home. When I got up, the chair was smeared with feces. Unfortunately, Señorita Adela was standing next to the chair. She peered at the mess, incredulous.

"*Ay, niña,*" she exclaimed. "You are behaving so badly these days."

Luckily, Ana Maria had just arrived. I inched away from the chair and out the door. "Tell Cecilita's mother I must speak to her," Señorita Adela called after us. But by then, I had skipped outside and straddled the fence, arching backwards so that my hair—as well as my skirt-- fell toward the ground. Ana Maria ran over and tugged me off the fence, hurrying us home.

"*Vamos, que vienen los comunistas,*" she whispered that the communists were coming. I didn't know who they were, but I figured they were the ones shooting people against the big wall, the *paredon.*

On March 16, 1960, Cuba's Communist Party issued a resolution asking for arms from the friendly socialist countries. The next day, in Washington, President Eisenhower accepted a recommendation of the Central Intelligence Agency to arm and train Cuban exiles for an attack on the island. Then, our government froze the bank accounts of about 400 Cubans accused of collaborating with Batista.

On March 28, the chairman of La Habana's hair-dressers' association was sentenced to three years in prison for writing anti-communist slogans on walls. The regime took over CMQ, the most important radio and television center on the island, but not before the owner, Abel Mestre, delivered a tirade against Castro on the air and escaped into exile. The government took control of the College of Journalists and the printers' association. The U.S. Embassy protested each time American citizens were placed under arrest but received no response from the government.

One by one friends and neighbors left their homes and went abroad--to Spain, Mexico, Puerto Rico, Venezuela, the United States. One day Guillermito did not come back to school. Next door, my friend Cristy did not answer insistent calls. School functions, however, continued as before. At a holiday performance, my teachers chose me—despite my disciplinary track record-- for the lead role in a ballet adaptation of *Snow White*.

"She has the darkest hair and the darkest eyes of all our students," Señorita Adela told Señorita Rosa, the second in command.

I looked around and, sure enough, I saw that the rest of my classmates had hair the color of straw and eyes the color of the sea. Mine looked just like our book's representation of Snow White's. No one challenged me, and I was the most important person at school for months.

For the performance, my mother's seamstress designed a long dress with a vibrant blue skirt, white bodice, black puffy sleeves and a flowing red cape. I wrapped a red headband around my dark chin-length hair, which I wore with squared off bangs just above the eyebrows.

Up on stage, on the evening of the ballet, with my lips painted scarlet and my eyes lined with my mother's dark brown eyebrow pencil, I lay down on a soft mat of shredded green paper and, surrounded by fake paper bushes, I waited for my prince. The dark eyes that had secured me the role roved around the stage and down to the audience, refusing to stay shut. I looked at the fairies dancing all around me. I looked straight into the eyes of the prince slowly approaching.

"Close your eyes," Señorita Adela hissed from behind the curtain.

"Keep them closed," added Señorita Rosa. But I kept my eyes opened, holding the gaze of the prince who pretended I was asleep when he came to kiss me awake. His face came up to a fraction of an inch from mine, and I saw that his pores were wide open, scrubbed red by a strong soap. I turned my face, and he kissed my cheek. He took my hand and helped me up. I stepped on the hem of my skirt and wobbled before we began the dance we had stayed after school to perfect. We waltzed up and down the stage in a scene I would reenact throughout my life: a constant dance that went nowhere.

A month later, I was once again in the spotlight. Not only did I have the darkest hair and eyes, but I was the tallest of my classmates. My height thrust me in the lead in an Alsatian circle dance thought up by the teachers to teach us European geography. In fact, I was so tall that my dance partner had to be brought in from outside the school. He was Señorita Adela's nephew, a ten-year-old with green eyes and copper freckles that spread over both cheeks and down to the base of his neck.

This time, I wore a dress with a wide flowered skirt and a blue and silver sequined apron around my waist. A handkerchief tied over my head and under my chin. My partner wore knee-length pants and a cap at a rakish angle over one ear. He towered above me. He held one hand behind my back and the other one poised just at shoulder level as we circled the stage to the music on the record player. The next week, my mother took me to a photo studio wearing the Alsatian outfit.

"Do you know that the *Alsacianas* do not have the money to wear such finery?" asked Elsie, when I presented her with the photograph. "They are poor country people and cannot afford a dress like this."

"Who are the Alsatians?" I asked.

"Let's look it up in the dictionary."

Elsie brought down a bulky brown book, and I flipped the pages until we found the word. A long paragraph explained that Alsace was in the northeastern region of France. The last line that Elsie read held both our attention: "a Bohemian or adventurer."

"What does this mean?"

"It means someone who loves freedom, despises oppression and works to end the poverty of the little match girl."

Elsie searched for a nail in a kitchen drawer, hammered it into a wall and hung up the picture. It was another lesson in progressive politics that I surreptitiously absorbed.

11.

A boil on the side of my left calf erupted. The top layer of skin ballooned out like a tent and then drew aside for a flow of pus to leak onto the bedclothes. This festering boil signified that departure was near: it was the side effect of the smallpox vaccine all Cubans received just before they were granted exit visas. The night of the injection, I lay shivering from the fever it caused under the mosquito net draping my bed.

I now knew I was going to the United States, and I pictured it as a big beach where my father was sailing his yacht along the shore. The fever raged until morning, and I saw shapes coming in and out of the wall. The toy chest holding Cinderella and Minnie Mouse loomed in a corner like a menacing giant. The Disney characters jumped off the shelves and ran around the room. My dolls, with caps of golden hair, joined them in the fracas. Only the porcelain figurine of a Chinese woman stood immobile on a shelf. One of her hands was missing. My mother had taped it to the doll's side when Fidel rode into La Habana the year before.

"I'll put it back once she grants my wish," she had said. I squinted into the gaping hole where the hand should have been, fascinated by the idea. I never discovered what my mother had wanted, and the figurine later got lost in our many moves.

No one in the neighborhood trusted anyone else.

"*La mama de Oscarito* has denounced her husband to the government," Ana Maria told my mother.

"I heard that Marcelino turned in his own sister too," she answered.

No one dared speak out against Fidel. When I marched with my classmates around the Colegio Kopi playground, keeping pace with Sousa's march, I sensed a split in loyalties in the neighborhood families.

"To whom does our flag belong anyway?" one mother asked another when they came to pick up their children. Some talked of our colonial past, our Spanish governors who gave way to the *independistas* following the Spanish-American War in 1898; others mentioned the brief colonization by Great Britain; still others discussed the even briefer occupation by *los Americanos* before a congressional amendment blocked them from annexing the island as they did in neighboring Puerto Rico.

"Yes, but all our presidents have been dictators," someone else complained. "Maybe Fidel's ideals of equality and justice are what we need." While many celebrated Fidel's revolution, a steady flow of emigrants continued to leave quietly: businessmen, ranchers, Batista sympathizers, men without families, families without men. At Colegio Kopi, a student disappeared every day.

"*A los Estados Unidos,*" whispered Señorita Adela and Señorita Rosa.

Elsie shook her head at the departures.

"How can you justify taking money out of the country?" she asked my father before he left.

"It's my money," my father had answered. "Castro should not be interfering if I want to make a bank transfer."

After a week, the boil burned into a round permanent depression that looked like a gray moon crater on the side of my left leg. "Why did the doctor inject her in the leg?" Ana Maria examined the deflated wound.

"Because I didn't want a scar on her arm," my mother answered. "It won't look as bad on her leg when she grows up. She can always wear pants."

I recuperated and went back to school, but at home I was lonely. All the children in the neighborhood were gone. I played with my dog Negrito, but he had to stay outside on the patio. So I took as my companion a baby chick dyed blue my mother had bought me for Easter. The blue dye was falling off now and he grew daily, following me everywhere. Sometimes I stepped on his toes without meaning to because he was so close. When that happened, I ran for the bottle of Mercurochrome, the antiseptic that cured all, and painted his injured toes red. I used the Mercurochrome freely on myself as well. My mother's anger often meant blows on my arms, thighs, hands. When she hit me, I painted all the "injured" places with the tincture.

"Now go stand in the corner," she said after I finished the curative measure.

But when she wasn't looking, I edged over to the big black telephone and dialed random numbers. I liked the way the metal wheel felt against my finger. My mother, immersed in her thoughts, never heard me converse with strangers in low tones, something I did regularly to ease the loneliness and make up for her lack of attention.

"*Hola, como estas,*" I whispered into the handset. "*Yo tengo un pollito y un perrito.*" How delightful to hear these voices talk back to me and ask about the baby chick and dog!

After Easter, Russian oil began to arrive in Cuba. In May, Russia dispatched an ambassador to La Habana. Fidel closed down *El Diario de la*

Marina and its editor fled to the Peruvian Embassy. The government took over *Prensa Libre,* claiming the paper was attacking "truth, justice and decency." The archbishop of Santiago issued a pastoral letter denouncing relations with Russia. The literacy campaign began in earnest with 800 teachers dispatched to teach the peasants in La Sierra Maestra. Revolutionary students staged a takeover of the University of La Habana. At the same time in Miami, the CIA persuaded Cuban exiles to organize against Fidel. Those who agreed were sent to Nicaragua to train for an invasion. Texaco, Royal Dutch and Standard Oil refused to process Russian oil. So in June, all U.S. oil directors fled, and the government took over the Esso and Shell refineries. Sugar dropped to its lowest price, and, if the United States didn't buy it, we could starve.

The heat in La Habana occupied space like a closely fitting oxygen mask as my mother opened her umbrella to shield us from the hot sun between the bus stop and our destination. My father had sent word that I needed to have aerosol treatments before we left: my upper respiratory infections were severe now and left me weak. The usual clinic had shut down, and a private doctor offered the treatments in his living room in a neighborhood three stops away from home.

I sat in a chrome and leather chair and placed a tube in my mouth from a machine that held the clear mentholated liquid. I inhaled and exhaled forcefully. The steamy concoction filled my lungs. I did this for an hour twice a week in the months before our departure. The goal was to allow me to breathe at night. The doctor gave me a prescription for a ten-day course of tetracycline. Nobody knew that tetracycline—taken before the second set of teeth have come in-- condemned a child to a lifetime of permanent yellowed teeth no whitening agent could bleach. But for then, my six-year-old teeth glittered like pearls.

A week later we had the most important errand to run downtown. I walked behind my mother's swinging hips to the bus stop. Inside the crowded bus, I sat on my mother's lap so she didn't have to pay the fare for me. Then, a few blocks and we were in the business district, next to what looked like a vast warehouse. Inside the building, under interminably high ceilings, government officials scribbled on documents and shuffled papers on heavy wooden desks lined up in straight rows.

My mother, dressed in a dark blue, tailored Coco Chanel suit with her legs wrapped in the most translucent silk stockings, did not speak nor explain why we were there. Other families waited too, standing against the walls. Finally, it was our turn. A man dressed in a white, wrinkled *guayabera* with a brown stain on the collar summoned us to his desk with a wave of his hand. He brushed aside a long clump of hair to reveal a bald scalp. He looked over our papers.

Then, eyeing my mother up and down, he stamped down heavily, imprinting the government seal that gave us permission to leave our home. He handed back the file with a dismissive flick of his wrist.

We walked away, my mother gripping the documents, and made a detour to a lunch counter at the far end of the building. I stepped up carefully, feeling dizzy, distanced, as I always do when I enter a hostile world, and sat on a stool. All the workers here sympathized with Fidel, and we were the hated *gusanos.* Only *gusanos* tried to leave the country at this time.

"*Les puedo servir?*" May I serve you? The waitress, a young mulatto woman, wearing a tight net around her hair, scowled at my mother.

"*Dos coca colas, por favor.*" Two Cokes please.

As I held the glass up to my lips, I glanced inside. There, in the brown thick cold liquid, two cockroaches swam toward me. All twelve legs rowed in slow motion on the swirling river of brown cola. I placed the glass on the counter. I looked at the waitress, who laughed openly. My mother had seen the insects, too. She put her glass down, along with a few coins, and we left without a word. After that, we never left the house.

With the documents tucked away under a pile of linen in a drawer, my mother began to pack in earnest. She shipped our mahogany dining room set to a Miami warehouse. She stuffed wide boxes with embroidered linen sheets and cotton towels, a set of English china etched in 24-carat gold leaf that had belonged to her mother, and a collection of high-ball glasses illustrated with the drawings of French artist Henri Toulouse Lautrec. Smaller boxes held my white baptism gown, baby clothes, the Snow White costume, a Spanish dictionary-encyclopedia, an elaborately illustrated volume of European fairy tales, Fanny Farmer and Betty Crocker cookbooks, family photographs from the 1800's, a wooden darning egg, and remnants of my grandmother's trousseau.

My father sent a telegram saying he had left Mexico City and had obtained a job at a hospital on Miami Beach with the help of a friend, David Cohen, a car dealer whom he had met in La Habana in the early 1950s. In the last weeks before departure, I read, played school and spent a lot of time watching our black and white television set. On the news, I saw people still yelling in the streets, "*Cuba si. Yankee no. Pa' rriba, pa' bajo, los yankees pa'l carajo.*" Upwards, downwards, to hell with the Yankees. But cartoons and other programs still came from what Fidel referred to as the *imperialistas* of the north, *los norteamericanos.*

I loved the show *Ozzie and Harriet.* I had a crush on the youngest son, Ricky Nelson. This boy could really move and could he sing! When he rocked down low with his guitar and looked into the camera straight at me, I felt faint. With Ana Maria watching worriedly, I jumped up and ran out. Ricky Nelson sang to me as I stood hiding my face in the corner against the wall. "Aayyy, Reekee Nel-son….*Me gusta mucho.*"

One particular cartoon show fascinated me. I watched nervously as Popeye threw a can of spinach into his mouth seconds before he ripped thick ropes from around his girlfriend Olive, tied to the train tracks. I liked Popeye's muscles bulging out of his white sailor suit. "Help. Help. Help," Olive cried.

"He-o. He-o. He-o," I yelled. It was the first English word I uttered, a version of "help" that would come in handy later as a Cuban girl lost in America. However, most of the aid I received in our new land was self-help, as my mother continued the plunge into schizophrenia, and my father extricated himself from our lives.

12.

The day we left La Habana, I woke up on wet sheets. It really wasn't a matter of controlling my bladder: I didn't want to stop the hot liquid in the middle of the night because it felt good, like a comforting bath that helped me sleep better. I lay in bed, fiercely sucking my thumb while Ana Maria and Amparo pulled open the curtains and set aside the mosquito net.

"*Hora de levantarse!*" Ana Maria said brightly. Time to get up. She bent down to hug me, and I squirmed in the wetness. The sheets were plastered to my rear end and back, hard and scratchy and reeking of urine and sweat. But this morning Ana Maria, her wide flowered skirt swaying around her ample girth, didn't mind that I had wet the bed. Amparo, dressed as usual in a light blue uniform with white cuffed sleeves, hovered right behind her. As soon as Ana Maria released me from her arms, Amparo scooped me up in a tight hug. I clung to her neck, sitting up in the squishy moisture, both of us sniffling.

"*No te olvides que siempre seras la hija de mi corazon,*" Ana Maria whispered as she set out my dress, matching socks and shoes. She didn't want me to forget that I was the daughter of her heart. I dragged out of bed, and Amparo picked up the wet sheets. She wiped away tears from her face with the dry corners.

How do you remember love from your early years so you know when it's the real thing later? I stood there absorbing this feeling. I knew love because of Ana Maria and Amparo, poor and illiterate, with calloused hands rough on my skin and uneven nails that snagged my clothes. They were there, solid, accepting, while my mother and father led separate busy lives. If memory is hunger, like Hemingway's wife Hadley said in *A Moveable Feast*, then it, along with loss and regret, started here.

Ana Maria opened the window and door that led to the back patio. The hot humid air trapped in the bedroom eased out. It was wet outside. A quick crackle of thunder had ushered in an early spurt of rain. The previous night, thunder exploded like bombs, making us scream and bringing a torrential downpour. Down the hall, a white sheet still covered the hole in the wall by the maids' quarters and my mother now slept in a chair at night, guarding the entry into our third floor flat. Shots rang out often, mostly at dawn, from the spooky open space behind our building.

The island entered a state of military alert. A group of lawyers in militia uniform took possession of the Bar Association headquarters in La Habana. On July 6th, President Eisenhower reduced the sugar quota for Cuba by 700,000 tons, saying that this action amounted "to economic sanctions against Castro." Khrushchev retaliated by announcing that Russia would take the spurned sugar and, if need be, that artillerymen would defend Cuba with rockets. In La Plaza de la Revolucion, Castro spoke for hours on U.S. economic aggression. In the meantime, government officials ordered the owners of more than 600 American companies to present sworn statements showing their inventory, the first step toward nationalization.

"Hurry up and get ready," Ana Maria said, "you're going on a trip today."

"*A los Estados Unidos,*" I said. What an adventure! And then I'd be back home with Ana Maria and Amparo. Of course.

"There's a lot of packing to do still," Amparo added. I splashed in and out of the tub, then struggled into a dress and pulled on socks and shoes.

"Yiya is here," my mother called out from the living room.

A tall woman with a loud voice and broad hips, Yiya was a friend of the family. She came into my bedroom with a leash in her hand. She kissed everyone hello and went out into the patio where my dog lay in the sun. Yiya walked back in with Negrito in tow. He looked at me with sorrowful brown bulging eyes. His ears lay flat, his tail limp.

"Where's he going?"

"Negrito needs a new home for now," my mother said. Ana Maria stood next to her, frowning. "He can't stay here alone."

"Why, why," I cried, "can't he go with us?"

Yiya hurriedly waved good-by, and Negrito was gone before I could hug him. My mother, Ana Maria and Amparo continued a flurry of last minute packing. The baby chick, now fully grown, fluttered around my legs, no longer blue and yellow, but white and brown. I picked him up, but my mother took him from my arms and handed him to Ana Maria. "Here. For fricasee."

Ana Maria accepted the chicken, tucked it under her arm, and went back to last minute packing. What did that mean? Fricasee? There was too much activity to stop and get answers. "*Te queremos mucho, mi hija,*" Amparo said. "Write to us." I ran for the address book and scribbled their names and addresses.

"I will never forget you." And I never did, setting up a two-way stream of letters that forged a bridge to the island. Decades after my caregivers' deaths, I see their words – carefully saved treasures in an old wooden box -- as proof that love exists.

That afternoon, at the airport, I walked with my mother down a long hallway flanked by glass windows. My paternal grandparents, Amalia and Rafael, whom we hardly ever saw since my father left, leaned against the wall on one side and my mother's stepmother, Elsie, now a declared communist and family outcast, stood by the other. No one explained why we were leaving. No one shed tears. No mention was made of when we were going to see each other again. We waved good-by, walked out onto the tarmac, up the rickety steel steps and into the plane.

Up in the clouds, I looked down on the island sprawled like a sleeping crocodile on the Caribbean Sea. It got smaller and smaller and then disappeared. I opened my purse and retrieved a pad of onion skin paper. I wrote:

Querida Elsie,
A little girl on the plane left her gold bracelets in the bathroom when she went to wash her hands. They say that the Fidelistas sitting in front of me stole them. They're dressed in green uniforms and have big beards. Why would they do such a thing? Everyone is silent because they don't trust them. Why is that? I miss you so much already. Will you come and visit me for my birthday?
Te quiero mucho, Cecilita.

Elise never answered my questions. In her steady flow of letters, she steered clear of any mention of politics, nor did she describe the transformation of our island. Relatives told my mother that Elsie had remained a staunch communist until her last days.

UNSETTLED IN
LOS ESTADOS UNIDOS

All this, I said, is exceedingly clear…simple and explicit.
— Edgar Allen Poe

1.

My father waved his jacket furiously from side to side as he stood on the parapet of Miami International Airport that sultry, early evening on the 20th of July, when the air sat like a box around us, just six days short of the first official anniversary of Fidel's revolution in Cuba. The sun was bright orange and sinking, and the light started turning gray. Shadows fell from the air traffic control tower in the distance, and I descended the stairs from the airplane and stepped onto the tarmac. I walked toward my father as if on air, the last rays of sun reflecting off his thick aviator glasses, against a backdrop of tiny blinking lights.

Now known as the Gateway to Latin America, the airport opened for business in 1928 as the Pan American Airfield just south of the city of Miami Springs. Steady growth led to a massive expansion and, the year before our arrival, the airport added hangars for Eastern, National and Delta airlines. No one knew then that those first flights bearing Cubans in 1959 and 1960 would usher in a flood of refugees who would dramatically transform Miami's demographics, not only with Cubans but − later -- with thousands more disaffected and troubled immigrants from the rest of Latin America and the Caribbean attracted by the city's Spanish-speaking culture. Today, MIA ranks first in the nation by percentage of international flights and second by volume of international passengers, behind only New York–JFK.

Perched on that open balcony of the airport, my father had no idea that he was a pioneer in the overwhelming rush of immigration into South Florida, and one of the first to build the area into the international mecca that it is today. He was simply a happy man welcoming his family into a foreign land where he thought he would eventually make his fortune. It is this image of him smiling and shouting for joy that I see when I tell others what my father felt about me then because it expresses an emotion I want to keep alive. I suppose it was love, and it was directed at me, so that meant he once loved me. It is important to me to know that and to write it here.

He did once love me.

My mother and I stepped up to a long narrow counter. She wore an elegant two piece suit. The agent stamped our passports, eyed my mother and gave a low whistle. Then we followed the crowd into the waiting area, crossing an invisible barrier so palpable it suspended my breath. That evening in its early darkness, I moved into a place that irrevocably altered my life.

It felt as if I had thrown off my mosquito net and the light changed, as if I were coming up for air after a long submersion into a turbid sea, like cutting through a sticky spider's web, or stepping into a waterfall. It was as if I had peeled off a strip of adhesive tape from a piece of writing and the letters came off, imprinted backwards. As imaginary as it was real, that line separated Then from Now. Stepping over it, I tell you again, was such a distinct step I can relive it over and over again and it always feels the same. In this new world, I began to love my father and hate my mother then love my mother and hate my father. The long walk on the tarmac toward the airport marked a transition from proper doctor's daughter to someone I had to work hard to define.

"*Pelonita!*" my father shouted when he was close enough to touch. It was his pet name for me that meant, literally, hairless one. (Several months before he left Cuba, my mother had shaved my head as a cure for thin hair. But by now it had grown to almost chin length.) His grinning face sparkled in the twilight of that early evening. When had he first used that term of endearment? I felt the same warmth I did when I read his inscription on a framed photo he gave me before leaving La Habana: "*Para la hijita mas linda del mundo, del papito mas lindo del mundo.*" To the prettiest daughter in the world from the best looking dad in the world.

He certainly did look handsome in the picture: horn-rimmed glasses, white shirt, tie, dark gray jacket, and the smooth olive of a freshly shaved face. Decades later, we would stop speaking. After everything that was to come, it was better that way. But at the airport that night, with the runway behind us and the sun now completely hidden, he pulled me from my mother's melancholic silences and into the world of the living. I clamped my arms around his legs, fiercely, while he hugged my mother as best he could. Did we cling for long minutes, waiting for the frozen grief of separation to melt as we curled inside of a hug? No. Here we were, reenacting a family reunion like the one so many thousands of Cuban families experienced, yet each one of us was poised on the brink of a separate adventure where our lives would intersect on brief occasions and then take different turns. Did we know that the unspoken grief which lingered had to do with mourning the past and struggling to accept that nothing would ever be the same?

The adventure in America began when we climbed into my father's battered white Chrysler that smelled of wet leather and drove to the sleepy resort city of Miami Beach. On the way, colorful neon signs screamed unreadable words from doorways, sides of buildings, billboards. My father pointed to yellow flashing words. "Pick'n Chick'n," he read. "And those over there, the red words, are Joe's Hot Dogs." The signs were set off impressively against the night. We crossed the Julia Tuttle Causeway, a bridge where the water below churned in a mass of black waves. I smelled the salt and heard the slap against concrete pilings. Hundreds of art deco hotels greeted us on the other side, squatted short and stocky along tangled narrow streets. Decades later this area would be listed on the National Register of Historic Places, boasting the world's largest collection of Art Deco architecture erected between 1923 and 1943. Our destination, The Fontana Hotel, crouched alongside them on Collins Avenue, trying to look dignified but needing a coat of paint.

"I'm not making a lot of money now," my father said. His friend David had helped him secure a spot as a resident at Mount Sinai Hospital. He planned to revalidate his credentials as a physician and specialize in surgery. Taking our luggage inside the room, he stood by the door, ready to leave. "We'll look for an apartment tomorrow. Something small."

"Aren't you staying?"

"I have to go back to the resident's hall at the hospital," he said. "I'm on call." My mother hesitated, and then her face relaxed into resignation. Why hadn't he swept my mother off her feet and into his arms? Why did he leave so soon? His hand lingered on the doorknob, but my mother turned away to unpack.

"I have to live in the resident dorms for the next three years," he said. "There's no surviving otherwise. They'll pay me extra."

My mother accepted his explanation as the truth. I didn't know it yet, but we were already a broken family. For my father, this was the beginning of something big. For my mother, the American Dream was too difficult to imagine.

2.

Our first home was a sparsely furnished, one-bedroom apartment in a pink and white low-rise building in North Miami Beach, an affordable Miami suburban city of five square miles home to a large observant Jewish community. Today it is the fourth largest Haitian enclave in the United States with scattered pockets of Dominican, Peruvian, Jamaican, Bahamian and Cuban residents. The buildings are just as unassuming today as they were back in the sixties. Ours, as many are now, needed a new coat of paint. Rust streaked the shaky balcony railing. Most of the varnish had been scuffed off the wood floors. A brown water canal flowed alongside the street, its banks overgrown with weeds, chopped off tree roots and brambles.

Slow-cooking black beans and *lechon* were not a part of our new life; we had no maid, no cook. Instead, my mother served nightly TV dinners: meatloaf, fried chicken, mashed potatoes, corn, apple muffin all packed tightly in place on aluminum tins I collected to use as toys. Sometimes she scrambled or fried eggs and scooped them onto a plate of rice. Her plantains, scorched pieces of overripe banana, dripped with oil.

"I never had to learn," she said, "because I always had a cook. And I hate cooking."

My mother made do with a few cheap plates and pots she bought at the Pic 'N Pay. All of our furniture, china and glassware, locked away in a warehouse, waited for an apartment big enough to house them. Eventually my father sold the mahogany dining room he had shipped, but the china, glassware and books, including a handsomely bound dictionary-encyclopedia in Spanish, made their appearance several years later in a house my parents bought in Miami. These items inextricably bound me to Cuba, and I still cling to them, reminders of a previous identity forced into a metamorphosis with which I would never be truly comfortable. Like my parents, I, too, had one foot on the island and one in the new land, a situation that to this day refuses to go away.

I wish I could say my mother kept up with the relatives, writing long letters at our rickety dining table, placing desperate calls to the island, waiting anxiously for each new arrival as most Cuban families did in those early years.

Instead, she wrote a few times and then stopped altogether. As the years passed, she met the news of the arrival in Miami of her sixteen aunts and uncles and thirty-two cousins with a shrug.

"I'm too busy trying to survive," she said, struggling with a plastic basket filled with dirty laundry. "I don't have the energy to visit anyone."

During the day, she diligently practiced at a rented typewriter or a cash register in the hopes that she could get a job in an office or a store. At night, she lay alone on her double bed, staring at the ceiling, hugging her pillow. I slept on a twin bed shoved against the wall next to hers.

When I was sick with a sore throat, which was often, my mother sat on the edge of my bed writing on yellow pads the stories I dictated in Spanish and English about fairies, Santa Claus, reindeer, and dogs. These stories flew into my mind out of nowhere, and I created characters and scenes with joy. It was at this time that I can say my literary aspirations were born, the feeling all mixed up with the love and closeness of my mother, the bond of sharing language in isolation. After my mother wrote down the stories, I stapled them together with a title page and created a table of contents. These were my first books.

My father remained on the periphery of our lives. We saw him only on Sundays when we drove in our old station wagon to pick him up at the hospital. I missed his vibrant, loud voice in contrast to my mother's quiet one.

"Why can't you live with us?" I often asked him. My mother never did.

"I'm always on call. I can't leave the hospital," his answer always the same.

During these outings, my parents barely spoke to each other and never touched. Could it be that my father was there only to see me? Looking back, I see a man who had already started marking the time to his next departure, maybe planning to make his getaway with me in tow.

The Sunday ritual, magical when all three of us were together, included fishing off the bridge in Crandon Park which occupied the northern part of the island of Key Biscayne, east of Miami and south of Miami Beach. Crandon, an 800-acre urban park once the largest coconut plantation in the United States, housed a zoo and skating rink, both later demolished. On the southern tip of the island, the small village of Key Biscayne was then and is now considered to be one of the most exclusive communities in America with multi-million dollar homes owned by Fortune 500 executives and celebrities. In 1969, President Richard Nixon—renowned for his Cuban connections in the Watergate scandal that led to impeachment, built his Florida White House there facing the ocean.

On the bridge, while swinging bait and tackle over his head, did my father ever dream he would live on Key Biscayne?

But on these Sunday outings, my father contentedly concocted an oatmeal paste, threw it into the water and then lowered a wire frame that held rows of thin hoops. Within minutes, we caught dozens of sardines. He cut them up and used them as bait to catch bigger fish. While my father and I scurried up and down the bridge, happy in the sun, my mother fixed her gaze on the horizon.

"Maybe I'll see Cuba," she said. It was the only indication that she missed her home, her relatives, her job. My father grunted, ignoring her. As for me, I dove headfirst into our new life; everything was exciting, dazzling.

When it was time for lunch, my father threw all the fish back into the ocean. He took a bag of charcoal and dumped it into a park grill planted in the ground. After sprinkling it with lighter fluid and setting a match to it, he barbecued three huge Porterhouse steaks he had stored in a cooler. He read medical books as he waited for the meat to cook. My mother sat still in her aluminum chair. After our meal, she dropped my father off at the hospital, and we drove back home. She never hugged him good-by or complained, never argued, stoically bearing the separation. What was she thinking? Why didn't she tell him she was lonely? Why didn't she see what was coming?

3.

We weren't alone in our North Miami neighborhood. My best friend Cristy, from the balcony next door in La Habana, had left the island with her family some months before we did and now lived in a house nearby.

"Cristy, Cristy," I yelled with joy as we hugged.

Then, she skipped to her room and came out with two hula hoops. I stepped into the smaller, pink one and furiously churned my waist around with no success. Cristy swung the large blue hoop into the air and moved to a rhythm only she could hear. The hoop twirled around her steadily.

"Let's do the Twist," her teen-aged sister Pilar shouted, turning on the radio and pumping the volume. "This is Chubby Checker. Let's do it!" She shuffled her feet from side to side and swung her arms at the same time. I abandoned the hoop that refused to twirl around my waist and copied her movements. This I could do! I twisted back and forth and even down low almost touching the floor with my knees. There had been nothing like this in La Habana!

Pilar switched to a new station and changed her step: "And this is the Mashed Potatoes," she exclaimed. She made one foot fly to the left and the other to the right. I copied the move and in five seconds rocked along with her while Cristy, not a good dancer, hula hooped with fervor. On the radio, Elvis Presley shouted "you ain't nothin' but a hound dog," instantly supplanting Ricky Nelson as my new hero! In the kitchen, my mother and Lena, Cristy's mother, oblivious to the effects of rock and roll on us, talked politics, shaking their heads at the new developments on the island.

"*Ese desgraciado*," Lena cried, referring to Fidel as the disgraced one. Her tirade burst through the music.

The Cuban telephone and electric companies, the oil refineries and sugar mills now belonged to the state. And, during the First Congress of Latin American Youth in August, Che Guevara told the group: "Our Revolution has discovered by its methods the paths that Marx pointed out."

"How can we ever go back?" my mother exclaimed in despair.

But I didn't care about going back. I was too happy playing with Cristy again and enjoying all the new sensations of my new world. Living in *los Estados Unidos* was going to be just fine.

However, in a few weeks, Cristy's family – the only people we knew from Cuba -- left. "Cristy's father got a job in Puerto Rico," my mother said. "He and Lena couldn't learn the language here. It was too hard for them. Puerto Rico is a lot like Cuba." But even if my mother wanted to leave, she – dependent on my father – did not have this option. Before they departed, Cristy's father, a TV salesman, brought us a used black and white set. It did not replace Cristy, but it filled the evening emptiness: Friday night with Mitch Miller, Saturday morning with the Three Stooges, Dale Evans, and the Lone Ranger, Sunday night with Lawrence Welk.

The TV set helped my mother purge emotions.

One night, I found her sitting in the dark, the TV as the only light in the room. She inched closer to the screen, transfixed by the final scene of the movie *Imitation of Life*. On the screen, a young woman screamed with anguish and pounded her fists on the casket bearing her mother away.

My mother sobbed and wailed something indecipherable. I held out my arms to comfort her, my palms sweating, but she collapsed on the couch, burying her face in tightly crossed arms.

I didn't understand then the bewilderment, loneliness, pain, and fear of my mother, an orphan and abandoned wife, far from the comfort and security of home, with few friends, no job, and no way out of the trap into which she had willingly walked when she left the island. If my father didn't want to be with my mother, why didn't he leave her in Cuba? Was it me he was really trying to rescue from a system he believed would enslave anyone who stayed?

4.

With Cristy gone, David Cohen and his family moved to center stage in our lives. David had been instrumental in helping my father leave Cuba. He ferried my father's yacht to South Florida, helped him sell it, transferred money from the island into a U.S. bank account for him, and pulled strings to get my father the position as a resident at Mount Sinai Hospital. David, a car salesman doing business in La Habana, met my father in the early fifties. My father bought a shiny 1955 Chrysler from him, and the two men hit it off. Later, I heard, but had no way of proving, that David had ties to Meyer Lansky, a reputed South Florida gangster rumored to control much of Cuba's nightlife. Without David, my father's start in America might have been a lot harder. My father lived with him before he moved to the "resident's hall," and now the loyal friend opened his North Miami ranch-style house to my mother and me. We became frequent visitors.

Many years later, my father stopped speaking to David at the urging of a jealous third wife. He became a forgotten friend, just as I turned into a forgotten daughter. It was a pattern my father played out as he discarded people who stood in the way of his new, affluent – and romantic -- life in America. But in the sixties, David was my father's best friend. And my father relied on him to keep his wife and daughter out of trouble.

I was forced to learn English to communicate with the Cohens. That first summer, the English language felt like the harsh taps of a hammer on my head. That was when I was listening. When I wasn't, the words sounded like the hum of bees, simply a background noise. Then, suddenly, miraculously, before the summer was over, I spoke English.

"Stop it! Stop it!" I yelled at David's daughters who were poking me with their fingers. The twins Sherry and Elise, curious six-year-olds just like me, were bewildered at the Spanish I spoke. As Sherry and Elise jumped on me, David scolded them.

"Nothing will happen to you," he told me. "I'm your second father."

I understood those words and fell in love again, forgetting Ricky Nelson and Elvis Presley. Tall, with a shock of slicked-back, black hair that fell softly over his eyes, David laughed with joy and stormed in anger at the same time. His hooked nose made him look like an elegant Middle Eastern prince. He talked to me and hugged me often, both of which my father rarely did.

"David, look after my daughter when I'm not there," my father said once.

"But Rafael, she's your daughter," David had answered.

"I can't do it right now." But it was not just a momentary solution while my father toiled as a resident. David told me later that throughout the years my father would ask him to keep an eye on me, saying he was not fit for the job, and that my mother was not either. Today, David looks eagerly at a picture of my mother stretched out on a lounge chair at his home back then. I can see a gentle romantic gleam in his eyes. "She was so fragile," he says in a low voice. "So fragile."

The opposite of my father. David remembers him as driven, resilient, diligently working to regain his professional credentials, envisioning a future of material wealth and emotional freedom with his mistress, one – when he realized I was too unruly to control -- where I did not prominently figure.

At the Cohen's, since I had never seen wall to wall carpeting before, I stepped carefully, afraid to stain what seemed to be soft luxurious fabric. Central air-conditioning, rather than wall units, cooled off the house. Heavy draperies covered all the windows and made it dark inside. In the family room, a bar laden with bottles of liquor stretched across three walls. Two giant poodles, Onyx and Calypso, guarded a locked cabinet filled with rifles in one corner, and, in the backyard, a pool glistened under the sun. The smell of dog hair, cigarette smoke and dampness hung over everything.

It took ten minutes for my mother to drive us to the Cohen's home from our apartment in her newly acquired car, a used olive green Ford station wagon that looked like an army tank. David, who became my mother's confidant and intermediary in my parent's marriage, had helped her choose it from his lot. The leather was splitting on the seats and rust was beginning to corrode the chrome handles on the doors, but the price was right.

"Sit in the back and don't talk," my mother ordered from behind the wheel. This was the first time she had driven a car. She drove slowly and carefully, stopping at every sign and looking at all the corners several times before she accelerated. "David gave me lessons in the parking lot and said you were safer in the back seat." There weren't seatbelts then.

Each morning, we picked up the twins and headed to the summer morning movies at the 163rd Street Shopping Center, a thriving open air strip of stores built in 1956 that included Burdines, Richards and Woolworth. Now it is an enclosed mall with colossal metal arches and translucent canvas ceilings housing a variety of discount stores. David's wife, Sheila, a slim woman with jade green eyes and a cloud of dark hair, never let me go without offering me a drink of water.

"*Agua?*" she asked.

In the afternoon, we headed to Victory Park. It resembled a small forest. Pine needles and pine cones covered the ground. A merry-go-round, swings, and slide formed the centerpiece of a small clearing. My mother sat on a bench while the twins and I climbed to the top of the monkey bars, shouting and laughing. One afternoon, another family came to the park. The children spoke in Spanish to each other. They pointed at me. I spoke English to the twins who were on the other side of the slide and hadn't seen the new kids.

"Look at that girl," one said. "Her blouse looks funny on her. It's too small! We can see her stomach! Ha, ha, ha. She looks stupid!"

I stared at them. *I speak Spanish! Can't you see that by looking at me?* I screamed inside my head. I felt a strange sense of separation from myself. The two Spanish-speaking kids hadn't realized I spoke their language. I remained invisible, as far as they were concerned, part of the American world they were still trying to figure out. Did that mean that the English words I had just exchanged with Sherry and Elise were free of the Cuban accent? Could they even tell the difference yet?

I ignored them, feeling absolutely no connection. It was a sensation I would often feel later, as new arrivals tried to befriend me; however, I had already sailed beyond on the continuum of the melting pot, the ruthless assimilation process into America, and did not want to be friends.

5.

In the fall, I walked into Mrs. Abel's first grade class at Fulford Elementary School, named after a Coast Guard captain who – sailing home from the Spanish American War in 1897-- spotted what became North Miami Beach and staked out a homestead. All the students stared at me. They laughed when I tried to pronounce words I couldn't get quite right. I wanted to make new friends, be accepted, so I laughed, too.

The teacher handed me crayons and pencils as thick as two thumbs, and paper that felt like newsprint with three inch spaces between the lines. I added, subtracted and wrote block letters with ease. At Colegio Kopi in La Habana, I had black and white copy books and long, slim pencils and elegant pens.

"I think we should move her to the second grade," Mrs. Abel told my mother two weeks later.

"No. I do not wish that to happen. I don't want my daughter with older children."

What! I couldn't believe it! I wanted to be with the older group. "*Mami,* the teacher thinks I'm a good student, better than the others," I protested, "and the children in the second grade have a lot more fun in the cafeteria. I want to go to the second grade."

"The schools are better in Cuba," she answered, curtly. "That's the only reason you know more. It's dangerous to be with kids who are older than you are."

With that, my mother sealed my fate. The next day I returned crestfallen to class, glancing with longing at the second graders who filed past at lunchtime. If only I were one of them, I sighed. Since that disappointing beginning to my school career in America, I've often wondered if, had I been placed a year ahead, I would I have skipped the turbulent years in school. Already, my first report card pointed to trouble. Next to a row of As, the teacher had checked off the "self-control" column. Despite struggling with the new language, I talked to everyone who sat around me and laughed boisterously in the playground.

One day, rather than spend the time to walk around on the sidewalk, I climbed the wall that separated my classroom from the playground to get out to the fun more quickly. The teacher, watching, promptly called my mother.

My mother, once again at a parent-teacher conference, didn't know what to say.

"It's obvious your daughter is bored," said the teacher.

"She has high spirits," my mother answered.

Nothing could move my mother to advance me to second grade, and she reiterated her points firmly. I realized later that one advantage of having a mother who speaks English is you never have to translate. A disadvantage is that she doesn't need you to survive in a foreign land. Years later, I noticed that the families of my Cuban friends constantly called upon them to help negotiate important matters with American neighbors, store clerks, or government workers. I saw that they enjoyed a closer bond with their parents, while I was dispensable. Even so, I felt proud that my mother spoke English and navigated the school system like a professional. Language, like a lot of other things, is a double-edged sword.

In this new land, students commonly practiced leaving the building in case of fire. We silently lined up outside in monthly drills. Then we learned a new procedure. The teachers announced we were going to practice how to survive in case of a bombing. When the bell clanged, they instructed us to file into a large room, crawl underneath a desk and stay there until given a sign. None of the students knew my country was connected with the events that spurred these bomb drills.

But I knew. David Cohen had told my mother that Cuba and the United States were getting close to a declaration of war. While I couldn't totally comprehend the concept, I felt nervous. Did war mean my relatives in Cuba would be bombed? Or that my parents and I would be the victims of the bombing?

That September, Castro announced he was accepting Russia's offer of rockets to repel a rumored invasion from *los Americanos*. In October, presidential hopeful John F. Kennedy accused President Eisenhower of creating "communism's first Caribbean base" in Cuba because he was soft on Fidel. Eisenhower countered by announcing a ban on all U.S. exports to Cuba. Fidel showed his muscle by taking over nearly 400 private enterprises, including all the banks and sugar mills, 18 distilleries, 61 textile mills, 16 rice mills, 11 cinemas, and 13 stores. My father shook his head. News about Cuba plunged him into foul moods, making him pace up and down or smash his fist into his hand.

"I did the right thing to leave Cuba," he said, "Our country is lost, totally lost, LOST!"

I, on the other hand, felt a big wall going down on everything I had known before on the island. While I reveled in my new experiences, I wanted to feel connected with my relatives and friends. It took weeks for letters from Cuba to arrive. In the last letter, our old housekeeper, Ana Maria, explained the fate of Negrito, my Boston Terrier. Squinting at Ana Maria's wobbly printing, I realized that she could barely write. She had been one of the peasants who Fidel wanted to help. I didn't consider this then, but I wonder now: how could a man with brilliant ideas such as a national literacy campaign – which gives voice to the people -- be capable of snuffing out the individual freedoms of an entire island? Must progressive ideas ultimately end up in a repressive system of government? These questions haunt me.

"He went crazy without you," Ana Maria wrote about the dog. "The woman who took him over tied him up outside on a tree, and he went crazy." I felt desperate because I wanted to find out more, but calls to Cuba were not allowed at that time. I was isolated from all the relatives, my father was never home, and conversations with my mother were limited. Most of the time, she lay in bed with her face toward the wall.

"Maybe we could communicate by telegram!" I offered.

"Too expensive," said my mother. She stood by the window, silently staring out, something she did when her depression overwhelmed her. Eventually, I just left her alone at these times.

6.

Orange and black paper streamers hung down from the ceiling in Fulford's cafeteria. Pumpkins with carved out faces and candles inside pushing out the darkness stood on tables alongside punch and popcorn. Students jostled each other, showing off painted faces in multicolored streaks. I stood in the center of the action dressed in the Snow White costume I wore at the Colegio Kopi ballet performance in La Habana the year before. The sleeves gripped my arms, and the skirt trapped my legs.

That October, 1960, at my first Halloween party, I looked longingly at the many first and second graders dressed like "Beatniks:" black tights, black turtleneck and a cigarette held in a long ivory holder. I sensed that this costume made a statement about personal freedom. I later learned that the attire represented the 1950s Beat Generation – including writers Allen Ginsburg and Jack Kerouac -- predecessors of the Hippie Generation that would have such an impact on me.

How different I looked from my fellow students. But only on the outside. My spirit had taken flight already to a place my parents could never go. I wanted to feel safe in this new country, but I also wanted to explore and do new things. The beatnik get-up appealed to my desire to be grown up and live an exciting life.

That evening, I ran from house to house in the Cohen's neighborhood. What joy to get handfuls of candy for simply yelling "trick or treat!" The twins wore "Beatnik" costumes and ran a lot faster than I could in my long dress, so I hiked up the skirt around my thighs and tied it in a knot. My father said he couldn't leave the hospital for the occasion, but my mother and Sheila, the twins' mom, rushed to keep up and waited on the sidewalk while we filled our bags at each door. *Next year I'll be a Beatnik, and be free and look mysterious and grown up*, I thought. I instinctually understood that I could do what I wanted in the presence of my constantly distracted mother.

In November, after Kennedy's election, my mother's depression lifted over the possibility of the United States ousting Fidel from power. We heard rumors that Cuban exiles were training secretly in Guatemala for an invasion. Small guerilla bands of Cubans on the island still resisted the regime, skirmishing with Fidel's troops deep in the Escambray Mountains with air cover by Cuban piloted American planes. While the details buzzing around in my parents' conversations didn't form a concrete picture in my head, I sensed danger and turmoil and felt nervous. My father once again used these new incredible developments to justify his decision to come to the U.S. and start over.

"Fidel will be there for life," he told David as we sat down to our first Thanksgiving dinner. "The important thing is that no one takes my money again. I lost everything. I'm going to stay in this country and be a physician. I have to work hard because I am not a rich man. I'm not thinking of going back like all the other exiles doing nothing with their lives, just waiting for Fidel to fall."

David brandished huge knives above his head and carved a 20-pound turkey while Sheila brought in brimming bowls of corn, mashed and sweet potatoes, cranberry sauce and biscuits. How different from our roasted pork, black beans and rice! The twins' grandparents were visiting from New York, and everyone laughed and talked, including my parents who sat side by side giving no indication of their personal troubles.

Suddenly the two poodles, Onyx and Calypso -- right under my feet -- jumped at each other's throat in a maelstrom of roars. I could feel their breath on my ankles. I didn't move, hoping their jaws wouldn't clamp down on my flesh. Trembling, I slowly got up from the table. Everyone else laughed. "It's just a father and son fight," David said about his dogs. "You have to toughen up. This isn't Havana where everything was easy, you know." I thought of my spacious apartment in Nuevo Vedado, my doll house, my dog, our two loving housekeepers. Things were easier back home, I agreed. But this America was interesting.

Later that night, David disciplined his daughters with a belt. They had uttered "curse words"-- words I couldn't make out at all. I looked in horror at the long strip of leather David pulled from his waist. He took the girls upstairs to the bedroom. I heard the sad moans from the girls. It was a terrible ending to the festivities. I felt lucky; my mother's slaps were nothing compared to the strap.

Christmas Eve – *Noche Buena* -- this first year of exile was the coldest on record in what were usually warm winters in South Florida. No one we knew from Cuba was here yet and the Cohens were Jewish, so for this holiday my father picked us up for an outing that was just the three of us: a trio of Cuban immigrants, packed next to dozens of tourists, riding the trolley in the halcyon days of South Beach's Lincoln Road, a once favorite vacation destination for my parents. A trendy shopper's delight in the Art Deco district, Lincoln Road featured luxury department stores like Bonwit Teller, Saks Fifth Avenue, and even Cadillac and Packard car dealerships. The pedestrian walkway showcased gardens and fountains reflecting the Miami Modern Architecture, or "MiMo," style that architect Morris Lapidus pioneered in the 1950s.

But the 1965 opening of the trendier Bal Harbor Shops, a few miles north, lured away big name retailers and the area declined into a poor retirement community, nearing total disintegration. In the late 1980s, however, savvy investors began to rebuild South Beach. Now, it is an international tourist attraction and the world's top choice for night life.

On the trolley, the cold air whipped my face, and I hid behind heavy plastic curtains installed by the doors against the elements, trying to stay warm in a thick hooded red coat my father had bought at the Goodwill outlet. This was a new kind of cold, nothing I had ever experienced in La Habana. We got off to look inside the windows of the different stores and then jumped back on for warmth. We did this for the entire length of Lincoln Road. I chatted nonstop with my father; my mother kept silent. Once when I asked my mother why she so seldom spoke, she answered: "that's who your father fell in love with." If tension existed between my parents that night, I was oblivious. The lights flooded the streets, and we watched the tourists from the north strolling in the chilled air as if it were summer. *"No tienen frio?"* I marveled that they weren't cold.

On Christmas Day, my father drove from the resident hall to share a few hours with us. He sat in a chair watching me play with what Santa Claus had brought: a record player, a record by the popular Kingston Trio and a baby doll with a stroller. The record player was the best gift and soon, when the Beatles took my new world by storm, it was always on with "I Wanna Hold Your Hand." That year no one said anything about Los Reyes Magos, our traditional Three Kings celebration on January 6. I left my shoe out anyway, but no presents greeted me when I woke up.

The trappings of our island life were being shed, layer by layer.

7.

This is why I liked my new home better than La Habana: birthday parties at Greynold's Park – the site of an old rock quarry and Seminole Indian trading post -- with paddle boats on a lake, minnows swimming right off shore, ducks walking around and a rock castle on a hill; the Barnum and Bailey Circus; the school play *A Midsummer Night's Dream* where I was a fairy; an arts and crafts program where I received first place for a nifty bowl and spoon I designed out of clay; blond, blue-eyed fellow student John Kelly; a playground potato sack race; a second hand bike I painted pink in the utility room of the apartment building, then rode just to the edge of the brown water canal, veered to the right and fell into a heap of weeds; and the Beatnik costume I finally wore on my second Halloween.

I was a busy seven-year-old in 1962, but I still found time to write long letters to my relatives in La Habana, detailing my new life while holding tightly to my old world. Unlike my mother, I looked forward to hearing about the activities of our two housekeepers, Ana Maria and Amparo, my mother's stepmother Elsie, my mother's Tio Cesar, and my paternal grandparents, Amalia and Rafael. All answered my epistles, showing the much needed interest that my parents did not, could not, provide.

In La Habana, my parents lived intense lives that often did not include me, but all the other people around me readily filled the vacuum. Here in this new land, my parents' lack of attention translated into a silence sometimes impossible to overcome. I read the letters over and over, committing them to memory: Ana Maria's big sprawling pencil handwriting and Elsie's tight fountain pen cursive. All spelled love. Once, Elsie even included a tiny card with stick figures she had drawn. For the skirts, she pasted miniscule shells from the sea. Captivated by her imagination and full of longing, I didn't know she was circumventing the lack of greeting cards for sale on the island because of the U.S. embargo.

By writing to my relatives, I practiced Spanish that, without knowing, quickly took a back seat to a new language. We did not discuss Fidel, but I later learned that Elsie championed Castro's campaign to redistribute agricultural land while my paternal grandparents condemned the regime for forcing the editor of *Bohemia,* the island's main cultural and political magazine, to flee after he accused Castro of submitting to "Russian vassalage."

My father continued his tirades against Elsie and my mother scolded me when she saw me writing to her. But my need for love overcame political ideology. I remained unmoved and kept writing.

"Politics make me sick," my father declared. "I don't want to know anything more about Fidel."

In Miami, the U.S.-sponsored Cuban invasion was no longer a secret. On April 14, 1961, Brigade 2506, named after the serial number of one of its members who died accidentally during training, set off by sea from Nicaragua's Puerto Cabezas to land at Playa Giron. Luis Somoza, the country's dictator, watched from the quayside. In the early hours of April 15, U.S. planes began bombing Cuba. But then Kennedy abruptly cut in half the number of B-26 aircraft bombers to be used in air support, and hundreds of Brigade 2506 either died or were taken prisoner on Playa Giron. History tells us that, from the beginning, Kennedy didn't like the idea of U.S. military intervention. He wanted Castro's overthrow to appear to be the work entirely of the exile community so that he could deny U.S. involvement. But White House CIA Director Allen Dulles and Chief of Operations Richard Bissell realized strong support was essential to the success of this mission: if U.S. air craft did not support the Cuban brigade from the air, and if no U.S. battleships floated offshore ready to back up the exile fighters, then the invasion would fail.

That's exactly what happened. Dulles and Bissell did not tell Kennedy that with 200,000 troops and militia at his disposal, Castro would have no trouble overpowering 1,300 volunteers, most of whom had no battlefield experience. Later Kennedy admitted to his brother he wished he had permitted the use of U.S. ships to back up the exiles. In less than a year, believing Kennedy to be a weak president, Soviet Union leader Nikita Khruschev and Castro began installing nuclear missiles on the island —only ninety miles from Florida—a decision that precipitated the Cuban Missile Crisis and brought the world to the brink of nuclear war.

"*Es un comunista,*" my father declared about Kennedy. "Communists are everywhere in the world." As a result, I reinforced my belief that communists were dangerous people who not only took our homes but also wanted to kill us. My father often reminded everyone that, had he not left Cuba when he did, the communists would have killed him in his office.

Even my mother came out of her lethargy. "*Es un sin verguenza,*" she said, calling Kennedy shameless for not supporting Brigade 2506. "He doesn't know what it is to lose his country."

As for me, the talk about Cuba conjured images of death. Were people we loved going to die? Were we safe here in the United States? The frowns and silences of my parents did not offer a clue, so the tension and fear continued to feel like the familiar burden of a mosquito netting hampering every move. But our political situation diminished in importance compared with the personal emotional turmoil that was to come.

8.

The springs of the back seat in the station wagon pushed through the padding and into the small of my back. I plumped up my pillow and twisted into a new position. My mother, at the wheel, accelerated across the Julia Tuttle Causeway connecting Miami to Miami Beach and turned into a dark side street off the parking lot of Mount Sinai Hospital. I glanced out the window: spotlights swept the black sky like slow-motion windshield wipers. At eight years old and already well versed in cold war ideology, I readily understood when someone at school explained the lights were trying to uncover Russian enemy aircraft. I knew it had to do with Cuba.

"Twinkle, twinkle little star," I whispered. I wanted to pray, but all that came out was "I wonder where you are." Was God up there? Was he watching over us?

"The communists are going to take over the world," my father said. "They've already moved into our homes back in La Habana and want to move here, too." The sweeping spotlights in our new country, he said, had to do with Russia installing missiles in Cuba pointing straight at the United States. I later learned that throughout the summer of 1962, Russia had been sending surface to air missiles to Cuba: a U-2 reconnaissance plane had captured aerial photos of 42 ballistic missiles with a 2,000 mile range.

That year, President Kennedy called for the mobilization of 150,000 reserves to fight the Russians in Cuba. For a second time, he had to decide whether or not to attack the island by air. Meanwhile, he dispatched a naval blockade -- 16 destroyers, three cruisers, an antisubmarine aircraft carrier and six utility ships -- to stop Russian vessels from reaching Cuba. While these details were unknown to me then, the atmosphere of tension and anxiety that surrounded my parents when they watched the news or listened to the car radio is vivid in my mind. Danger surrounded our home back on the island, and danger lurked in many corners in our new home, too. Was my father ever going to live with us in our apartment? Would we be safer if he did?

The old car shook to a stop, brakes screeching, then again crept along. My mother looked up at a building I couldn't recognize. She stopped, hopped out and peered through the bushes into a lit dining room. Her gaze slithered up to the second floor window. The curtains glowed from the inside. She jumped back into the car and drove off. She turned a corner, and I realized we were close to the resident dorms where my father lived at the hospital, just blocks from the spot where we picked him up on Sundays. Sometimes we went up to play ping pong in a vast recreation room overlooking Biscayne Bay. Other times, my father took a fishing line and threw it into the water behind the parking lot where we were stopped. My mother drove slowly up and down, sweeping each car with her gaze.

"Are we here to see *papi*?"

"*No creo que esta ahora.*" She didn't think he was here.

"*Porque estamos aqui?*" I had no idea why we had come. We had never just dropped in.

No answer as she swerved out of the parking lot and back onto another side street. The car rumbled a few blocks, bumping through potholes and over rocks. This time, she turned into the building's parking lot. She drove up and down the rows of cars until she stopped by my father's white Chrysler.

"*Esta aqui!*" I struggled into a sitting position. "Are we going to see him?" I sensed a new, rare energy in my mother, who, that night, had managed to throw off her habitual depression and embark on a fact finding mission against my father.

My mother dug into her purse and found a piece of paper. She tore a small square and scribbled something. She put it under the wiper. Then, she kicked the Chrysler's side door, muttering indecipherable words before jumping back in the car.

"I want to see *papi*," I shouted as we drove away.

Back home in our bedroom, I noticed my mother had ripped opened a letter addressed to her and flung it on her bed. She must have forgotten to put it away. At this late hour, my mother sat in the living room talking on the phone in English. I slipped a sheet of onion skin paper out of the envelope. I looked at my grandmother's cursive flowing in rich blue fountain pen ink. I read in Spanish: "*Don't let any woman take your place. Remember you have to fight for your family. Carinos, Cuca.*" Did this letter have anything to do with my mother going to check up on her husband? Was she trying to save her marriage?

I folded the thin paper and put it in the box with all the other letters from Cuba, missives that keep me connected to all that went on before. Why hadn't my mother knocked on the door of the apartment? Was there someone there with my father? I never found out the answers.

9.

My mother's secret life of woe and despair leaked out in bits and pieces. She befriended an American neighborhood woman who lived in a house that smelled like talcum powder and moth balls. Gladys was as tall as my father, six feet tall, with wide hips set off by a tight belt at the waist. Her red hair fell in ringlets to her shoulders. When I was around she spoke Spanish, -- she learned the language as a child in South America -- but on the phone, the conversations between her and my mother were in English, just like with my step-grandmother Elsie in La Habana. My mother didn't remember that I now had an excellent command of two languages.

"I don't know what to do," my mother moaned.

I heard only half her words as I watched The Three Stooges pummel each other. But the tones of frustration and anger held my attention.

"What do you think he was doing there? I think it's the same woman. She is so cheap, so low class. Who is she? You're asking who she is?" my mother cried into the phone. "I know exactly who she is. She was the nurse in his office in La Habana. He brought her here to this country!"

Even then, I found this piece of news shocking. How could my father have dared? Did it mean that he loved this woman more than he loved my mother? Did it mean that he would never come home and spend the night? It was an unsettling thought.

Gladys visited us often in our apartment, and this cheered up my mother. She always brought over records of lively music from the twenties and thirties. When she came over, my mother shoved aside the typewriter and cash register that she practiced on and set out sparkling glasses. She squeezed four limes into water and ice and scooped in three teaspoons of sugar each. My mother energetically stirred the potent mixture, laughed and talked and gave us each a glass. The atmosphere became light and festive, and I joined in the conversation whenever I could, telling stories of my days in school. By then, I wrote all these school stories in multi-colored notebooks my mother bought at the Pic 'N Pay and saved them in a pile on the floor of the closet.

"Let's listen to this," Gladys cried gaily. She opened up my prized record player, adjusted the speed from 45 to 33 rpms, and placed the arm of the needle in the middle of a heavy black disc. "I used to dance to this when I was a girl."

Gladys swayed over to the center of the living room floor, and, wildly swinging her arms, she lifted the right leg, threw it in front of the left, leaned forward and then kicked it back. She did the same with the left leg.

"Come on, I'll teach you!" Her reddened freckled face creased with laughter.

I jumped up and copied her movements.

"This is the Charleston," Gladys said. "We did it in the South where I went to school. The men were wild about me. Don't you just love this song: *Ain't she sweet. See her walking down the street. And I ask you very confidentially, ain't she sweet!*"

I grabbed my rag doll, the one as tall as me that we had brought from Cuba. I strapped her feet to mine with the ribbons from her ballet shoes. Holding her close, balancing the merrymaking with the sorrow I could feel in my mother's heart, I danced wildly up and down the floor while Gladys kept up a steady rhythm with the Charleston step. The record stopped, and I tuned into the Lawrence Welk Show on the TV. We waltzed up and down in imitation of the dancers on the show.

My mother, watching us from a chair, laughed exuberantly, and I would have danced all night just to keep her laughing.

"Good night ladies," Lawrence Welk called out from the dance floor, as bubbles rained down from the ceiling.

10.

"What about Jim?" Gladys asked my mother one afternoon as we stopped at a gas station.

"I don't know." My mother smiled in a way that she never smiled at me. I saw her profile from the back seat of the station wagon. She climbed out and waited. A man wearing grey overalls with the name "Jim" stitched over his left front pocket walked up to her.

"I miss you," he said. Gladys turned around and talked to me loudly about my tests in school, but I wanted to listen to my mother's response.

My mother, dressed in black pedal pushers and a flowered sleeveless blouse, looked fresh and relaxed. Jim took the gasoline hose from the tank and started to gas up the car. She murmured something, and he looked her up and down. I frowned. Was Jim my mother's boyfriend? Did he want to marry her? I felt something eerie in my heart. Maybe I should tell my father that my mother had a boyfriend. What would happen to all of us if this were true? I didn't want my father to go any further away than he was already. I wanted him closer. Back with us.

"Here, take these." My mother handed me two small white pills when we arrived home. "You have a sore throat."

"I do?"

"Yes, you don't look well. You need to lie down to get better."

I took the pills.

When I woke up, my mother and Gladys were gone. In a daze, I stared at the ceiling. Shapes danced all around me, speeding up and down the wall and out the window. Then the door opened, and my mother looked in. I could hear Gladys in the background. The phone rang, and she walked back out.

"It's your father," my mother called from the living room. "Are you well enough to get the phone?"

I moved to the living room on a cloud.

"Who's there?" my father asked.

"It's Gladys," I whispered. My mother and Gladys had gone out to the hallway and were laughing about something. I struggled into full wakefulness.

"That witch. She's putting ideas into your mother's head. She is always talking bad about me."

"No, she's not."

"She is. I just know it. Women are all the same."

"Not me, *papi*, not me"

"No, *tu eres muy dulce*." My father always said I was sweet.

"But," I lowered my voice even more. "There's a man." For one confused moment, my loyalties split. If my father had a girlfriend, why couldn't my mother have a boyfriend? I wanted my mother to have a boyfriend. The feeling had something to do with evening up the score. I didn't want her to be a victim. But shouldn't my father know? I wanted to warn him my mother might leave him for Jim! But what if my father left her for whoever my mother always talked about on the phone? I couldn't decide what to do, and my stomach rumbled in protest.

"What?!"

"Jim. Jim is his name and he's ... he's *un americano*." I thought this astounding revelation would spur my father to reclaim his wife and patch up his marriage, but it did not. I never witnessed any exchange of words on the topic.

My mother tugged on the leash and led Onyx, the Cohen's black giant poodle, out of the station wagon. "Cecilita, don't open the door to anyone," my mother instructed me. "I have to go on several errands. Onyx is staying here with you to make sure nothing happens. Read your books. I won't be long."

By now, I had an impressive collection of books, Grimm's and Andersen's *Fairy Tales* my mother had picked up at a garage sale, short stories called *Habia Una Vez* Elsie had mailed from Cuba, and a set of The Bobbsey Twins and The Happy Hollisters. Writing my own stories, I tried to copy the styles of the authors of my new English books, Laura Lee Hope and Jerry West. I had collected most of these books by tricking my father into buying them.

"Please, *papi*, buy me these," I said, mesmerized at the shelves of books in the discount Met store on Coral Way. "I need them."

"We don't have money for anything but the basics!"

"But they are required in school," I lied. "I'll get bad grades." Incredibly, he believed me and purchased a new volume each time we went to the store.

Onyx hobbled up the stairs after my mother and limped into our apartment. He lay on his side next to the bedroom door and stretched out his legs, breathing deeply.

"What's wrong with him?"

"David says he had an operation," my mother leaned down to pet Onyx. "But that he will be all right. David says he is a good watchdog and that you will be safe with him. Gladys is out of town and Sheila and the children are traveling, so we're going to take care of Onyx."

But David was home. He had just called my mother on the phone. Could she be seeing David and Jim at the same time?

I petted Onyx, but he didn't move. He looked nothing like the lively dog snarling and barking at his son Calypso under the dining table that frightening Thanksgiving night.

"Here, take these pills. They're vitamins. And lie down to read."

"They look like the ones I took for my sore throat."

"No, they don't. Hurry up. I'm late. Come on, lie down."

I went to bed and took the pills with a glass of water my mother set down on the night table. She took up *The Bobbsey Twins at the Seashore* and handed it to me. I settled in bed with the book. Hours later, I woke up in a dark room. Dizzy, I moved slowly out of bed and to the hall. No one was home. Dimming light filtered through the living room window. I kneeled down next to Onyx, and he struggled up, panting, tongue out. He tried to stand on all four feet, but could not. He sat on his haunches and then slumped back down, unable to hold up his weight. A pool of blood had collected on the wood floor in the spot where he had been sitting.

I screamed.

The sound echoed throughout the apartment. Onyx whimpered and stretched down on the blood. My mother opened the front door. I turned toward her and saw her dark silhouette against the last light of the afternoon, blazing around her like a halo.

After that, my mother never left me alone again. Where she went and who she saw are still mysteries. I later realized that my mother used these tranquilizers to keep me out of the way while she took care of her complicated life. She could have been meeting Jim or David or my father. She could have been negotiating something: her future in this new scary land. Soon after, Gladys moved back to her Alabama home, and we never heard from her again. My mother did not return to the gas station, or, that I know of, try to date. More alone now than ever, she sank deeper into isolation.

As for Onyx, in a few weeks he felt well enough to dive into the Cohen's backyard pool, fetch balls and leap into the air.

11.

Our old station wagon bumped steadily south, turned east toward Miami Beach and shuddered to a stop in the parking lot of the Rascal House just before the road swept up into the 79th Street Causeway. The restaurant anchored a run-down, nearly abandoned, shopping center in a declining neighborhood, but this was my father's favorite breakfast place. My mother and I jumped out into the early morning heat-drenched air, laden with the moisture that signaled the end of school and the beginning of 1963's summer reading. I was nine, excelling in school with an active social life of friends and beach outings.

"Aren't we going on vacation? Isn't *papi* picking us up at home?"

"I'm going to make a stop here first."

"Why? We already ate!"

"Don't talk now."

I followed my mother inside to a back table. As if by magic, there sat my father, and next to him -- the mistress. Who knows how I knew? Something about this new land made all secrets erupt to the surface.

Back in Cuba, my father's infidelities were but unintelligible murmurs in a stream of loud conversation. In contrast, for these first three years of our lives in America, my mother and I had tangibly lived in the shadow of my father's mistress, a threat that lurked unseen but with the strength of a million ghosts. Now she was real. I shrank back, staring. My mother stared, too.

The woman had the blackest hair I had ever seen, slicked down with oil. Her face, a pale brown, revealed the angry traces of adolescent acne. Thickly painted black arches served as brows over eyes that never met mine. Her lips burned red, full and parted. She and my father sat before a feast of eggs sunny side up, bacon and ham, grits, hashed brown potatoes, a basket of muffins and pastries and coffee. Neither one moved.

Were they expecting us?

My mother pushed the table with her thigh, a quick hip movement I had never seen. Dishes clashed against silverware, and water slopped over glass rims. My mother shouted insults at my father. Her pain echoed throughout the vast dining room, attracting everyone's attention. My father spoke soothingly and slipped slowly out of his seat. He signaled to a waiter, dropped some bills next to his plate, took my mother by the arm, and propelled her outside. I stood by the table, alone with the mistress.

La querida. The loved one.

I looked at her eyes, but she was staring intently at something on the other side of the room. I backed away, fearful, bewildered, and slammed out of the restaurant and into the parking lot. My mother shouted outside; my father spoke softly. She banged on the hood of the car with her fist. He moved in closer as if to restrain her.

"We were supposed to go to New Orleans today!" my mother exploded.

Would she slap him?

"It's our vacation! Aren't your three years up as a resident in that terrible, terrible hospital? Aren't you going to come live with us like you said?"

Why didn't she slap him?

"Go home, and I will pick you up in a few minutes. We'll be on our way very soon. She's just a nurse from the hospital. I had to discuss a difficult case." Even when caught, my father denied any wrongdoing, and, my mother, wanting to believe, didn't call him a liar.

Instead, she placed her hands on her head and squeezed, eyes tightly closed. I looked at my father reproachfully. He stepped back onto the sidewalk, ignoring me. With an exasperated shrug, my mother turned, still holding her head, and threw herself into the driver's seat.

Why didn't my mother demand answers to her questions?

I slid into the back seat, and we drove home, humiliated. On that early morning drive, I bonded with my mother in ways I didn't understand. My mother, betrayed and defeated, now had ocular proof of my father's infidelity. Never me, I promised. In this, as in many other disasters in my mother's life, I absorbed her pain, her loneliness, the frustrating feeling of futility with which she lived, and the imagined – but real for her -- powerlessness that forced her into inaction. My protectiveness toward her grew with every new crisis, while resentment against my father expanded exponentially. These are the moments that define a child's adulthood, always irrevocable, unforgivable. Never me.

In less than an hour my father pulled up at the apartment, and we climbed into his car for the drive to New Orleans. I wrote in my diary, a shiny red travel journal with a key, about everything I saw out the window. However, I suppressed all details of that event, already written irrevocably into the notebook of my memory.

What would happen next? Would my mother leave my father? Could she?

"Aren't we going to get an apartment for the three of us?" my mother asked again.

"*Si, papi por favor.*"

How was it that my father could get away without answering any questions?

We drove all the way to New Orleans, that summer day of 1963. My father picked out a hotel on Bourbon Street, and we entered a room with a king sized bed. It was way past midnight. I plopped down to sleep, exhausted. My father lay on one side of me and my mother on the other, turning their faces to the wall.

12.

The bell rang. Hundreds of children spilled out of classrooms and into the playground at Fulford Elementary. Close to the street, parents struggled to drag bundles of newspapers out of their cars to a covered shelter, the hub of a newspaper drive that afternoon. My mother, parked on the curb, waited for me to help her take piles of papers from the car. I ran to get one bundle, struggled back with it and placed it in a corner at the same time and place that Billy dumped his papers. We bumped bodies. Loose papers under my feet acted like a sheet of ice, and I almost crashed to the floor.

"You Spic," he shouted, running off. A few children stopped and laughed. Another one echoed, "you Spic." Then another. I had never heard this word before. It sounded ugly, like "spit," but no one was spitting. The new word reverberated all around me, like echoes. I knew it meant to degrade. I stumbled over the newspapers and fled to my mother's car.

"They called me Spic," I said, giving vent to loud wails in the back seat. "What's a Spic? They yelled at me and laughed at me. The boy with the Bugs Bunny teeth started it. Am I a Spic?"

In those early years, my mother sometimes did think on her feet.

"It has something to do with being Cuban. *Pero no te preocupes*," she said. "Don't worry. *Los Americanos* don't know a thing about grammar. Just tell them that you know English better than they do."

Why hadn't I stood up to Billy? The shock of being socially ostracized with one short, swift word had been overwhelming, and I never forgot it. The experience forged forever my sense of being different, an unsettling sensation I would harbor throughout my life, a feeling of never having really arrived no matter how successful I became. And even when, decades later, my daughter graduated from Princeton University, and I sat in the audience next to the cream of the American elite – many the descendants of the first immigrants to this nation when the United States boasted only thirteen colonies -- my difference from them remained strong and palpable, disconcerting, regrettable. It defined me as a refugee from Cuba in the sixties, and it defines me now.

After that hurtful afternoon at Fulford, I didn't hear the epithet directed at me again, not because of any fundamental enlightenment on the part of the community at large but because the schools quickly filled up with Cuban children, the new majority. The American kids disappeared, their families running away to northern Florida or other states in a social phenomenon called "white flight," the large-scale migration of whites of various European ancestries from racially or ethnically mixed urban areas to more homogeneous regions.

But racial tension extended beyond the Cuban arrivals. This was 1963, during the time of the protest march from Selma, Alabama, to Washington, D.C. and Martin Luther King's speech, *I Have a Dream*. A Ku Klux Klan church bombing had killed four black girls in Birmingham. Students staged sit-ins at lunch counters, and civil rights workers organized voter registration drives throughout the south. School desegregation battles raged in the news.

The next day I got into a fight in the playground. But it wasn't with Billy. It was with Laverne, the first and only African-American student at Fulford Elementary. My mother didn't want me to be her friend, but I spoke to her anyway because I liked her. I thought it was neat that when she scratched her legs with her nails, she left big white streaks on her black skin. Every night I dialed her number on our "party line" -- often narrowly beating to the phone those with whom we shared it -- since we couldn't afford regular service.

That day, in line after lunch, we argued over a candy bar. I slapped Laverne and took hold of her neck. She kicked me, and we tumbled to the floor. One of the teachers ran up screaming. Another teacher rushed over, and they pulled us apart. One took me by the arm, the other grabbed Laverne, and they marched us into the principal's office.

I knew instinctively that as a white child, I would have no trouble convincing the authorities of my innocence. I used this knowledge to gain the upper hand.

"Who started this?" the principal demanded in a no-nonsense voice.

"She did," I answered, pointing at Laverne who hugged herself tightly with her head bowed. The principal looked at Laverne with an "I knew it" face.

"What do you have to say for yourself?"

"I dint," she whispered. "I dint do nothin."

"Yes, she did. She hit me first," I lied, "and grabbed my neck."

"Young lady, I will call your mother right now," the principal addressed Laverne. "You will not be able to come to school for a few days. Cecilia, go back to class."

Laverne sat next to me in Mrs. White's fourth grade class. Her voice floated above the rest when she joined in the Lord's Prayer in the morning. When she came back from being suspended, prayer had been banned in school after a Supreme Court ruling declared it unconstitutional. For me, it was just as well.

At catechism class on Saturdays, the Lord's Prayer ended with "and deliver us from evil, Amen," the Catholic version. But at Fulford, everyone kept on praying until "the power and the glory, forever and ever, Amen," the Protestant version. I felt disloyalty to something I couldn't name, so I stopped at the word "evil," stealing guilty glances at my classmates.

That first day back at school, Laverne showed courage. After the Pledge of Allegiance, she placed her palms together and whispered the Lord's Prayer all the way to the end. Then she sat down. The teacher ignored her, and the students laughed. Laverne did not look at me again for the remainder of the school year. I had many other friends, so I quickly forgot her then. But I remember her vividly today. Thoughts of the racial prejudice reenacted that day in the principal's office still bring forth shame and regret in my heart.

Days later, at lunch in the cafeteria, more trouble. I cradled my head in my arm and huddled in a corner. Loud laughter, the clattering of trays and scraping of chairs came in and out of hearing as if someone were playing with the volume of the radio. Was I crying? Was I sleeping? All the students filed outside and went back to class, but I stayed immobile. A deep sorrow had taken hold, and I couldn't push it away long enough to get up from the table. A teacher roused me from the trance and walked me into the principal's office for the second time that week.

The secretary called my mother, but it was my father who came to pick me up. It was his first time – and only time – that he went to school. My always too-busy father left all matters of disciplining and schooling to my mother, knowing full well, I later understood, her mental and emotional condition made her unfit for the role. Caught up in his personal visions of grandeur, and just as powerless as my mother, he could not stem the tide of family destruction. Tense, he sat in a chair, smelling of cologne, wearing a white shirt, tie and a pair of dark slacks. My father never went anywhere without a tie.

"Wha' hah-pen?" my father's English was not as good as my mother's.

"Your daughter seems to be having a problem," the principal said.

"She's just tired," my father said. "She's pooped."

"Maybe there's something bothering her?"

"I'll see about it."

"*Papi*, please move in with us," I said, as he led me to his car.

"*Pronto, pronto,*" he answered soon, soon, extending hope, and we drove away.

Not long after, a week before Thanksgiving of 1963, the country buzzed with the news of the president's assassination. The principal, gasping for air, announced over the public address system: "Boys and girls, President John F.

Kennedy has been assassinated in Dallas, Texas." We tried to make sense of those shocking words, sitting in silence for a long time. Mrs. White, so obese she rarely got up from her desk, lumbered slowly up and down the rows picking up scraps of paper or pencils as if to set something aright. She smelled of grease and sweat. We sat stiffly until the bell rang, and school was dismissed. It was November 22, my saint day, the day of Saint Cecilia, the patron of music, and my mother and I did not celebrate at dinner.

"This is worse than in our country," she commented, setting out white rice and *picadillo*. "There is no law and order here. Even Fidel, who is hated, cannot be killed in broad daylight." These words impressed upon me the invincible nature of Castro. I felt glad we were beyond his grasp, but a bit shaken up about safety in the United States. Later, I connected my mother's comment to a truth about the immigrant experience: no matter how corrupt or oppressive it is, there is no place like home.

13.

A band of kids screaming in Spanish swarmed all over the Carlyle Hotel at 1250 Ocean Drive, and I was one of them. As a ten year old in 1964, I didn't know that the abandoned, gutted Carlyle – with condos there selling today at more than a million dollars -- symbolized the rapid decline of South Beach, visible everywhere in our new neighborhood.

"Ra, ra, ra," we shouted, running up and down stairs and in and out the front door and all around the dilapidated, musty 1941 building. We carried plates of cookies and jugs of Kool-Aid to the once glittering hotel and threw raucous parties on the veranda, the radio – plugged into an outside wall outlet -- blasting "I Saw Her Standing There," "I Wanna Hold Your Hand," "It's All Over Now," "Where Did Our Love Go."

A door down from the Carlyle, Mudda and Fadda, owners of our new home, two squat 1934 buildings joined by a center courtyard, sat on the porch and spoke in Yiddish to each other. Mudda wore a loose print dress and flip flops, and Fadda sported baggy gray pants that pleated over a belt holding them up. His shirt buttoned all the way up to the neck. Oblivious to our noise, -- at more than 80 years of age and possibly hard of hearing -- they looked up every once in a while and answered garbled English questions from their tenants, most of them newly arrived Cuban families now flying into Miami by the hundreds. The couple -- part of a predominantly Jewish retirement community that began settling in South Beach after WWII—had purchased the Ocean Front Hotel with their lives' savings.

Today, throngs of revelers drink and dine on the veranda of the Carlyle and a hostess waves passersby to a table at the Ocean Front's exclusive Italian restaurant on the same porch where Mudda and Fadda sat alongside my parents, my father studying for his Foreign Board examinations, my mother gazing out to sea.

My father's stint as a resident at Mount Sinai Hospital had come to an end, and, still not making much money, he chose this beach-front, run-down Deco apartment because of the low rent and proximity to his new job as physician assistant -- a position his friend David helped him obtain. Miraculously, my father had kept his word, and my wish had come true: all three of us lived together again. I felt happy and secure. My father worked long hours, but he came home every night now. They still didn't display much affection, but my parents appeared more relaxed, engaged in quiet conversations and never argued.

Despite the new family peace, my father appeared restless and yearned for more. "I can't get any other jobs," he complained bitterly. "They don't hire Cubans in the hospitals. But Dr. Gray is giving me an opportunity. And it's all right for now. He's a very good physician." The dream, simply deferred, burned in a secret nook in his mind.

My mother interviewed for several jobs as a teacher's aide, but so far no one had called her back. "I'm glad because I have no one to leave you with," she said, so she lounged around Ocean Drive, internationally known today as fashionable, glittery Deco Drive, strolling on the beach or sitting in the breeze. No fashion models or tourists disturbed her, the streets nearly empty.

That summer of 1964, our adopted land was going through convulsions that kept everyone talking. The Civil Rights Bill passed the U.S. Senate, riots erupted in New York, New Jersey, and Puerto Rico, three civil rights workers registering poor blacks to vote disappeared, police arrested Martin Luther King Jr. for eating in a Florida restaurant, Malcolm X founded the Organization of Afro-American Unity, and the number of troops in Viet Nam rose to 21,000. My father added his voice to the upheaval, vociferously supporting Barry Goldwater – a staunch anti-communist known as "Mr. Conservative" -- for President.

In my world, school started again and each morning my mother walked me to Ida M. Fisher Elementary on Washington Avenue, past boarded-up, abandoned hotels like the Carlyle and a few bustling ones like the White House, the Netherlands and the Tide. "I can't believe I'm back here now after all these years," my mother said one day as we walked by the Tide Hotel, where she and my father honeymooned in the forties. "Your father and I were out on that balcony." She pointed upwards.

Struggling in school now, I tried to adjust to new teachers and classmates. Slowly, the academic advantage I had from starting school early in Cuba slipped away. One day, the teacher divided the class into teams for a math race. It was my turn. I ran breathlessly to the board, wrung my hands, chewed on the chalk and looked back at my team members for inspiration.

"Come on, you know the answer," one student yelled. But I didn't. I slowly wrote down two numbers. Wrong. "Boo!" my team members shouted. I walked back, hiding my embarrassment with a stiff smile. The next day, the teacher demoted me to a slower team. In math, I could no longer keep up with the more advanced students.

What about my literary talents? In this area, I still excelled, constantly called upon to read aloud since I miraculously knew all the long, hard words and did not stumble. My essays always received high grades. But one day I wrote a poem, and the teacher slashed it with red marks. Apparently, she wasn't impressed that I had emulated a poet in my English book. Why did the poet in the book get away with repeating lines in alternate stanzas and I could not?

After school, my mother and I went to the beach. Sometimes I pulled an over-sized black inner tube with me into the water and drifted far out to sea, bobbing up and down on the waves with never a thought for sharks, my mother watching from the shore. In the early evenings, one neighbor, sixteen-year-old Iraidita, raced her collie up and down Lummus Park, the grassy embankment that separated the street from the sand. The sleek collie streaked through the twilight, his coat shining from vigorous daily brushings. Mirtica, a twelve-year-old who lived downstairs and suffered from cerebral palsy, grunted wild sounds from a wheelchair, her mother and grandmother standing guard. She reminded me of my cousin Cesarito.

As the sun moved west, leaving only a trace of light, couples leaned on a low rock wall bordering the sand that stretched for blocks down to the sea. White sand, cool in the dusk, dredged from the bottom of Biscayne Bay when tycoon Carl Fisher designed his island paradise back in the early 1900s. "Not quite as fine as in Varadero," my mother said, making a circle in it with her toe.

The ocean crashed against the shore just beyond. Some days, the sea churned with rage; on others, it was calm *como un plato,* like a plate. That evening, my mother wore a silky blue dress splattered with flowers. Pink lipstick contrasted with a set of perfectly even shiny white teeth and frothy hair set in soft waves. She walked away from the sand, over the grass and into the front patio of our building. She sat down in a plastic chair, next to my father, reading a medical textbook by the light of a lamppost. Mudda and Fadda nodded sleepily in their chairs as screaming kids streaked by. My father looked up and met her gaze; a touch of desire leapt from his eyes.

My heart jumped. To a child, ignorant and lonely, hope is reality. I clutched greedily at this reversal in my fortune, a respite in the march of my parents toward family disintegration, and didn't question it. After all, how could he compare my mother with the acned, plump woman we had seen at the Rascal House? My father placed his arm lightly around her shoulders. At night, lying on the living room couch – my makeshift bed -- I stared into the sky with its riot of stars and sang "Twinkle, twinkle little star, I'm so lonely and so far" while my parents buzzed in conversation in the bedroom.

That fall I caught pneumonia. My father walked me into Mount Sinai Hospital where the nurses installed me under a huge plastic oxygen tent. I stayed there ten days, contentedly reading and drawing with a new set of soft lead colored pencils I had cajoled my father into buying. My mother drove to see me each morning and afternoon. On one of those drives, she got into an accident that totaled our car. She had whiplash and wore a huge cushion around her neck for months, never complaining or asking for anything, and I didn't care if we had to walk from then on. Unbeknownst to me, my crafty father – setting aside his marital troubles for the time being --had negotiated a substantial accident settlement that would move us out of our musty Miami Beach apartment and place us squarely into the center of the immigrant's longed-for American Dream.

14.

Battered boxes bulging with the remnants of our life in La Habana littered the yard and leaned against each other on the porch, some blocking the entrance to the front door. Here stood stacks of the old English china carefully wrapped in newspapers. There, under a pile of white linen bed sheets, peaked the fancy highball glasses. The ones imprinted with Toulouse-Lautrec's posters luring revelers to the *concert bal* at the Moulin Rouge. All had survived a ninety mile journey from the island and several years of warehousing, shipped hurriedly to Miami before my father's swift, and, to him, death-defying departure. Now the china and glasses sit prominently on my own kitchen shelves, symbols of a tenacious nostalgia for a life whose memories refuse to dissipate.

"Ah, to begin anew after all I've been through," my father exclaimed, fingering gold filigreed liqueur cups with one hand and tousling my hair with the other.

"I thought I'd never see this again." My mother – depression undetectable now -- lifted up a sterling silver tray with ornately carved sides and curved feet, the very same tray that years later she pawned for the money to buy sleeping pills. Outside, the driver of the Modernage truck backed out of the driveway and drove away after depositing new furniture all through the house.

I gleefully ran in and out of the rooms and around the yard, then out to the middle of the road to join a group of kids playing kickball. I had never lived in a house before; all the open spaces invited the neighborhood kids -- Lola, Elizabeth, Marilyn, Maritza, Aurora and I – to play outdoors day and night. Rebellious underground tree roots pushed up sidewalk slabs, tripping the elderly on foot and kids on bicycles. In the heat that made breathing difficult, gardenia bushes and mango trees kept the air sweet and wet. The terrain was similar to the Cuban landscape: sensual.

The harmony tentatively taking root in our South Beach hotel still reigned between my parents. The mistress had receded into the past. My father wanted a second chance. My mother forgave and forgot. Both celebrated our good fortune that, immigrants for only three-and-a-half years, we laid claim to The American Dream.

Our new home, a small 1940s house on Northwest 29th Avenue and Ninth Street, just north of the Cuban neighborhoods and south of the black communities, sat on a stretch of road that looked like a crooked thread running through a garment. I was now in Mrs. Chambers's fifth grade class at Kensington Park Elementary School, just across the street.

The area, known as Little Havana, extended immediately west of Miami's downtown and served as the focal point for Cuban exile political and social activity. Long before Castro's Cubans arrived in this slice of low-rent South Florida, thousands of exiles from Batista's dictatorship settled here, offering a Spanish language cushion to the new immigrants.

Today, Little Havana, the capital of Cuban Americans, is the site of the famous Calle Ocho Carnaval that each March attracts a million revelers. Although most Cubans have moved out and Central Americans – particularly Nicaraguans and Hondurans -- have moved in, it is still a low income community, a haven for new immigrants, where everything is cheaper in the *bodegas* and coffee costs a quarter at some cafeteria counters.

Despite bums picking over the garbage and the run down aspect of much of the place, the forces of gentrification that revitalized many American cities forge ahead: old, dilapidated buildings lock arms with upscale restaurants and luxury condominiums, popular because of their proximity to Brickell Avenue, the Wall Street of the South. Each second Friday, Southwest Eighth Street, the heart of the community, hosts an artwalk, showcasing not only trendy galleries, but also the Bay of Pigs monument on Thirteenth Avenue and Maximo Gomez Park, called Domino Park, on Fifteenth where old Cuban men play dominoes, chess and smoke cigars, still ranting against Fidel.

My mother picked our neighborhood because the houses boasted an elegance that reminded her of home. Many, like ours, sported hardwood floors and faux marble fireplaces. Our house, white with yellow trim and a flat shingle roof, showcased tall, dense emerald-green fir trees that flanked the entrance to the red-tiled front porch. During hurricane season, wide, white awnings with yellow stripes closed their lids above jalousie windows to protect us from rain and flying objects.

It was a typical early 1960s South Florida neighborhood, just beginning a radical transformation as thousands of young Cuban exiles, obsessed with ousting Fidel, began to move in next door to retired Northerners living there since after WWII. The elders wished for quiet, unable to understand the passions of their new neighbors. In 1959, they had watched the black and white newsreels of Fidel triumphantly entering La Habana, then news film of the Bay of Pigs invasion in 1961 and the Missile Crisis in 1962. I heard them say that the newcomers caused chaos in the nation. They asked us: didn't Castro liberate Cuba from the tyranny of a dictator? Isn't he teaching the poor how to read?

"He's a communist," my father answered.

Every Cuban in the neighborhood wanted to go back to the island, insisting their stay here was only temporary. But my father said that would never happen. Cubans were here to stay. He pointed to a development earlier in the year as proof: Castro had signed an important sugar agreement with Russia, now the island's main military and commercial ally, ensuring Cuba's enslavement to the United States' giant communist enemy. As a professional with a bright future, my father felt motivated to swiftly assimilate into American life. He believed he could make a lot more money in the United States than he could back in Cuba.

Our Cuban neighbors, on the other hand, skilled workers with limited knowledge of English, believed their lives would be less stressful back home where their relatives clamored for their return. Most of my parents' relatives were in Miami by then, and my father – given to outbursts of joyful whistling during this time -- had already begun the process of bringing his own parents to America.

The old timers, only a few befriending us, also lived absorbed in the past. They were tired of life but afraid of death, and formed a framework of stillness around the noise in the Cuban houses. Suspicious of the racket outside, they ran to the window at the slightest sound in the street. Only the widower who lived at the top of the slope seemed indifferent to the new Cuban neighbors. His was a gray, two-storied house with a chimney. Nobody knew his name, but gossip had it that he went crazy after the death of his wife. He boarded up his front windows as if waiting to die. Cats sunned themselves on his sidewalk, yard, porch, and roof. The Animal Control officers came out once but didn't do anything.

That Halloween, we knocked on his door, yelled "trick or treat," and looked the other way when he came out on the porch to fill our bags with candy. On a dare, I summoned up courage and broke the silence. I wanted to hear the widower talk.

"What's your name?" I asked him, holding out my trick or treat bag and averting my eyes underneath the angel mask I was wearing.

"Jim McCoy." His tone, like an echo bouncing from the walls of a tunnel, disturbed me.

We stood there motionless, taken aback by the sound. Underneath my mask, I felt exposed to the resonance of his voice. I wanted to peek out of the eyes of my mask, but I couldn't. Instead, I felt rather than saw a form dressed in black, with a beard covering skin whiter than egg shells. We continued to stand there until the widower took a step forward.

"Let's get out of here," one of my friends yelled. "He's spooky."

I ran, following the trick or treaters down the stairs of his porch, confused about my desire to look into the widower's face. What did I want to see? Perhaps I needed to check the reflection of my own sadness in a stranger's face. Or imprint the look of surrender in my mind, so I could avoid it. I fought constantly, not only with my mother, but with myself, and with anyone else who made me angry. Sometimes I was tempted to retreat, lock myself away just like the widower.

15.

My father didn't last long at our new address. It seemed nothing could hold him. Not our beautiful house, my more relaxed mother, his growing daughter. In December, he announced he had a new job at Edgewater Hospital in Chicago. He bought thermal underwear and a thick woolen coat down to his knees from the Sears catalog. "It's a good opportunity for me," he said. Just as the year slipped away, he was ready to go.

"In a few weeks, we'll be together again," he said. "You're moving to Chicago as soon as your mother rents the house."

"Are you sure?" I asked.

He nodded.

One morning before dawn, he jumped in his car, waved good-by and drove off.

My mother immediately went back to bed. I stood at the door watching the lights from his car dissolve into the dark, like a lump of white sugar swallowed by black coffee. I walked back to my bedroom, took up his picture from my night table and pressed it to my heart. I did not go back to sleep.

The next day my mother began the familiar ritual of packing: she wrapped all the English china in newspapers and the highball glasses in bed sheets. She arranged to ship all the furniture to Chicago and turned off the phone. A week later, the mailbox held my father's first letter.

Querida Cecilita,

I had a very good trip to Chicago even though it snowed the last two days. It hasn't stopped snowing since I got here and there are mountains of snow in the streets. I just got an apartment around the corner from the hospital. It's very small but good enough until we find something else better. I miss you so much. Can't wait for you to come. There's a school near the hospital.

Lots of kisses. Tu papi.

Silver and shining, the train shuddered and gained speed as it left behind the city of Miami. We sat in stiff seats, long wool coats draped in the overhead rack. My mother gripped a handbag stuffed with thermal underwear, woolen socks and scarves. We slept in a sleeper car and ate in the dining car, black porters and waiters closely attending our every move. Three days later, the train roared into Chicago.

I stepped out onto the platform, and the cold fell on me like a sheet of ice that March of 1965. I gazed in wonder at the drifts of snow piled higher than my head. I kneeled to examine the ice crystals that crunched under my new rubber boots. The thermal underwear felt tight and scratchy, but it barred the freezing blasts of wind from touching my skin. I never knew there could be such cold air even if the sun sparkled and made the day clear and shining.

My father, standing by the tracks, held me in his arms, somber and distant, not at all like the father who had greeted us at the airport nearly five years before. He was a different man from the one who had sat on the porch of our South Beach hotel and whistled and laughed as he put away china and crystal in our Little Havana house. What had happened to that light of love I had seen? Had I imagined it?

"Rafael," my mother said. She reached out, her hand arrested in midair by my father's disdainful words. She stepped backwards. My father's face twisted, and he gesticulated with his arm as if waving away a cloud of pesky insects. My mother clutched her scarf around her neck and shivered in the icy cold, voice pleading, face crumbling.

I stood miserably squirming in my heavy winter coat, the cold and the coat bearing down like weights on my shoulders, distracting me from registering the exact words. But the tone conveyed the message: resentment, irreparable damage done.

"*Porque?*" my mother insisted. No answer.

My father drove to a small building in downtown Chicago and dropped us off in an overheated shabbily furnished apartment. He did not stay. My mother, tiring of her vigil at the window, dragged herself to the nearest chair and collapsed into it to spend the night.

The next day, angry and confused, I pulled on the hated woolen coat, staggering under its weight, and rushed into the snow. I was eleven-years-old and becoming more headstrong and independent. The white ice had packed itself into an unyielding terrain. I slipped and waded through the piles with determination. The soft snow sucked down on my rubber boots, reluctant to release my feet. I used all my strength traveling through the dingy frozen water. I rushed ahead blindly.

Then, there in front of me the Museum of Natural History rose up into the sky; its gray and brown bricks reflected the weak sunlight. I entered, entranced, jumping at the sight of a huge bear frozen in the act of clawing up to the ceiling.

I walked through the hallways, lost in the sights and silence of the musty museum. Hours went by. Dusk dropped fast, closing time. I pushed myself out into the snow. Now the snow reached almost to my thighs. Finally, I saw our apartment building and lights shining from the windows. My mother opened the door and said nothing about me being gone all day. Her face, swollen and wet from tears, bore no expression. I fell asleep with the radio humming "red roses for a blue lady."

My father arrived early in the morning to drive us back to the train station. We stood on the platform for an awkward minute. I cried and clasped my arms around my father who glided out of my grasp, kissed me good-by, and could not set a date when we would see each other again. My parents said nothing to each other. The train rumbled off for another three day voyage back to Miami. I sat dejectedly by the window. Bitter tears blurred the white landscape slipping away.

"Why did we leave so soon?" I asked in the sleeper car, hurt squeezing my heart.

"Your father said something to me that I didn't like." Then, she whispered a startling conjecture: "It may be possible to love two people at the same time."

That didn't make sense, then. Why hadn't she tried harder to keep him? Why didn't she get rid of the mistress, the cause -- I believed -- of this new rupture? I realize now that her energy level and emotional strength did not match my father's, and she retreated from battle. Once, my relatives told me, my parents had been inseparable. The idea ignited my always dormant longing for the past.

My spirits lifted the next day when I spotted what seemed to be a rock band sitting in one of the cars. I loved the Beatles and the Rolling Stones, and rock was part of my everyday life. It was the group Jay and the Americans, laughing, joking and smoking, instruments piled all around. One of the band members, was it Jay? started humming "the concrete and the clay beneath my feet begins to crumble but love will never die," and the others followed suit, breaking out in full song.

Soon the singing drowned out the dull whir of wheels on steel tracks. I sat with them when they went to the dining car, and they hummed through mouthfuls of mashed potatoes: "if I had a hammer, I'd hammer in the morning." I chattered while my mother sat silently next to me, pink lipstick glowing, hair smoothly in place, face like the porcelain China figurine with hand taped to her side that we packed into one of our boxes.

Several days later I tore open a letter from my father.

Querida Cecilita:
You don't how much I miss you. The snow is gone now and it's not that cold. I'm sending you ten envelopes with stamps so you can write to me. I'm also sending envelopes with 13 cent stamps so you can write to your grandparents in Cuba. Call me collect from your neighbor's house in the evenings after seven. We will be together again. Nothing can separate us.
Tu papiton.

The Chicago fiasco spurred an irreversible rift in my parents' relationship. That's when my father made up his mind that nothing would interfere with the reinvention of his life. He considered that our recently purchased Little Havana home would be a safe place to leave us while he pursued his dreams.

"I asked your father," David said years later, "How is Ceci? How is her mother?" The answer: "I don't want to talk about them. I just want to move on with my life. You know, have a good life. I've had enough trouble already. I'm going to be a physician in this country. That's all that matters. I'm going to have a new life."

I want to say that's when my mother saw an opportunity for personal happiness, and that, she, too, exited triumphantly into a better life. But that didn't happen. Here, in America, no one could stop my father's desire to leave us behind in pursuit of romance, wealth and social status, nor my mother's plunge into insanity and poverty.

16.

For my mother, the departure from Chicago signaled the beginning of crying spells and days spent in bed in a darkened room. Her silence stretched out so long and heavy that she seemed to disappear into the bed, walls, floor. Like a turtle barricaded inside the shell, she cemented each opening against the world. It signaled the beginning of a cycle of poverty and dead-end jobs and a horrifying downward spiral into madness. As for me, I blamed her for letting my beloved father, the link to a vibrant, happy world, get away.

"Are we ever going to live with *papi* again?"

"No. I've called him many times, and he won't take my calls or call me back."

Later, our family friend, David, tried to explain. "I told her to be sexy with him, to act more like a woman to him, but I couldn't reach her," he said. "She just sat there shaking her head, as if she didn't understand. She always seemed so fragile, so delicate."

No father. No rules. It was summer now. I went to sleep and woke up when I wanted. Neighborhood kids ran in and out of my house all day and all night. We skated, biked and played freeze tag on the streets. At night we played *cuarto obscuro*, hide-n-go-seek in a dark bedroom.

I turned the volume on the record player full blast. I listened to "The Jerk" and the Lovin' Spoonfuls' song about how summer made your neck feel gritty. The music blared out the front door, open to catch a breeze because the air conditioner was broken, and my mother didn't have the money to fix it. Fans oscillated in my room and living room. My mother placed a small one on her dresser. It was hotter inside than outside.

The Grosse Pointe Public Library a few blocks away on Seventh Street offered a break from the heat. I walked there daily and read 26 books that summer of 1965, winning first prize in a reading contest. The librarians posted my name and the titles of the books on pieces of colored paper on a bulletin board and rewarded me with a certificate.

Despite her emotional state, my mother occasionally did some surprising things. She took one look at the certificate, walked across the street to the elementary school and signed me up for a creative writing class in the afterschool program. It was life changing. I walked into the portable the first day of class and felt a thrill I had never experienced.

"Boys and girls," the teacher said, "I want you to let your thoughts run freely and write down whatever pops into your head."

I waited for ideas to strike. Then pictures blazed in my imagination, similar to when I had dictated the Santa Claus stories to my mother. I took up my pencil and went to work, creating a cartoon strip that told the story of a struggling student.

The teacher, impressed, shared my work with the class. I went home elated.

Visionary moments were few for my mother. She didn't notice when, in our back yard, I first lit up a cigarette at age 11. She didn't know that Conchi across the street relentlessly beat her niece, Aurora, who cowered in a corner. She didn't witness the horror of Rosa, two houses down, as she struggled to pull her father off her mother, whom he had stabbed repeatedly with a kitchen knife. She didn't see the despair in the eyes of Enrique, Conchi's husband, who planned failed military maneuvers in the Everglades trying to get his country back.

My mother was oblivious to all of it; but I took it all in. I knew she was thinking about my father, but I also knew she was drifting unanchored in a new country that so far had offered only disappointment and loneliness. Sometimes, she talked to visitors on the porch, but when I went outside, nobody was there. At night in her bed, she talked to someone by her bedroom window.

"Go away," she said, angrily. "Stop bothering me."

Rummaging through the closet one day, I found my father's revolver in an unpacked box. I rubbed its cold sides. I opened the cartridge and saw it had no bullets. But a thought sprang into my mind. I would use it against burglars and the invisible visitors. I reasoned that the mere sight of it would scare anyone. I tucked it under my pillow, feeling safer already.

The next time I heard my mother's voice, I pulled out the gun, tucked it under my pajama top, and rushed to her room. I was terrified of burglars after our next-door neighbor, Mrs. Lockliar, told me a thief had crept into our kitchen through the back door just before we bought the house. For weeks I imagined what I would do if I had to face the same situation. I kept the gun out of sight, so my mother wouldn't take it away, and stood guard. But it wasn't a burglar I confronted; I didn't know it was a much more dangerous foe.

My mother jumped out of bed and leaned out the screen-less window.

"Get out," she shouted.

"Who's there?" I asked, peering into the darkness with her; not a leaf stirred.

"No one." She dove under the covers. I went back to bed, confused.

Who were the people outside her window? I don't know when I realized they existed only inside her head.

From the sidewalk, we could see the widow Lockliar pruning rose bushes on the side of her house painted pink inside and outside, including the awnings. A yellow scarf kept her white wispy hair away from her face. A flowered jersey dress spread like a tent over her massive body.

My mother and I walked up to her front door. My mother knocked sharply. I stood just behind her. "I don't want you to talk to us anymore," my mother said in a soft almost imperceptible accent when Mrs. Lockliar, breathing hard from rushing inside, opened the door. My mother, the only Cuban mother in the neighborhood who spoke English, stood proudly on Mrs. Lockliar's porch with shoulders back, wearing dark glasses that hid swollen eyes from all the crying. She looked glamorous, like Jacqueline Kennedy, in a knit, teal blue, Chanel suit and white patent leather pumps with bows on the toes. I had my journal and a book under my arm; in case things got boring, I wrote stories or read to pass the time. But there was nothing boring about this confrontation. Would my mother slap our neighbor?

Another widow, Mrs. White, chubby and short, who lived in a duplex – also painted pink -- on our other side, sat in the living room drinking tea. Mrs. White smiled gently, her eyes not entirely focusing. Mrs. Lockliar, an imposing figure, said something to Mrs. White, paused and slipped off her yellow head scarf. I could feel her thinking. Tall and wide, with a booming voice practiced in the art of protest, she turned around, walked to the back and slammed shut the screen door, complaining about the mosquitoes and ignoring my mother. Heavy curtains covered the windows; thick area rugs blanketed the wood floor. Shelves laden with glass figurines lined the walls from ceiling to floor. In the backyard, fruit trees oozed a sugary steam into the heat of the day, the pungent odor mixing with the still air inside. Each night, before going to sleep, I smelled the sweetness, and, when I woke up from burglar nightmares, the smell was still there and calmed me.

"I don't know what I have done to offend you," Mrs. Lockliar said. My mother did not move from her position by the door. "All I told you was that you can count on me if you need anything."

"I don't need your help."

I felt anger at my mother's rudeness. I feared that Mrs. Lockliar and Mrs. White, both frowning, wouldn't let me play with their Siamese cats.

"Do you understand what I am saying?" my mother continued.

The widows stared.

"*Vamonos*, Cecilita. Let's go." She turned to go as if she were a queen. I rolled my eyes. All I wanted to do was play with the cats, have fun with my friends and stop being afraid of burglars. My mother had no reason to battle the kind widows. She displayed one personality some of the time and another personality at others. Light and dark.

I spent those early years in Miami running after the tiny spark of light in my mother's eyes. That light meant she was OK. But most of the time, just like in La Habana, the light would turn off before I reached her, and then I rushed terrifyingly into a black pit. This was one of those dark moments. Mrs. Lockliar and Mrs. White wiggled their fingers at me in a sign of good-by as I glanced at them before closing the door.

17.

In September of 1965, Hurricane Betsy approached the Florida Keys. The news warned of wind gusts reaching an estimated peak of 160 mph with landfall expected by midnight. The sun scorched the neighborhood, but the wind was picking up already and it was only noon.

"Why don't you come and wait out the hurricane at our house?" Marilyn asked. "We'll have a lot of fun and my cousin Manny might be there."

Marilyn was my best friend now. She lived across the street with her parents, Conchi and Enrique, two sisters, Maritza and Marlene, and two cousins, Aurora and Felicia. From my window, I enviously watched relatives come to visit every weekday, every weekend. They lined up their cars on the front yard: cousins, aunts and uncles, nieces, nephews in old Fords and Chryslers. I fervently wished I had a brother or sister, leaving notes to the long-legged stork my mother said delivered babies. I never got an answer, so I contented myself with adopting the family and becoming part of their daily routine, filling the ever expanding void in my life.

"Ok, I'll ask my mom." I liked her cousin Manny, and I was always ready for fun. I really didn't ask my mother; I now just did whatever I wanted, my mother giving up any attempt at keeping order. But when I went home, my mother told me Conchi had already invited her to spend the night. I was surprised that she accepted. Maybe she felt friendlier toward Conchi than toward Mrs. Lockliar or Mrs. White because Conchi was Cuban and closer to her age. Maybe they recognized the mutual sadness in their eyes when they talked about Cuba. Whatever the reason, I was happy to have company that night and helped my mother gather flashlights, batteries and a transistor radio to take with us.

Back at Marilyn's, I went into Conchi's bedroom to call my father collect. My mother had not yet called the telephone company to connect the phone since coming back from Chicago.

"It will be nothing," he said. "We've gone through so many hurricanes in Cuba and we're still alive. The news is making too big a deal out of it."

"*Papi*, I feel very alone. *Mami* never speaks. When can I visit you in Chicago?"

"I'm going to Texas to work in a private office next month," my father said. "I'll arrange for you to come as soon as I'm settled. It's near the beach and the weather is much better than here in Chicago."

I heard a click on the phone.

"Did you hear someone pick up the other line?" I asked. "Maybe someone is listening to our conversation."

"No, I didn't hear anything."

"When can I have a boyfriend?"

"You can't have a boyfriend until you're fifteen."

"I also want a car."

"That won't be for a long time."

"I want a red or green car," I insisted.

When I hung up, Conchi waited for me by the door. "I don't care what you have to say to your father about cars or boyfriends," she screamed, cornering me against the wall. "I wasn't listening on the other line. Do you hear me? It wasn't me listening!"

I nodded, afraid of the crazy look in her eyes, bulging black, rolling around. If she wasn't listening, then how did she know what I had said to my father? I usually went to Rexall's Drugs on the corner to use the pay phone, but it was a lot easier to go across the street. Conchi marched outside where her husband Enrique, cousins and uncles boarded up doors and windows, and peeled out of the driveway in her car. When she came back, loaded with canned food and candles, she didn't mention the incident. Maybe Conchi was sick, like my mother?

Still hours before the hurricane, everyone was in a party mood. Already, boxes of mangoes lined the walls in the living and dining rooms. Three mango trees bloomed in the back yard, and the house was always filled with the gooey fruit. Relatives started arriving. My mother crossed the street and sat primly on Conchi's couch. The sun set, and we settled in for the hurricane. We played Parcheesi and cards. We ate ham sandwiches. At midnight, a funnel of wind sucked up the heat and cooled off the air, pounding on the windows and doors with the roar of a runaway train. Layers of rain wiped the dust off the sidewalks and furiously pelted the walls and roof of the house. No one said anything for several minutes. Then, the giant sleepover began. Everyone rushed to a bed or sofa and got comfortable. Marilyn had to sleep with her two younger sisters, so I was stuck with a cousin, Magda.

"Move over." I shoved Magda, whose ample body squeezed me close to the wall. The boards nailed to the windows strained against the wind. Someone in the living room shouted that water seeped inside.

"Grab some towels and place them next to the door sills," Enrique yelled. "Stand back from the windows!"

The house trembled as if coming down with a chill.

Was my mother still on the couch? Did she go home to her bed?

"*Mami,*" I called out.

"*Estoy aqui,*" she answered from the living room that she was there.

The next morning, I woke up to the scraping of Enrique's hammer as he pried the nails out of the boards shuttering windows and doors. An overcast sky met us outside but no more rain and a lot less heat. The hurricane moved fast to the west coast of Florida. The electricity came back on, and we piled into the dark, cool, family room to watch *American Bandstand* on TV. My mother went home. As the air gusted in small swirls outside, in that magical time when the light lingers before night, we started a game of freeze tag. Our shrieks echoed up and down the block.

The curtain at Mrs. Lockliar's window fluttered and fell back into place. Ostracized by my mother, she had spent the hurricane alone with Mrs. White. I felt sorry for her, but, almost tagged by Marilyn, I turned back to the game, and the elderly women promptly faded from my mind.

18.

Traffic whizzed by an open window on Northwest Flagler Street, the air thick with the immovable heat. It was October 1965, and I was inside an office building in downtown Miami. My shoes squeaked on slippery hallway floors. Heavy unvarnished wood doors stood silently guarding the entrances to tiny offices on both sides of the hall. The doors were rough to the touch: you could pick up a splinter if you rubbed them. Tarnished brass plates bore the names of those ensconced inside. We knocked, walked in, and a secretary ushered us to seats next to a desk stacked with papers in the center of a cramped room. The humidity made everything sticky.

A man, bald and stocky, rushed over from an adjoining office. My mother extended her hand; he gripped it, flashing yellow teeth. Ice hung in the air.

"I'm here to sign the papers," she said.

"Ah, yes," he grinned again.

I was in that awkward stage just before puberty. I danced the "monkey" to Roy Orbison's "Pretty Woman" and admired myself in the mirror. The Beatles triggered pandemonium with their music, ecstatic fans fainting at their concerts. My friends and I sang along to "All My Loving" and "She Loves You" and tried to figure out which Beatle was singing. Was it Paul? No, it must be George. I learned from a classmate that Santa Claus didn't exist. What a letdown, but I wasn't going to tell my father, so he could still buy me presents. As I gained knowledge about the world, I began to understand the consequences of divorce. I worried that it would tear me away from my father forever, and that I would probably have a step-mother, maybe one as hateful as Cinderella's, whose story would later mirror mine.

In the tiny office, the edge of the desk dug into my ribs, no room to move back. The man across the desk, a lawyer my father had hired, pushed a messy pile of papers in front of my mother. Resplendently dressed, with fresh lipstick and cloudlike wavy hair caught back, she looked like the film actress Hedy Lamar. But inside her head, the swirling sorrow wasn't an act.

She held her head high, struggling to look dignified as she read the contract.

My mother didn't have her own lawyer, a clear conflict of interest that my father used to his benefit. Possibly feeling shame about the divorce, she didn't ask anyone's advice. Not our friend David, nor her aunt and uncle Carmela and Manolo, who had recently moved to Miami from New York, nor my step-grandmother Elsie or my paternal grandmother Amalia. She signed the papers and sat back.

The contract stipulated that my mother could never ask for more money. My father, whose career as a surgeon was on the verge of skyrocketing, offered her $150 a month for alimony until she remarried and $150 a month for child support until I reached eighteen. My mother could keep the house. After all, it was her money from the accident that they used for the down payment. Did she know the full consequences of the terms? Did my father ever consider her mental state when he drew up the papers with his lawyer? No. I believe that my father, a physician who boasted he had taken a special course in psychiatry, had long ago diagnosed my mother's mental illness and mercilessly took advantage of her condition.

"Now you are free," the lawyer chuckled.

"He is a degenerate," my mother said. "You, too."

My heart pounded; my gut cramped. I pushed back my chair; it slammed against the wall like a drumbeat. The lawyer stood up. He was about my height. I felt danger. I was afraid. He spread cracked lips into a smile. I could see through the opening of his cavernous mouth a deep dark pit without end.

"Cecilita," my mother reached out to hold me back.

I squirmed away and freed myself from the chairs. I gripped the door knob, but it was stuck. A sharp tug and I was out on the slick hallway floor. My saddle shoes clung to the smoothness. The silent, shiny hallway stretched out on both sides. I turned and ran to each door, checking for signs of the bathroom.

Finally, there it was. I pushed inside and felt a ripping motion in my stomach that paralyzed me before I could reach the toilet. There, on the floor, this one a rough, dirty one with tiny tiles in a black and white pattern that came in and out of focus, I squatted and relieved myself of diarrhea.

A week later, my mother sent me on an errand to Rexall's Drugs on the corner. I walked to the phone booth, sat down inside and closed the sliding door. I clutched the receiver, dialed the operator and asked for a collect call to Chicago.

"*Papi*," I said when my father accepted the charges.

"*Sí*, Cecilita."

"We don't have any money left. My mother says…."

"I know your mother put you up to this. I send enough money to her."

"No, it's the truth." My father had not yet signed the divorce papers, but he was already sending my mother less money.

"I said no."

"When am I going to see you?" Tears slid down my arm.

"I'm going to arrange for you to visit as soon as I'm settled. But when you are twelve you can decide if you want to live with me or your mother. You can live with me if you want to. That's what the law says you can do."

I paused, shocked, loyalties divided. Did that mean I would have to leave my mother? I craved the energy and excitement of my father's life, but felt responsible for helping her.

"Then we will never all live together again?"

"Is that what your mother wants to know?"

I placed the receiver softly back on its hook, angry that I had failed at my mission of getting what my mother needed, what we needed, and confused about what I knew to be true: the imbalance of power between my parents and its resulting injustice was slowly destroying my mother.

I believed the mistress was with him in Chicago, and that she prevented him from sending us money. I feared that he would take her to Texas as well. I pulled out a dime, and dialed my father's friend.

"David, will my father marry the other woman?" This is how I had heard my mother refer to the mistress.

"No, he never will," David assured me. "She is just a passing thing."

Emerging from the phone booth, I was not persuaded. I frowned, sighed. I realized I had to become my mother's protector, a state of affairs my father understood and deplored; his own jealousy -- as he sensed me pull away -- spurring him to seek revenge on my mother and on me.

TRAPPED IN LITTLE HAVANA

Everybody's youth is a dream, a form of chemical madness.
— F. Scott Fitzgerald

1.

The Freedom Flights immigration agreement came on the heels of a daring move from Fidel Castro. In October 1965, he opened the port of Camarioca – east of La Habana -- to anyone who wanted to leave for what he called the "Yankee Paradise." When their exiled Miami relatives came to pick them up in small boats, nearly 3,000 Cubans jumped aboard and sailed to Key West. The Camarioca exodus, a forgotten blip in history, foreshadowed another, more momentous boatlift fifteen years later.

In 1980, five desperate asylum seekers crashed a bus into La Habana's Peruvian embassy. Castro seized the opportunity to bid good-by to all malcontents on the island and – as he had done in Camarioca -- opened a port, this one in Mariel. In the ensuing boatlift, 125,000 Cubans escaped: the refugees rushed onto the vessels – some owned by relatives, others chartered -- alongside mental patients and criminals who the dictator forced aboard. This international crisis served as the backstory for Al Pacino's character Tony Montana in the 1983 film *Scarface*.

But in 1965, President Johnson erroneously believed the unprecedented Freedom Flights airlift he had agreed to would operate only as a temporary measure until Cubans returned to their homeland. Beginning that December -- and for the next eight years -- charter flights known as the "Vuelos de la Libertad" left twice daily from Varadero Beach to Miami, transporting nearly 300,000 Cuban political refugees to the United States. This airlift transformed South Florida into the Latin American capital that it is today.

In the mid-sixties, the extraordinary growth of our community caused us to become increasingly isolated, "ghettoized," from mainstream America. The new refugees crowded into crumbling tenements and old houses, seeking work in hospitals, hotels and on the streets selling fruit and flowers. English vanished, Spanish signs displayed everywhere. Café brewed in every restaurant and in every office, and salsa dance music blared from Miami Beach hotels and government auditoriums. White flight sped up, and soon, Cubans pushed out to the western and southern borders of Dade County, into Westchester, Sweetwater, Kendall, leaving behind a decaying Little Havana. The decline did not faze my father. His money could buy his way out, but he insisted Miami was the only place for us.

"Anywhere else, you're just another damn Cuban," he said.

As hard-working, sleep-deprived parents closed themselves off, feeling protected, speaking a common tongue and facing a common foe, many of their children began to realize there was much more out there, beyond the borders of their community.

2.

My father drove hurriedly toward his medical office in a suburb of Beaumont, a small Texas town south of Houston and north of Galveston, leather-gloved hands clamped on the wheel. Out the window, I watched fleeting houses glitter with Christmas lights, freshly painted with lawns closely mowed unlike those in Little Havana. I was visiting for the holidays, the first time without my mother. Outside, before sunrise, everything appeared swathed in shadows, including the woman who waited for us on the sidewalk by a bus stop, gripping an overstuffed handbag and a battered briefcase.

"This is Beba," my father said carelessly, coldly. He slowed to a stop, reached behind and pushed open the back door of the car. "She's my nurse." He waited for her to get in, silent, moody, looking straight ahead.

The woman, whose face still had not emerged from the shadows of the cold dawn, wore a starched, white uniform over which she had pulled a baggy yellow sweater. She climbed into the back seat. I snapped around to look into her face, illuminated for just seconds by the light in the car before the door shut and we went back to darkness. I glimpsed a hint of a smile, eyes lowered, long lashes brushing acne-marred cheeks, hair grease-slicked on the sides.

An image pushed itself up through years of trying to forget. Was this my father's mistress? Had he brought her out here to live with him in Texas as I had feared? Maybe this woman just looked like the other one. In the silence of the ride that December morning of 1965, with the tires crunching scattered ice on the road and the heater whirring in the background, certainty spread slowly into my brain. The woman in the back, bouncing up and down from the potholes of a deserted Beaumont street, was the same one who had eaten breakfast with my father at the Rascal House the day we drove to New Orleans.

On that humid summer morning, Beba had looked away, with neither a smile nor a frown, as my mother and I came up to their table. I remembered the greasy hair, slicked back on the sides with heavy hair cream smelling slightly of rust. That same aroma wafted up to the front where I struggled to cover up my anguish.

Now I knew who had been in the apartment near the Mount Sinai Hospital resident hall that midnight when my mother and I found my father's car parked outside. Was Beba the same woman mentioned in the anonymous letters my mother received just before our departure from the island? Or were they about some other woman?

The jolt of the brakes ended the thinking. My father inched forward into a small driveway, hopped out of the car and threw his gloves on the seat. The building was a simple, concrete structure with two windows taking up the entire front wall, flanked by trees whose branches leaned against the roof. No houses around for a least a few blocks. I held my red and black angora sweater tightly around me and slid inside. My father did not look at me; he turned on all the lights and made for his office, not offering to show me around. Beba walked down a hall and into a back room, delivered herself of the handbag and briefcase, and began sterilizing speculums in a heavy iron boiler. She arranged syringes in a row on a chrome tray and filled glass containers with cotton and Band-Aids.

I resisted the desire to throw up. I picked up a stethoscope and wrapped it around my neck. I went into an examining room and rearranged the vials of gauze, tongue depressors, and swabs. I ran my hand across the cool shiny surfaces of the steel table and glass cabinets. The odor of disinfectant clung to the air. I leaned against a wall, picturing my mother back home alone in Miami, lying down, crying, pointing at people I could not see in the doorway, at the windows, her smooth complexion puffy from grief, sad eyes closed. I thought of the leaky roof, the broken air conditioner, the bum scavenging garbage at a corner dump.

And here was my father, just six years after leaving Cuba, reinventing himself with another woman, ugly, fat, with greasy hair and acne scars, in a neighborhood whose residents looked anchored, not bothered by the relentless din of Little Havana. I didn't know yet how far he would turn away from me in his new life. But already I felt a distance between us, an estrangement I couldn't identify. "You're the only thing I have," he used to tell me on the phone when he first moved away to Chicago and during the first few months in Beaumont, and I looked adoringly at his framed picture on my nightstand.

A slamming door pushed away the memory. A woman with short, charcoal hair and round blue eyes stomped her way to the front desk. "Good morning!" she shouted. My father and Beba repeated her words absent-mindedly. They were huddled together, going over patient charts, ignoring me.

"This case reminds me of the one in La Habana," my father said.

"Do you think he needs a biopsy?" Beba inquired, a hand on his arm.

The new arrival looked at me standing uncertainly in the hall. "I'm Luann, the receptionist," she said, as she settled into the chair. "Come up here with me, baby, and keep me company." The phone rang and patients started walking in. I knew she felt sorry for me because she kept patting me on the hand in-between making appointments while I sat next to her, filing charts.

"I have a daughter just your age," Luann said. "Maybe you can come out to the ranch some afternoon. We have horses and a lot of dogs."

I nodded, warily watching Beba ushering patients into an examining room, chart in hand, taking vital signs. My father had promised I would assist him, but she had taken charge, pushing me out of the way. In less than six months since my father's arrival in Beaumont, he had a thriving practice. He had set up his office with two other Cuban doctors, Wilfredo Garcia and Raul Reyes. Dr. Garcia, who had not passed the revalidation medical exam, was a silent partner. His sister was Dr. Reyes's wife.

"Garcia used to be a pharmaceutical rep in Cuba," my father said. "He was never a doctor. I don't know what he's trying to pull. He doesn't know anything about medicine."

Garcia, Reyes, their families, my father, Beba, and an older couple, the only Cubans in Beaumont, formed a tight community that played dominoes on Saturday nights and cooked *lechon* and *congri* on Sundays. I bonded with the kids, Mary, Carmen, Machito, Lila, and Raulito, and we took several car trips together to Galveston and Houston in the two weeks that I was there, my father sometimes responding to my persistent hugs.

That Christmas Eve, everyone crowded into my father's small first floor apartment, one of many in a row of freshly painted gray buildings clustered in a circle. He set up a barbecue grill on the tiny porch and threw on a long strip of beef tenderloin, cooking it slowly while we kids played freeze tag in the cold air. Beba, in the kitchen, stirred a pot of black beans and smashed cloves of garlic for the boiled yucca, a white starchy vegetable.

"This is chauteaubriand," he explained to Dr. Reyes, pointing to the meat. "They make it at a French restaurant in Houston. I thought we might try something new with our rice, beans and fried plaintains." As he cooked, the talk circled excitedly around the new immigration agreement, the Freedom Flights.

"More Cubans are expected to arrive soon," Dr. Reyes called out.

After the Christmas Eve meal, my father peeled over-ripe bananas and placed them in a concoction of butter and sugar melting in a frying pan. He cut up Sara Lee pound cake and scooped vanilla ice cream on each slice. Then, he spooned the hot banana mixture over that. "This is Banana Royale," he announced, pouring an orange liqueur from a bottle and setting a match to the whole thing. The flames leapt up from each small plate to exclamations of "ooh" and "aah" from the group. Beba made café Cubano and brought it out to the grownups in tiny cups. The other kids and I sat on the floor playing cards.

I did not notice any romantic overtures between my father and Beba, but I sensed that everyone in the group accepted her and felt comfortable with my father's arrangement. I didn't know then that, in a few years, she would become a permanent fixture in my life. The transition my father had dreamed was now real. Did I realize then I had to create an even stronger dream – a dream of my own – so I could survive in Little Havana?

3.

We lined up in a square with one couple on each side. Bowing and curtsying to our partners, we gripped hands and skipped in a circle to the rhythm of a screeching fiddle.

"Do si do your partner," yelled the "callers," two teachers with microphones plugged into speakers. Tapping their feet to the beat, they prompted us through the sequence of steps of America's famous folk dance, nothing like the wild hip thrashing salsa movements. The afternoon square dances on the basketball court at Kensington Park Elementary gave boys and girls a chance to touch.

We locked elbows with our partners, rotating in a circle. My body tensed expectantly against Eddie's, then against Aldo's – two of the cutest boys in sixth grade. I was twelve in 1966, fully aware of the power of sexuality. Clasping hands and grazing shoulders with boys turned into hot explosions inside me. I discovered that I could be driven toward a boy with the force of the moon pulling at the tides, but then had absolutely nothing to talk about with him.

In our neighborhood, the old timers began disappearing. One day, an ambulance came by and drove off with the widower McCoy. Mrs. White and Mrs. Lockliar moved north to be with their children. More and more Cubans moved in, our ethnic enclave hermetically sealed. Some of the streets now had piles of garbage that the city did not haul away. On a side street near the main drag, next to a strip shopping center filled with repair shops, a beauty salon, and a few empty stores, a pervert masturbated in his car.

Outside Little Havana, life in America existed on a faraway planet for me, my friends and their families. Viet Nam, student protests, race riots, women's liberation: nobody cared. Issues before the Miami City Commission or the Dade County School Board made no impact on Cuban parents too busy rebuilding lives and careers; however, they did find the time to take note of Cuban news. They celebrated when President Johnson signed a new law, the Cuban Adjustment Act, which exempted Cuban immigrants from general

U.S. immigration laws. Any Cuban who reached the U.S. since January 1, 1959 was eligible for permanent residency after two years. Some 123,000 Cubans immediately applied for permanent status, among them my parents.

Besides Cuban politics and daily survival, gender issues obsessed Cuban parents. They made sure to reinforce the stereotypes and impress upon their children, experimenting with romance in their language of choice -- Spanglish -- that sex was wrong outside of marriage.

"A boy will never marry you if you have sex," they said. "He will never respect you."

Unlike my friends Marilyn, Lola and Elizabeth, I had no father at home to terrify me into submission. Not only that, but my mother had little interest in drilling me about the rules. Parental neglect gave me the freedom to listen to what my body said and dodge the brainwashing.

"I now am able to bear children," I told Marilyn the morning after I saw the blood on the toilet paper. A classmate had punched me in the stomach the day before while we horsed around on the playground, and I figured the cramps were the result. But when I saw the blood, I thought with excitement: I'm a woman now.

"A good reason why you shouldn't have a boyfriend," Marilyn said. "You could get pregnant."

"Too smart for that," I said. "And I'm not waiting to have a boyfriend until I'm 15, like my father thinks." I had cut out a picture of a cute boy from a magazine and placed it in my wallet. "See, this is Ruben." No one guessed he wasn't real.

"You have too much freedom," Marilyn said.

That spring, the divorce between my parents became official. I read the settlement – a stack of papers on the dining table outlining the money my father had agreed to pay for child support and alimony. I didn't know those figures wouldn't cover our expenses, and I was too preoccupied with my own life to brood over our broken family. I cared only about reading, writing and romance. I signed up for The Book of the Month Club to get discounts: ten books for ten cents. I read *Gone with the Wind*, mesmerized by Scarlett O'Hara, my new role model. A vivacious, beautiful woman, she made things happen. I wrote poems about love and stories about bordello madams, making up sex scenes. I recorded my life in a journal. I stored all my writing in boxes, thinking I would develop these fragments later.

I now missed my father only sometimes. I was emerging from a place where my parents acted upon me, to a space where I was the principal actor.

"I'm glad *papi* doesn't live with us," I told my mother. If he had, I knew he would have sent me to Catholic school where students wore ugly blue and white uniforms like Lola and Elizabeth, forced me to do my homework and not allowed me out of the house after dark.

"Hm," my mother answered, lying down.

One afternoon at Rexall's Drugs, a quiet, cool place to escape the afternoon heat, I sat with Marilyn, Lola and Elizabeth at the soda fountain. The menu offered seven layer cake and pie a la mode, but we ordered ice cream sodas and paid for them with a row of As on our report cards. The pharmacist, an old man with drooping whiskers and smelling of stale sweat, joined us on a stool. I looked at the ringworm on my hand.

"Is there a cure for this?" I asked. Marilyn and Lola wrinkled their noses.

"I have something on the shelves," he said. "I'll show you the new games I just stocked, too." Marilyn and I, wearing shorts and frilly blouses, followed him to the back room where chemicals stored on shelves reached the ceiling. Lola and Elizabeth, known as "goody-two-shoes" and dressed in their Catholic school uniforms, stayed behind, probably thinking we shouldn't talk to strangers. Neither girl was allowed to say "bad words" and had to be home by 5 p.m. They could not even look at boys when the parents were around.

Just as I entered the back room, with Marilyn a few feet ahead, a hard object pushed into the small of my back, hard but yielding in places. The pharmacist pressed his body forward again, rubbing himself on my butt, side to side. I sped up to get away, but so did he.

"These are great," Marilyn exclaimed, pausing to admire the Parcheesi and Password. I pushed past her, fear rising. I walked back out to the stool, sat and swiveled to face the pharmacist. I felt powerless and struggled to pretend nothing had happened. This was different from the romantic fantasies that I thrived on every day. The pharmacist took his place behind the counter, never making eye contact, slipping pills into bottles, the ringworm ointment forgotten.

"What's wrong?" Lola and Elizabeth asked at the same time.

"Nothing," I told them, but I'd learned that there could be a dark side to sex.

4.

"*Papi,* I'm boy crazy!" I greeted my father when I emerged from the plane at Houston Municipal Airport – now known as George Bush Intercontinental -- ready for summer vacation. At 12, I looked like a woman. I wore shorts and a scarf top that tied around the neck. Men whistled and hollered at me everywhere I went. But Texas wasn't Little Havana. Around me, sedate men in cowboy hats and silver-spurred leather boots walked arm in arm with women crowned by piles of teased hair and wearing flowered dresses. The men carried briefcases, and the women gripped straw purses. Teenaged boys and girls with dazed expressions and hair down to their waist – I didn't know they were "hippies" -- milled around in old, scruffy clothes, some with flowing threadbare robes, all with overstuffed packs strapped onto their backs. I looked at them with interest, noting the peace signs, the long necklaces, the bell bottoms I would later include in my wardrobe.

"*Ah, si?*" He looked at me in surprise.

"I want to have a boyfriend here in Texas," I said. "I had a great time at my sixth grade prom and every boy liked me. I wore a beautiful pink, green and white dress!" My hormones rolled along at a quick pace. "I can't wait to start seventh grade in the fall! Do you think we can go buy new clothes and make-up and a new bathing suit?"

"We'll go tomorrow."

I had just read the book *Sex and the Single Girl* by Helen Gurley Brown published in 1962. Brown offered straightforward tips about catching boys in her magazine *Cosmopolitan,* which I always read from cover to cover. The stories talked about empowering women and supporting their desire to shape their own lives. I agreed with every word. I wanted the exciting life of my father and not the narrow, silent one my mother led at home.

Already a feminist, I just didn't have the word for it. I abhorred the greater power of men that defined my community and, I realized, the outside world. Inwardly, intuitively, I resolved to systematically destroy all constraints on me as a female. Never was the time more appropriate for my personal liberation. That summer of 1966, the National Organization for Women denounced the federal agency charged with upholding the Civil Rights Act and agitated for greater gender role equality, Timothy Leary told the nation to turn on with LSD, anti-war protestors marched on dozens of towns and cities across America, and Stokely Carmichael launched the Black Power movement.

The Generation Gap shaped itself into a powerful force, with millions of young people – myself included -- proclaiming they wanted to defeat an encrusted Establishment of elders. We were the famous Baby-Boomers, half of the U.S. population under the age of 25. While most Cubans in Little Havana ignored the upheavals in mainstream America, many of their children did not. I became increasingly interested in the world outside Miami. One day, I heard on the news a sixteen-year-old girl declare, "Everything is phony and the world's all a mess. I guess that's why we are revolting so." I nodded in agreement, knowing exactly how she felt.

My father – oblivious to the rebellion brewing inside his daughter -- drove for nearly an hour to his apartment in Beaumont. The town had changed from when I first visited last December: now bright light from the sun bounced merrily from trimmed hedges and flowering bushes, and a slight smell of salt floated in the air. We drove past fields that disappeared into the horizon, with horses and cows, heads down, tearing at the grass. We zipped through quiet streets with small houses. Then he turned into his gray brick apartment complex.

"Here we are," my father said, kicking the door open.

I dropped my bag in my room and went to the kitchen to prepare *empanadas*. My father loved to cook and eat, and I had a keen interest in my grandmother's recipes, which she sent tucked in her letters from Cuba. I followed the instructions written with a fountain pen in elaborately artistic cursive and threw flour and water together, molded the *empanadas*, chopped up some ham, placed it in the center, folded over the dough and dropped them in a frying pan with olive oil.

"It's the only oil that doesn't cause cholesterol," my father insisted. "Crisco, Wesson, UGH! How can you get oil out of corn? It's nothing but automobile oil, that's what it is. In this house, we only use olive oil."

I placed the *empanadas* on a plate, but my father wasn't interested, nervously walking around the living room. I noticed a record album that I hadn't seen before: "A Taste of Honey." In his bedroom, he made a phone call, mumbling into the phone.

"Well, let's go to the store. Didn't you want a new bathing suit?"

"Let's go," I jumped up and down, imitating a ballet dancer.

"Beba's coming with us."

I stopped in mid jump.

"She moved to the apartment upstairs. I wasted too much time in the mornings picking her up to go to the office," my father said. "She's lonely. She's here all alone without her family. They are all still back in Cuba."

My parents had signed the final papers on March 7, so – technically -- there was nothing wrong with my father dating Beba. Was he going to marry her? For one guilty, disloyal minute I considered that maybe I could choose to live with my father and have a normal family life with Beba around. But the shame of betraying my mother made me dash the thought away. I kept my face expressionless as Beba came down the stairs from her apartment and climbed into the car.

On the silent ride to the department store, I peered intently at various styles of bathing suits in the new issue of *Cosmopolitan*. When we got there, my father walked off to the sporting goods section, and Beba came with me up and down the aisles packed with beauty supplies: hand creams, night creams, eye creams, daytime moisturizers, nail polish, polish removers, shampoo, conditioners. I placed the carefully-chosen bottles in the shopping basket, and we walked to the swim-wear section. In the dressing room, I tried on one two-piece after another. Finally, the red one seemed just right. I stepped out into the hallway.

"You have no waist!" Beba exclaimed.

"What?" I looked at the mirror in horror. I saw how the curve moved in from the middle portion of my body and out to the hip. Maybe Beba needed glasses?

"Strap on a belt each day and tighten it as far as it will go," Beba said. "That way, maybe you can mold yourself a waist. I had a twenty-two-inch waist at your age." Her square frame turned, and she walked off, the mounds of her hips blocking the aisle.

I understood later that her outburst signified the beginning of a jealousy that would further erode my relationship with my father. When I complained, my father responded: "Her family is stuck in Cuba. That's why she is so negative." In my father's eyes, Beba could do no wrong. And I was the pest who refused to accept his new life, clearly, he often said, brainwashed by my mother.

It would be a long two months.

When we got home, Beba said good-by and went back up to her apartment. I organized all my new stuff in my bedroom. I hung up the clothes and arranged the bottles of cream on the dresser. My father paced in the living room. I heard two quick thuds from Beba's apartment. My father looked up toward the ceiling.

"What's wrong?" I came out of my room, frowning.

"Nothing." But he was ill at ease, even nervous.

"What do you have with that woman?" I pointed my chin at the ceiling.

"Nothing." My father sounded aggravated. "There's nothing going on. I am doing nothing illegal or wrong. This is all about what your mother is pumping into your head." He did not mention he and my mother were divorced, and he had all the freedom to do as he liked. Neither did I. Our struggle centered on the past.

Didn't he see I had known all along about the mistress? His outburst made me angry, and I shuffled back into my room and sat on the bed. The bottles of cream and shampoo caught a spear of sunshine from the open window and sparkled for a moment before the water from my eyes made them go out of focus.

Before bed that night, I tried on my new red two-piece bathing suit and examined myself in the mirror. I posed this way and that, looking critically at my waist. I applied eye cream, night cream and hand cream. I pulled off the suit and pulled on baby doll pajamas. I turned off the light. In what seemed seconds, someone pounded on the door. I jumped from bed. My father was already outside, engaged in a heated conversation with a neighbor.

"Peeping Tom?" my father exclaimed. "What is that?"

"Yes, Peeping Tom!" the neighbor answered. "Looking through your window. I saw him. When I came up, he ran over there behind the bushes."

My father stalked toward his room, emerging with the rifle he used at the gun range, face red, eyes wild. He threw himself out the door and jogged in a circle around the apartment building, gun at his side. Heart beating, I turned off the light to my room and watched through the window blinds as he ran toward some bushes and poked at them with the rifle. He ran to another set of bushes and did the same. He jogged back around to the front door and called the police. I buried my head under the covers. This was the last time I remember my father coming to my defense.

The next morning, a letter arrived from my mother:

Mi Querida Cecilita.

I was very happy when you called me on the phone. I am sending you the headband you left behind and a teen magazine. I haven't been feeling well. The doctor said I have anemia and gave me sleeping pills. But it's one o'clock in the morning, and I still can't sleep. I feel so alone. I sent you a record I heard on Saturday Hop. It's called Help Me Escape From Cuba. Did you get it?

Muchos besos de tu Mami.

I read the letter several times and muffled my weeping into the pillow. I missed her. That summer, I began the slow and painful process of closing my heart to my father, realizing that I preferred my mother's silences to his angry, cold gaze. Distant now, he was no longer the affectionate parent who whispered on the phone that he loved only me. Soon, I stopped going to the office. Instead, I asked him to drop me off at Dr. Garcia's house. I spent most of my time with the Garcia kids, Mary, Machito and Lila, and Dr. Reyes's two children, Carmen and Raulito. Every morning their mothers drove us to the pool, the movies, the mall, the beach. In the afternoons, we played 45s on the record player and practiced the swim, the monkey and the latest move.

O Sweet Pea, come and dance with me….come on, come on, come on and dance with meeee….

On weekends, all the families met at the gun range so the men could practice shooting. We drove to Houston to eat deer in a fancy restaurant. We went to breakfast at the Toddle House. We traveled to Galveston and walked out on the pier, sometimes throwing in a fishing line.

One Saturday, my father asked me if I wanted to sleep over at Mary's house. "Yes, what fun," I cried. I packed my bag, and my father and Beba, who went everywhere with us, dropped me off. I wasn't fooled. I knew he wanted to be alone with Beba, but the thought of staying up all night talking and dancing with my friends soon made me forget them.

After the music, the popcorn, the dancing, we finally went to bed as the sun was coming up. I dropped into a deep sleep only to awaken minutes later with Mary's hand caressing my breasts, the other hand in my pants. I can't say I felt shame at the time, just surprise. I lay still for a minute, trying to decide what to do. I didn't want my first sexual encounter to be with a girl! I shifted away, but, on her knees she forcefully took my face in her hands and lowered her mouth to mine. I pushed against her shoulders.

"No," I said. "I reserve that for boys."

Mary scrambled up and screamed curse words. I pulled up the covers, nervous. She paced up and down, pushing chairs and kicking the bed. Mary's mother poked her head in the room.

"Mary, leave her alone."

Mary sat on the bed, burrowing her face in the crook of her elbow. Her mother motioned to me to get up. I followed her to another room and finally sank into sleep.

I never discussed that evening with my father, but I declined each time he proposed I sleep over at Dr. Garcia's. In his attempts to get rid of me for a few days, he suggested I spend the Fourth of July at the horse ranch of his receptionist Luann and her daughter Susan, offering another opportunity for sex education. It was a good idea.

Sitting on the edge of the bathtub, I shaved my legs for the first time that weekend. I rode horses with Susan in the mornings; we sat with her older brother and his friends in the family room in the evenings. One night, he had a party. Onion dip and potato chips sat on the counter. Beer and wine packed the refrigerator and the bar that extended along one wall. Ice clanged in every glass as girls and boys milled around the room. The lights dimmed and the stereo went full blast. Luann was nowhere in sight.

Susan and I sat on one couch, grinning stupidly. We looked longingly at the boys, but no one paid attention to us. Maybe Susan's brother had warned his friends that we were off limits? After a while, couples began to form and drift to various corners of the spacious room. For some time, we watched them sway back and forth, tightly pressed together, like grinding shadows. I thought of all my romance novels and tried, but failed, to make eye contact with one of the boys.

Disappointed, I wondered when I would lose myself in a boy's arms. Wasn't it about time?

5.

Lucio thrust a thick, probing tongue inside my mouth. It felt like a chunk of overcooked steak that I couldn't chew and wanted to spit out. I tried not to gag and stretched my mouth as wide as it would go, holding my breath until I felt faint. It was a rough kiss with no sensuality, the "French" version I had dreamed about and practiced so many times on the back of my hand. What a disappointment! It happened when I was thirteen and in the seventh grade at Citrus Grove Junior High, between one building and another, in a narrow grassy walkway opening up to the main drag, next to a tree that spread its branches to blot out the sun.

Today, the walkways, trees and grass are gone, and Citrus Grove Middle, as it is now called, with nearly all of its thousand students on free or reduced lunches, is one depressing, monolithic brick building with no windows. Boys and girls, dressed in uniforms, stroll around the school holding hands, kissing openly. No need to hide now, as I did that day in 1967, wearing a smart orange skirt and top from Lerner Shops, with Lucio, my boyfriend of two days, sporting a neat, long-sleeved maroon Gant shirt and black pants.

Cars sped by. I leaned back, propping myself up with my foot against the concrete. Lucio, bending down from six inches above me, flattened me against the wall as if I were in danger of falling off a precipice. I felt no flutters in my stomach. But Lucio, eager as a pup, lapped up all he could before it was time for me to go home. The sun was sinking, and I had at least twelve blocks to walk. I turned my head slightly, and, before I could disengage from Lucio, I locked eyes with the Spanish teacher sitting in her car out on the street. Mrs. Martinez leaned out of the window and waved me over to her. Her eyebrows formed a thick, black, straight line above her eyes and quivered in anger, face muscles tense. Lucio looked up, followed my gaze, straightened up and lifted his hand in a weak wave back. Then he jumped on his bike and sped off in the opposite direction.

I walked over to Mrs. Martinez. Guilt and fear choked me, but I held my head high, and, with a haughty expression, I climbed into the back seat. Martica, her daughter, in seventh grade as well, sat in the front. A "square," a boring, homely girl, she did everything her mother told her to do, unlike me who lived like I chose, coming and going while my mother worked or lay in bed, crying with the door closed.

No one spoke in the car. Mrs. Martinez, still frowning and now shaking her head, drove me home, pulled up into the driveway and jumped out of the car. Martica didn't move.

"I want to speak to your mother."

I felt anger now.

My mother had just landed her first job after the divorce: babysitting, from daybreak to sundown. But this afternoon, she was home. I opened the unlocked front door, and we walked into the living room. My mother sat on the green upholstered couch my father had bought at Modernage before moving to Chicago, along with a set of mustard-colored swivel chairs, wood side tables and a coffee table with little trays that opened out to hold a glass or cup.

"*Hola, como esta? Soy la maestra de español,*" Mrs. Martinez began on a strong note, but her adamancy flagged when she noted that my mother barely moved.

"*Si.*" My mother did not ask Mrs. Martinez to sit down.

"Your daughter," Mrs. Martinez paused, "your daughter was....." She cleared her throat. "She was kissing....a boy....outside the school."

My mother remained immobile, staring at Mrs. Martinez with sad eyes. I dropped into one of the swivel chairs and swung sharply from side to side. My lips puckered up and turned down at the corners into a scornful grimace.

"Cecilita, *es verdad?*" Is it true, my mother asked.

I shrugged.

"Thank you for telling me," my mother turned to the teacher, now at the door.

Mrs. Martinez walked out.

My mother's black eyes, puffy and red, shifted over to me. The dark glasses she used to cover them when she went out lay on the coffee table.

"*Es una estupida. No sabe nada.*" I declared Mrs. Martinez stupid and ignorant and stomped to my room. After reading for a few hours, I went out and found my mother still sitting on the couch. She had cooked no dinner. Was she angry? Punishing me? No. She wore that look on her face, the one that said "I'm not really here," and I worried she would start talking to the invisible people.

"*Mami, tengo hambre,*" I said I was hungry. She didn't answer, staring into space. I found a few quarters on her dresser and bicycled all the way to Zagami's, a 24-hour grocery store seven blocks away. I bought an *empanada* and carton of milk. When I returned, my mother had gone to bed. We never spoke of it again. Today I believe my mother's defense mechanisms prevented her from absorbing one more sorrow.

The kiss empowered me. It placed me on an unwavering road to revolt, buttressed by the goings-on in the outside world. In the news I watched the Black Panthers -- armed with M-1 rifles -- march on California's state capitol, race riots explode in dozens of cities, and draft card burners clash with police at the Pentagon. The Human Be-In, "a gathering of the tribes," especially attracted my attention. Some 20,000 hippies, antiwar protestors and Hell's Angels – among others -- organized a massive party in San Francisco's Golden Gate Park.

The explosive Beat poet Allen Ginsburg, a vocal advocate of LSD, opened the day chanting a Hindu blessing while the Grateful Dead and Jefferson Airplane rocked out playing psychedelic music. Everyone sat in circles, enjoying the day, kissing and smoking pot. From the news I learned that the national hippie culture made its home in San Francisco's Haight Ashbury neighborhood, flooded with middle-class teenage runaways and hardcore drug pushers. I longed to visit there and hang out with such interesting people.

America's social upheaval signified a freedom I craved: freedom from pain, but also freedom to stand up against authority and experience life fully. Later that year, I listened to snippets of the Monterey International Pop Music Festival, the first, large-scale outdoor rock concert with 90,000 people in attendance. I loved the wail of Jimmi Hendrix's guitar and the heartrending vocals of Janis Joplin, but also the pop sound of the Association: "Never My Love," "Along Comes Mary," and "Cherish," my favorite.

Cherish is the word I use to describe our looooooooove…..

My record player blared music at 6 each school morning. It floated out the open door and windows of my house, welcoming my friends Gloria, Sylvia, Helodia and Ibis. Marilyn from across the street did not join the group. As square as Martica, she adamantly opposed my new lifestyle. At the end of the song, the arm of my record player jerked up and moved over to the beginning of the 45, over and over again playing the same song while we applied turquoise eye shadow and hot pink lipstick.

I wore a black velvet band around my neck and hip huggers, "hippie-style" wardrobe, such as long flowered dresses and "granny" glasses, now part of my every day attire. My feet, however, had yet to be liberated. I pulled on brown ugly saddle shoes the orthopedic doctor had prescribed to straighten out a tendency to turn in my toes as I walked. He had told my father I couldn't ride bikes anymore because it would exacerbate the condition. I ignored his advice and rode my bike everywhere. It was enough that the shoes were an embarrassment, and I cringed when anyone said, "You look so good….but only down to your ankles!!!"

I ran to the record player and put on the Rolling Stones. "I can't get no satisfaction," we screamed along with Mick Jagger. Ibis and Sylvia lit up Benson and Hedges cigarettes. I took a puff and sneezed three times. We hustled out the door, which I locked, a latchkey kid. My mother left each morning before dawn to make the slow trek by bus to Miami Beach where she babysat for the Goizuetas, prominent Cubans who had left our country with part of their fortune. One of the family members, Roberto Goizueta, rose to become the chief executive officer of the Coca Cola Company.

As we hurried toward the bus stop, laughing and skipping, Cuban matrons peeked out from behind the blinds, bewildered at our apparent lack of concern with propriety. The bell rang at Citrus Grove Junior High at 7. We only had 15 minutes to get there. But we didn't care if we were late. We ran to the corner on Northwest 7th Street just as the bus pulled away. I spied an ice cream truck stopped at the red light.

"*Heladero*," I called out. "Can you take us to school? We're late!"

The ice cream man, who wore a dirty white apron and stained dungarees, nodded and waved for us to jump in.

"That's hitchhiking!" Gloria resisted.

"So what? It's now or never."

We jumped inside and hung on to a counter nailed to the center of the truck, the ice cream man laughing as recklessly as we did. He wove in and out of traffic, leaning on the horn and cursing out the window, and called back to us, "One day I'm not going to be here to help you out."

6.

We made it on time to homeroom. Reynaldo, a recent arrival on the Freedom Flights, poked me with his pencil. We whispered and giggled throughout a film on the damaging effects of nicotine. I looked up long enough to see a man puff into a handkerchief and display a brown stain that had spread across its whiteness.

"This is what happens to your lungs if you smoke," the announcer said. Fortunately, this piece of advice sank in, and I abstained when my friends smoked pack after pack. I sneezed uncontrollably each time they lit a cigarette, the allergic reaction helping me avoid this addiction.

"Any questions?" The homeroom teacher, Miss Fleming, by nature a silent, haughty woman, did not engage her students in conversation before or after class. Although she often chaperoned the "sock hops" in the cafeteria on Saturdays, she stood watch with a frozen smile on her face.

"Miss Fleming, I have a question," I called out to disrupt her lesson. "Why is it that boys like you more when you don't like them and the other way around?"

Unbelievably, she smiled. "That happens only if you're immature."

After homeroom, we had a test in Mr. Malone's math class. I hated math. When Mr. Malone turned his back, I grabbed the test of the boy in front of me, quickly copied down as many answers as I could and threw it back on his desk before the teacher could sense anything was wrong.

"Who are you?" Rene whispered angrily, gripping his test.

"Don't you know who I am?" I hissed. "I'm the most famous girl in school."

"Mr. Carrollo, are you cheating?"

"No, sir."

"Why are you talking then?"

I kicked Rene's seat.

"I…I…I'm not, sir."

"See me after class."

After that, Rene fell in love with me, and we remained life-long friends.

Not only did I hate math, but I also loathed science, social studies, and physical education. I absorbed what I could from the teacher when I wasn't talking to my friends, didn't do homework, and never studied for tests, confident I could cheat my way through. For the first time, my grades dropped. They ranged from A to F, depending on my interest that day and how much I hated or loved the teacher, with an unvarying 3 for effort and F for conduct. But what did I care? I lived for the moment.

"Don't you want to have a good job, get married, buy a house?" my mother asked, desperation in her voice and my report card in her hand.

"No, I want to live an adventurous life."

"But how will you ever have any money to live?"

I shrugged.

At Citrus, I began thinking about writing as a career. I joined the creative writing club, and there we drafted short stories and read them aloud to each other. One of my poems appeared in the school literary magazine, encouraging me to keep writing. At home in the evenings, I wrote romance stories that featured adventurous heroines. I thrived on my imagination, using it to create other realities and, in so doing, escape the trap of the empty, painful present. Creating images and stories provided not only a new level of reality, but an outlet to search for knowledge. Even to this day, I understand and savor life most powerfully through the written word.

Then an ad in a magazine caught my eye. It was for a correspondence course at the Famous Writers School. I sent away for brochures and went over the material they sent me. Sadly, the cost was exorbitant, and I didn't have the money. Even so, just having the pamphlets on my desk provided motivation and kept my dreams alive.

My focus on language was such that I even won the Seventh Grade Spelling Bee, beating out, as my mother pointed out, the American students whose first language was English. Unfortunately, the day before the Dade County spelling competition—sponsored by the *Miami Herald* -- I came down with the flu and could not represent my school. The lucky runner-up went in my place.

"That's too bad you couldn't go," said Mrs. Priore, the English teacher. "You know so many words because you always have your nose in a book." A flat-faced woman with hair teased into a high bun and draped in loose, long dresses, she taught her lessons sitting down behind a desk. "But at least you're quiet," she added.

I didn't answer, deep into the world of the novel I had just received from the Doubleday Book of the Month Club. I read, with tremendous speed, Kathleen Winsor's *Forever Amber*, Daphne de Maurier's *Rebecca*, and the Victoria

Holt "gothic" novels *Menfreya in the Morning, The King of the Castle, Bride of Pendorric,* and *The Legend of the Seventh Virgin,* mesmerized by the spirited heroines who overcame any obstacle. I picked up grammar rules and narrative techniques through osmosis. There was no pressure to do anything in Mrs. Priore's English class as long as I kept my mouth shut.

I loved my French class. I didn't take Spanish because I already knew the language, and, my mother, who had spent time in a Montreal convent as a teen, made French sound classy and sophisticated. Miss Banks, a warm, outgoing teacher, strode so fast shouting in French from one side of the room to the other that my eyes could barely keep up with her. My friend Ibis and I became her favorites, and she could never understand the reports of bad behavior from the other teachers. We meekly repeated after her and answered all the questions.

"*Celine, ou est la biblioteque?*

"*La biblioteque est ici. Vas tu a la bibilioteque?*" I kept up the conversation easily, and every class turned into a lively exchange because I learned all the phrases instantly.

But when a substitute walked into the room, anything could happen. It offered a great opportunity to attract the attention I didn't get at home. So I became the ringleader in rudeness and incited the class to uproarious laughter and loud, wild chatter. One substitute teacher, with blond hair so long it hit the backs of her knees, sat at her desk with her face in her hands. I threw crumpled paper balls into the air and across the room.

"Please, stop," she begged.

"Shut up," I yelled.

Then I orchestrated a book dropping session. On the count of three, everyone slammed his or her book on the floor.

The excitement I engineered in school not only provided an outlet for anger against my parents, but it extended power and status. When my classmates stared at me with admiration, I felt whole, happy; none dared do what I effortlessly pulled off.

7.

My reckless behavior attracted the attention of the police.

One afternoon, Gloria, Ibis and I boarded the bus to downtown Miami, the hub of shopping in those days: Burdines, Richards, Sears, Florsheim Shoes, the Seybold Building, rows and rows of fabric stores packed to the ceiling with bolts of linen, satin and silk. On the street, bums pushed shopping carts. Teenagers from Overtown, the adjoining black community even poorer than ours, begged for change. We slinked into McCrory's, a five and dime store where my mother now worked as a cashier, and strolled through the aisles of cosmetics and hair products.

I stared at the rows of shampoos, conditioners, hair coloring. Obsessed with pumping up my dull, brown hair into voluminous locks, I bought hair treatments every chance I had. But no matter how many products I applied, no matter how much beer I mixed in with the Dippity Doo gel I used to set my hair on Campbell soup cans hoping to give it thickness, my tresses remained flat and limp, unlike the stereotypical, lustrous "Hispanic" hair I wanted.

"I bet you won't put anything in your purse and walk out with it," Ibis whispered.

"Ceci, don't you dare," Gloria cautioned.

"Bet you I will." Seeking admiration from my friends with my daring, I placed two L'Oreal oil treatments for dried and damaged hair into my shoulder bag. "OK, let's go home." We rushed out the door and headed toward the bus stop, but before we had gone several steps a plainclothes detective flashed his identification card at us.

"Follow me," he said sternly.

Ibis and Gloria burst into tears, but I engaged him in an angry exchange of words, never thinking to take off running. I now see that I craved confrontations with authority figures, so I could prove to them, and myself, they had no power over me.

"Who do you think you are for stopping us?" I demanded.

"Young lady," he said quietly, "You're lucky you're under 16 because if not I'd put you in jail."

"Well, I don't care," I shouted. "You are nobody!"

I noticed that he was old; his hands trembled.

"Come with me. Up the escalator and to the right."

"Please, Ceci," Gloria begged. "Don't say anything."

Ibis wrung her hands.

We marched into an office where two security guards sat at a table doing crossword puzzles. "Call their mothers. They were shoplifting," the detective said and looked relieved that he was leaving.

Ibis' mother was the first to arrive. She took Ibis by the hand silently, cursing under her breath, and they walked out. Ibis burst into fresh tears, begging forgiveness. Gloria's parents arrived next. Her mother wailed loudly and called upon God to forgive her daughter. Her father narrowed his eyes at me. Gloria hung her head and wiped her eyes. Neither one of my friends pointed to me as the culprit, nor did I volunteer the information.

My mother arrived hours later. She had scraped together a down payment for a dilapidated Dodge Dart with cracked dashboard and holes in the floor, and drove very slowly, never taking any of the expressways that were beginning to crisscross Miami. I spent the time entertaining the guards by telling them my life's story, intertwining fact and fiction. We were good friends by the time my mother knocked timidly on the door.

"Cecilita," she whispered when she entered the security office.

"Don't worry," I said. "Everything is OK."

I waved to the guards who waved back.

My mother, in times of trouble, just let it be.

8.

The Cuban community had not yet begun to follow the Pilgrim's footsteps. But I never could pass up an occasion to celebrate, so, on this cold November day in 1967, I gathered my adopted family, Ibis, Gloria, Sylvia, and Cari, four friends bound together for survival in the exile confusion of Miami, and we cooked the famous Thanksgiving meal at my house.

Ibis opened a tin of meat called Spam, given out in huge quantities to Cuban refugees seeking asylum at the Freedom Tower in downtown Miami. Sylvia whipped up mashed potatoes from a box. Gloria threw a package of green beans into a pot of boiling water. Cari set the table, and I ran to the corner *bodega* for a small *flan*, since pumpkin pie was unheard of at the time. On this day, just another day off for most Cubans, my mother, who never prayed before meals, gave thanks to God for our food, and we ate a hearty dinner.

But even while we moved closer to assimilation, my friends and I felt inextricably connected to the island. We listened intently to any piece of news about our homeland. My mother, an avid radio listener while she lay in bed, kept us up to date: she spoke of the arrest in Marathon of 70 men allegedly plotting to invade Haiti and then Cuba. U.S. federal agents seized machine guns, handguns and knives. She talked about a U.S. Air Force pilot, who, after dropping arms and equipment for counterrevolutionaries in Las Villas province, was shot down and captured. She mentioned that CIA-backed Bolivian military forces had killed Fidel's fellow revolutionary, the Argentine Marxist Che Guevara.

Then she ridiculed a *New York Times* article, "Cuba: Eight Years of Revolution," that had spurred pandemonium in the community. Reporter Herbert Matthews, who Castro's forces had smuggled into the Sierra Maestra to interview Fidel back in the 1950s, wrote: "There have been improvements in child care, public health, housing, roads and the typical leveling down of the whole social and economic structure that accompanies revolutionary equality… Cuban Negroes, for the first time, have equal status with whites, economically and socially." Not entirely true. To this day, blacks and women, the target beneficiaries of Fidel's initiatives, play a deferential role as white males rule every realm of Cuban life.

"Matthews, the writer, is another communist," my mother said.

After dinner, she went back to bed, and my friends and I were free to do as we wanted, so – leaving the dishes in the sink -- we boarded the bus for a carnival at the Central Plaza on Northwest Thirty-Seventh Avenue and Seventh Street. The shopping center stretched out for three or four blocks, containing a variety of small clothes and shoe stores, Zayre's department store, Federal Discount Drugs, cheap counter restaurants, and a Winn Dixie.

The carnival took up the entire parking lot, packed with kids like ourselves. Food booths and games such as shoot-a-duck, throw-a-ring-around-a-teddy-bear, and smash-a-badger enticed the revelers. But we were interested mainly in the rides, and we rode them until midnight: tilt-a-whirl, ferris wheel, roller coaster. We needed family, parents who paid attention, but we made up for the lack by losing ourselves in the pleasure of physical sensation; the thrill of flying – our bodies tossed in the air and from side to side, then dropped a hundred feet or more —made us forget family pain.

9.

Here I write the stories of my four closest friends, stories I didn't know how to tell back then, but desperately wanted the world to know because of their inherent injustice. Similar to my friends, I struggled with insurmountable forces trying to destroy us all. My father forced my mother and me to live in Little Havana, but for my friends, the children of factory and service workers, it was just circumstance and bad luck. We, the pioneering first wave of immigrants from Castro's regime, maligned by Anglos and envied as privileged by numerous immigrant groups, were not that different from others seeking refuge in America, and, in reaching out to this new land to solve crushing problems, we, too, lost pieces of our hearts in the process.

For these stories, I go back into my journals and read the details I collected throughout those years. Unlike the cause and effect construction of a narrative plot, life is often random and ruthlessly takes its victims without explanation. Being a writer now means having an opportunity to showcase my friends' tales of heartbreak to those outside of Little Havana.

IBIS

Ibis lived in a wood frame house on Northwest Thirty-Fourth Avenue and Third Street, a mile away from my home. Concrete blocks lifted the house up, and the open space underneath became a wrestling ring where cats and rats matched strength all night, their cries terrorizing neighbors. Inside, wrinkled linoleum covered the rotting hard wood floors. In the kitchen, grease from years of frying formed a thin film over the walls. But the gas stove never failed to hold a pot of rice, a pot of *picadillo* and a Cuban espresso maker brimming with black sweet cold coffee. Always hungry, I ladled spoonfuls of *picadillo* from the pot into my mouth when no one was looking, my refrigerator at home empty.

Food smells mingled with cigarette smoke, perfume and the odor of mold. The front room, converted into a large bedroom for Ibis's mother and her boyfriend, contained a king-sized bed covered with tangled sheets and a crumpled bedspread, an ornate cream-colored headboard, a ripped up couch, and a table holding rows of perfume bottles and creams.

Ibis's room, in the back, barely fit a twin bed and a chest of drawers. The door had no knob, just a gaping hole in its place. On her narrow bed, we spent hours playing Parcheesi or cards, or comparing notes on the boys at school, Ibis always smoking.

Ibis had kinky hair, a "gift," she said, from an African ancestor. Despite her few extra pounds, she took great pains with her physical appearance. She meticulously ironed her hair to make it straight and smooth. She owned both a long hair and a short hair wig to change her "look" each time we went to a party. Every day, she carefully lined the rims of her eyes with a black pencil.

"My mother," Ibis said, "can do a lot better than that man Lepido. My father was a wealthy landowner, when she went to clean his house. He was engaged to a society girl, but my mother convinced him to marry her instead."

Just then her mother Graciela walked in. Short and slim, with a sensual raw energy in her eyes, she had been cleaning houses all day but still seemed fresh and vibrant. "Today, they asked me if Ibis is my sister," she announced, going over to kiss boyfriend Lepido, a swarthy, broad-shouldered construction worker sprawled on the ripped up couch. "That's how young I look!" Lepido pulled her on his lap and licked her mouth and face with a huge red tongue. Graciela screeched and bounced off into the bathroom. "I'm going to take a bath first, in the tub."

"Unfortunately," Ibis lowered her voice, "when Fidel came in my father refused to leave his mother in Cuba and so my mother, brother and I had to come to the United States without him. My mother says she doesn't care who she's with because she's angry at my father. She says she can't be without a man."

I stretched out lazily on Ibis's bed, and my hand slipped under her pillow. I felt two sharp objects. I pulled out a pair of scissors and a knife.

"What's this doing here?"

"Shshsh…lower your voice," Ibis nervously looked through the hole in the door and grabbed the scissors and knife. She slid them under the mattress and tucked the bedspread carefully around the area.

"It's to fight Lepido," she whispered. "He comes in my room when my mother isn't here." I looked through the hole, and my eyes halted with shock against Lepido's mocking gaze. He spread his legs wide and stared at me steadily while popping off the top of a beer bottle with his teeth. I wanted to break a chair on his head.

"Let's go to my house," I said loudly. "My mother is waiting for me."

But before we could tumble to our feet, Ibis's brother pushed open the front door. Miguel, two years older than Ibis, lived with an aunt because their mother couldn't afford to pay for the upkeep of two children.

"*Papi se murio,*" he cried, "he had a heart attack!" A diligent student and member of the high school band, Miguel had a part time job and a car and helped his mother with money whenever he could. Graciela predicted that he would be the only one to leave our Cuban ghetto. His announcement about their father's death brought Graciela leaping out of the tub wrapped in a towel. She started screaming. Ibis, wailing, threw herself into her pillow and kicked her legs on the bed. Lepido continued to drink his beer. I chewed my nails.

After the crisis had passed, the carelessness of Graciela, who Ibis loved blindly, struck me as cruel. Even she must have been aware of the sexual threat Lepido posed to her daughter. Lepido's attitude reinforced my resolve to allow no one to exercise power over me. Stories like this strengthened the sense of injustice Elsie had instilled in me. Injustice and revenge, I once heard a professor say, motivate the writer. They certainly fueled my fire.

SYLVIA

In Cuba, Sylvia's parents heard Fidel say that children belonged to the state, so, fearing Castro would send Sylvita and Rubencito out to work in the sugar fields or force them into the military, they deposited the siblings on a plane bound to Miami. The 1962 airlift, named Peter Pan, brought 14,000 Cuban girls and boys to the United States under a program brokered by Monseigneur Bryan Walsh of the Catholic Archdiocese. When the young refugees arrived, they went off to orphanages and volunteer foster parents. Some physically and emotionally abused their charges, or, as in Sylvia's case, the other children in the home beat them.

"I stayed in a girl's orphanage in Homestead for two years waiting for my parents to arrive from Cuba," Sylvia said. "There I learned how to fight with a switchblade. The black girls jumped on me and beat me. But I fought back." Rubencito was lucky. He went directly to a relative's house and escaped that devastating experience. Now the family lived on the top unit of a ramshackle duplex on Northwest Twenty-Ninth Avenue and Seventeenth Street. The parents, factory workers, struggled to pay the rent.

Sylvia – lithe, beautiful – suffered from mood swings and never left her room, which she shared with her grandmother. She lay in bed reading one book after another from the Doubleday Book of the Month Club. Her favorite author was Mickey Spillane because she wanted to be a police officer.

"Let's eat," I said one Saturday afternoon. I lay at the foot of the bed. At my friend's houses, I either was lying down since I was tired from staying up all night, or I was eating since there was never any food at home.

"*Abuela,* can you make tuna sandwiches?" Sylvia called out to her grandmother, an elegant woman with blue eyes and a solicitous manner.

"*Como no,* Sylvita," of course, her grandmother exclaimed, her voice full of love. She opened a can of tuna and mixed it with mayonnaise and chopped lettuce.

"I hate my grandmother," Sylvia said out of earshot. "I hate my father, my mother and my brother. My father is a wimp. He does everything my mother tells him. My mother only loves my brother. My brother gets everything he wants. And my grandmother is so irritating. I wish she would leave."

"Let's have a party," I said, changing the subject. "I'm going to buy a new tent dress at Three Sisters. Then we can make deviled ham sandwiches and big pitchers of Kool Aid."

"Yes, that's a great idea," she said not enthusiastically. "Really, all I want to do is read in bed, but I'll go to the party."

That night at home, I started the party list and figured out the cost of two loaves of sliced bread and several cans of deviled ham. The next day I went back over to Sylvia's house with list in hand. Her mother answered the door, eyes red from crying.

"*Que paso,*" I said.

"Sylvita's grandmother is dead."

"But I was here yesterday and…."

"They had a fight, and Sylvita went out to the balcony. Her grandmother followed her, and she lost her balance or maybe Sylvita pushed her. I don't know. She fell down the stairs. Sylvita is at her uncle's house, and her father and brother are making funeral arrangements."

I looked down the steep stairs and thought I saw spots of blood on the sidewalk below. I shuddered, horrified at the image of Sylvia's grandmother slumped on the hard concrete. The next day I asked Sylvia what had happened.

"She just fell," she answered coolly.

I dropped the subject, bewildered. I never learned the truth, but the story refuses to fade from my mind. I can still see the old woman holding the sandwiches, smiling with love in her eyes; she reminds me of my mother today. Both were victims. Would they have escaped their fates if they had not traveled to America? My father listed an array of tragic situations that would never have happened in Cuba. But he was one of the perpetrators of tragedy; what would he know? Back then, I carefully committed everything to my journal -- pondering over the role of random injustice in life.

GLORIA

Gloria's parents weren't Cuban exiles. Poor, they left Cuba in the late 1940s and moved to the United States for a better life. They spoke perfect English, and their four daughters were born and raised in Miami. Pepe, Gloria's father, a maintenance worker for National Airlines, saved enough to buy a modest Little Havana house with terrazzo flooring and brand new kitchen cabinets. The living room sported a comfortable wrap around couch and a bar.

New Year's Eve 1967, Gloria's mother, Katy, invited my mother and me to their party. We walked the few blocks to Northwest Thirteenth Street. Platters of roast ham, *congri* and delectable pastries covered every table. Salsa music blared from the record player. It was my first time exposed to that wild Afro-Cuban beat that made feet fly and hips churn. Music at home: the Beatles, Chopin's piano sonatas, and Lawrence Welk's "champagne" tunes, so called because a machine spouted streams of large bubbles across the bandstand; back in Cuba, it had been Rodgers and Hammerstein, an American musical theater writing team. But Gloria, poor and dark-skinned with a thick mane of hair, was raised on salsa. She already knew all the moves, and we danced -- falling over laughing -- with her boy cousins while the grownups sat on the couch.

Katy, a stout, outgoing woman, sat in a corner with her sister who kept her face buried in her hands, weeping. Katy patted her shoulder, trying to get her interested in the merry-making but to no avail.

"She's pregnant," Gloria whispered about her aunt. "Her boyfriend left her. He says he doesn't want anything to do with the baby."

I stared at Gloria's aunt, horrified, not wanting to suffer her fate. Determined I wouldn't. But the music of El Gran Combo wiped all thought from my head: the trumpets, maracas, and congo drums were irresistible.

That summer, the Department of Transportation expanded the expressway to cut through our poor and non-influential neighborhood and connect east and west all the way to Miami International Airport. Gloria's house stood in the way, so the government exercised its right to eminent domain and demolished it, giving Pepe a check for a new one. The action enraged my father, who, discoursing on his theory of a worldwide communist conspiracy, pointed out the similarities with Fidel's takeover of private property.

The family, heartbroken, packed their belongings and moved to a smaller, older house on Northwest Thirty-Fifth Avenue and Tenth Street. Pepe and Katy never stopped yearning for the wrecked home. Sometimes, they drove over to watch the flatbed trucks loaded with concrete blocks, flattening bushes and trees and scattering debris and dust all over. "The money wasn't enough,"

Pepe shouted, working even more hours at the airport for the cash to update the new house. "I had just put in kitchen cabinets and new bathrooms." Soon, the construction site provided a hangout for lonely kids, including ourselves.

A few months later, a fresh tragedy thrust Gloria's family into depression. A cousin died in battle in Viet Nam, one of 16,589 casualties in 1968.

CARI

Cari lived with her brother and parents in a battered duplex nestled against the side of the Miami River and in the shadow of the Twenty-Second Avenue Bridge. Heavy curtains made of cheap brocaded fabric kept the living room dark. A couch and two armchairs wrapped in plastic cluttered a corner. The neighborhood had no sidewalks, and the driveways looked like a mish mash of broken stones and gravel. Roosters roamed freely through yards, cats too old to chase them.

Her mother, Aurora, was in love with her sister's husband. And her father, Gerino, a devotee of *espiritismo*, similar to the religious cult of *santeria* that our maids in Cuba practiced, but without animal sacrifices, tried to get answers from spirits.

"*Ooooobaaataaalaaa*," he sang in agony. "*Porque, porque?*"

In the afternoons, Gerino sat in a back room surrounded by ceramic statues of Indians and the Afro-Cuban deities Obatala, Chango, and Eleggua, protectors in the Yoruba religion. He placed plates of food before them as offerings. He lined up cigars, incense, glasses of water, and palm fronds in neat rows on the floor. From the living room, I could hear him pleading for help in winning back his wife's love.

One day, I decided I needed answers, too, and Cari and I joined a ceremony. The palm fronds trembled in Gerino's hands, but he clutched the green leaves firmly, sweeping the room, body swaying. Dressed in black polyester pants and a thin, almost transparent light blue shirt, he slapped the floor, windows and walls. The long green fronds, much taller than he, weighed heavily in his arms, and he struggled for control. He stumbled to a chair next to Cari and collapsed into a trance, eyes closed.

"What do you see?" Gerino asked, rolling his hands into fists. The color of his skin started to change, the pigment deepening into a toast-brown.

"I see an Indian," I whispered. Cari said nothing.

Gerino nodded and took up a cigar. Without opening his eyes, he lit it and puffed smoke all around him.

"And now, what do you see? Look at Cari's hands. What do you see?"

His voice had lost tone, as if coming from a well.

I looked at Cari's hands, large, strong prominent bones and sunburned. The skin folded into wrinkles. The knuckles thickened, protruding like door knobs.

"I see an old woman," I gasped, frightened. "Look, look at her hands!"

"*Si.*"

"You're going to work like me some day," Gerino said. Cari slumped back in the chair, overtaken by deep sleep, her hands shriveling up little by little.

"*Ahora viene el espiritu,*" he cried out, warning that the spirit was on its way. Gerino's eyes rolled back into his head, and he spoke an unintelligible language. He jumped up, jerking his body around and bending over as if he were going to regurgitate. He extended his arms out at his sides as he took on the spirit of the dead Indian. He threw himself on the floor, thrashing around until he almost hit his head against the wall, all the while speaking in tongues.

Why was I here? All I wanted was the warmth of family in my cold world.

Coming down from his trance, Gerino wiped his face clean of sweat. Cari opened her eyes, but she acted like she knew nothing of what had gone on. Gerino took out the *caracoles* -- shells which he used to divine the past and foretell the future -- from a velvet pouch and scattered them on the floor. From the shells' haphazard configuration, spiritualists believe they can gain an answer. He asked questions about his wife's affair. We waited, the shells mute. Their position meant nothing to Cari's father. Sadly, he gathered them up and invited me to ask questions.

"Why did my father leave us?" I threw out. "Does he love me? Is my mother sick? Does she love me?" Gerino cast the shells on the floor. We waited; he frowned and cursed. He picked them up and shoved them back into the pouch, shaking his head. The lack of answers devastated me. I saw my mother and father drawing farther and farther away, becoming figurines on a shelf. Like most abandoned and neglected children, I felt rebellion and anger, and I developed a tough I-don't-care attitude that my father later diagnosed – relying on his psychiatry course -- as a method of overcompensating for lack of love.

After the experience with Gerino, I tried to fill my emptiness with the spirit world. I felt spirits everywhere and at unexpected times. One evening, I came home from a stint as a volunteer Candy Striper at Jackson Memorial Hospital. My mother was still working. I put the key in the lock, and, just before I turned it, I heard doors slamming inside. I ran back out to the sidewalk and paced up and down, wringing my hands. My mother arrived after a few minutes.

"*Tengo miedo.*" I told her I was frightened.

"Of what? There's nobody here," she said, and made for the bedroom. A strange response from my mother, but I figured she was in one of her "light" moments, in touch with reality.

The car swerved on the ramp of the newly constructed expressway connecting Little Havana with the sprawling suburbs out west. Gerino struggled for control of the vehicle. He gripped the collar of his wife's blouse and tugged with all his strength, steering as best he could with his other hand. Aurora, bleached-white hair in short layers around her face, black-lined eyes, and long silver-lacquered nails, pushed against the car door and tried to swing her legs out into the highway.

"*Quiero morirme*," Aurora yelled she wanted to die, fighting hard to jump from the moving car. The open door scraped against a concrete barrier. Gerino pulled harder, and Aurora collapsed back into her seat, crying disconsolately.

We were driving home from a bowling alley in Westchester, a booming suburb replete with strip malls containing an uncoordinated line-up of stores: liquor stores, tire outlets, pet shops, flower shops, motorcycle repair shops, in a vulgar display of commercialism gone awry. Cari and I clasped hands.

Gerino reached over, slammed down the lock and picked up speed.

"*Por favor*, Aurora," he pleaded. "Why can't you love me? I am your husband!"

Aurora didn't answer.

Gerino dropped me at home and drove off, all of them crying.

La Niña, Aurora's sister, knew about the passion Aurora felt for her husband Pipo. It didn't seem to bother her, and it wasn't clear if Pipo returned Aurora's feeling. La Niña, always in a buoyant mood, ripped out off-color jokes as she washed hair and swept the floor in the beauty salon where Aurora and Gerino worked as hairdressers.

"*Mamita, le dije a Maria*," she said she told her friend, "button up your blouse so maybe you won't have so many men yelling at you in the street!" Pipo, lithe and sunburned, with black greasy hair and a smirk that bespoke of a fun-filled past, ran errands for the business and took charge of the supplies.

Maria Antonia, La Niña's daughter, worked as the cashier at the salon. Strips of acne formed a scarred mask on her face. She walked around boldly, gait uncoordinated, and challenged everyone with a cold gaze. She wasn't pretty and blonde like Cari, but she had what her cousin wanted, a pale young man with a round face named Esteban.

When Esteban drove up to Cari's Little Havana duplex where La Niña, Pipo and Maria Antonia lived in the back unit, Cari hid behind the curtains and watched her cousin saunter out to meet him. "Why doesn't he notice me?" Cari cried into the curtain. "Why can't he love me? I'm going to tell my father to ask the spirits to make him love me."

"It may not work," I said, remembering the silent shells. "Let's find new boys of our own. Esteban is no good."

Cari, a year older than me, only had her restricted license, but she drove her mother's car anyway. We left the lovebirds on the front porch and headed to the beach. There we engaged some boys in a sand throwing battle, but Cari's heart was not in it, and she begged me to leave.

10.

Something seemed different about my father when he picked me up at home that day. It was spring, 1968, I was fourteen, and he had just returned from Beaumont, driving a strange car with an upside down peace sign on the grill. I jumped in the automobile, settling into the soft leather seats, sliding my hand over the smooth wood grained panels and inhaling the new car smell. He wore a blue tie and white shirt, the jacket of his dark blue suit draped over the back seat.

"Let's go to El Baturro for lunch," he said. He looked at my clothes and frowned. I was wearing brown crepe elephant pants -- hip-hugging bell-bottoms with extremely wide legs -- and had tied a silky brown scarf with beige polka dots round my head. I bought this attire with my saved-up birthday money.

"You look like a hippie," he said, wrinkling his nose and accelerating.

"These are the most fashionable clothes in Miami," I fiddled with the radio knobs. The Beatles blasted from the side speakers, making the car shake ever so slightly. "I adore the Beatles!"

"Don't you like classical music?" My father lunged for the volume.

"It's boring. It all sounds the same." I kept my fingers glued to the knob, shimmying in my seat.

He had no time to answer since right then, a black man ran across the street in front of us, causing him to swerve and lean on the horn. "You have to be careful, Cecilita," he exclaimed, "if you run over *un Negro*, you have to pay for him as if he were a white man. I'm glad they killed (Martin Luther) King. He was causing problems for this country." My father believed King, assassinated earlier that year, was a communist conspirator. He said that men like King were behind the Viet Nam antiwar forces that, by then, numbered in the millions in the United States.

My father switched lanes, slowed down and turned into El Baturro, a classic Spanish restaurant on Northwest Seventh Street, just a few blocks from home. Later, it was torn down to make room for South Florida's first Spanish-language television station, part of the Spanish International Network now called Univision.

At El Baturro, I ordered *caldo gallego*, a white bean soup made with collard greens and pork, and my father chose the *cocido madrileno*, a stew of ham, sausage, pork, cabbage and potatoes. I was ravenous. My mother had stopped cooking altogether, and I grabbed a meal wherever I could, mostly in scraps at my friends' houses.

"Cecilita, I now have more money. I'm going to give you $30 a month for your personal expenses." I nodded at the good news. The $300 he gave my mother each month barely covered the mortgage, utilities, bus fare and food. With the additional money, I could buy clothes, makeup and eat at McDonald's or Morro Castle every once in a while.

"I rented an apartment on Biscayne Boulevard," he continued, "I have a beautiful view of the bay, and there's a tennis court. I'll be starting my own practice here in Miami now. I saw an office in Hialeah that I like, and I'll have hospital privileges at Palm Springs Hospital. And...," he looked up from his bowl and held the spoon up in midair.

"Uh, huh," I said, ladling the soup into my mouth with quick strokes.

"I got married."

I felt a strange lifting sensation, as if I were floating to the top row of a stadium and watching a game from above. Hurtful words back then -- and even now -- never made an impact on me at the moment. To cope, I had learned to delay the effect of any emotion that threatened to crush my heart. I kept eating on a reflex, but noticed that the soup now tasted like unsweetened oatmeal. My father waited without eating. I put down my spoon.

I thought back to the day that I called our family friend David from the drugstore, crying about my father's mistress, the same day I phoned my father to ask for money. "He will never marry Beba," David had assured me then. He had been wrong, and now I had Beba for a stepmother, a situation I abhorred, and, I worried, would only take my father further away.

"I don't want to see her. Can we go home now?" I covered up the shock as best I could.

My father did not protest. He flagged down the waiter, and, while he paid the check for the uneaten food, I got up and walked outside to the car.

"And...Cecilita," he paused. "Your mother told me about the shoplifting. Please don't tell Beba if you do decide to talk to her."

Was Beba's opinion of me the only thing he cared about?

I looked out the window as we drove home and spotted my mother walking north on Twenty-Seventh Avenue. My father saw her, too. She wore a snug two-piece suit in a woven cotton material and mid-size black pumps. Her hips swung rhythmically from side to side. Had my mother ever been aware of the power of her beauty? But seeing her walking home alone – the old Dodge Dart in the shop -- lugging a gallon of milk while I sat in my father's new fancy car made me aware of something much more appalling. I thought of Elsie and the lessons she tried to teach me back in La Habana.

I understood now that there were people in the world who exploited another's physical or psychological weaknesses for their own benefit. My father, one of the exploiters, took advantage of my mother's mental state and cheated her out of much needed funds through an unfair divorce settlement. I realized I either had to learn how to battle people like him to get what I wanted, or, more importantly, make sure I didn't need anyone by relying solely upon myself.

That moment in the car proved to be pivotal, the strongest catalyst so far to spur a life-long anger against injustice and ruthless authority. My father's lack of sensitivity drove, inadvertently, my politics of rebellion, a philosophy he hated.

I grieved for my mother's mental and material decline, yet the vibrant presence of my father didn't allow me to completely identify with her. I felt an inner strength that matched his, and I wanted to escape to his much better world someday. My father had pulled himself out of Little Havana, but he wasn't yet callous enough to abandon me altogether as he began his step by step climb into the land of the wealthy Cuban elite.

From that day on, I understood that my mother and I would remain on the fringes of his community until I found a way out. We were the have-nots, and he made sure we stayed that way by only sharing an infinitesimal portion of his wealth. Had he forgotten the role my mother played in launching his career in La Habana? She supported him during medical school, and my maternal grandfather, a university professor, helped him obtain jobs through his personal connections.

"She doesn't look bad," he said softly, watching my mother until he turned left onto Ninth Street. He pulled into the driveway and turned off the ignition. "Be very careful, Cecilita," he lowered his voice as if he were taking me into his confidence. "There are drugs out there, and alcohol. Don't ever get in a car with a boy who has been drinking. If he is speeding, just lean over and turn off the car. It's very dangerous here in America for teenagers. They are turning into hippies. I'm back in Miami now, so you won't be so alone. I can help you more now. You can spend time at my house."

It came off as a prepared speech from a man who knows his duty but wants to keep his distance. This was a new version of my father. Decidedly, he was no longer my "*papi*ton," the adored father who had told me "you are all I have."

"I don't want to go to your house," I said. My father shrugged. I walked inside, and a punch of pain streaked through my lower abdomen. In the bathroom, I saw blood on the toilet paper. I slipped into the belt that held the Kotex pad with safety pins, the belts used before there were stick-on pads.

"I just had my period two weeks ago," I told Ibis on the phone.

"You can get it again in the same month if you receive a big shock," she explained.

11.

When I'm feeling blue, all I have to do is take a look at you and then I'm not so blue.

The music streamed out of Jaime's car radio, flooding the quiet street with sound. He slid into my driveway and honked. I ran out of the house and hugged him, fiercely.

"I have never felt so loved," he whispered into my tangled hair.

I climbed up on the hood of the battered 1962 silver blue Corsair and ordered him to drive me around, leaning back on the windshield and spreading my arms as if ready to fly. Jaime pressed on the accelerator, gathering speed at short intervals so I could feel the wind push me back onto the glass and then slowing down. We laughed, not caring what the neighbors would say.

"Marry me," he said once I glided into the passenger seat.

"OK." I was fourteen in 1968, all so simple. No talk about future college or career plans, money in the bank, compatibility.

It was early in the morning, and we were skipping school, our bathing suits underneath our clothes. Jaime drove to downtown Miami and parked on a side street. We climbed up the steep steps to Gesu Church and slipped inside the darkened, empty building. The smell of crushed, wilting roses fused with the still, dank air. Holding hands, we walked toward the awe-inspiring altar and kneeled on a pew. Jaime turned to face the cross.

"Here, in front of God, we are joined together as man and wife," he whispered. "We are married now. No one can separate us."

I stared at the crucifix. Ceramic blood poured out of Jesus's side. I looked up at the ceiling-high, stained glass windows. I watched the flickering candles in red glass holders. The varnished wood of the pew caressed my bare thighs, but I fidgeted uneasily, accepting a light kiss.

The church, built in 1896, is the oldest Catholic parish in Miami and on the National Register of Historic Places. It offered Cuban refugees an oasis of luxury and peace in rundown downtown. For a brief time in 1961, the adjoining school became the first U.S. site of Belen Jesuit Preparatory School, established in 1854 in Cuba but relocating to Miami after Castro, himself an alumnus, expelled the Jesuits. In the 1980s, Little Havana in shambles, the school moved out to the southern suburbs, hoping to attract successful Cubans who could pay for their kids' tuition. Belen is now one of the top 50 Catholic high schools in the nation.

That early morning, the heaviness of the church's atmosphere made me squirm on the bench. I gripped Jaime's hand and motioned toward the door.

"Let's go to the beach now," I said, weary of the somber mood.

Outside, our spirits soared, and I promptly forgot the stuffy church and Jaime's marriage ceremony. We drove to Tahiti Beach, a hidden enclave across a bridge adjacent to Dinner Key Marina in Coconut Grove. Developers had excavated this section of real estate and planned to build a luxury condominium called Grove Isle. We parked under a tree where the car couldn't be spotted from the road and spread towels on the sand. Jaime brought out a basket filled with meat and guava *pasteles* wrapped in paper napkins. In this narrow stretch of island, the water was brown and filled with jagged seashells that cut your feet if you weren't careful. We walked out to the deep part. Jaime dove in and out between my legs. I wasn't a good swimmer, so I inched over to the shore. Then we lay down on the towels, away from the relentless sun, in a maze of trees that sheltered us from sight. We were soon lost under the leaves, locked in an embrace.

After the church ritual, Jaime considered us to be inextricably bound; he often mentioned we were husband and wife. He told me couples he knew were driving to Georgia to get married, since no barriers existed there for under-aged teens who did not have parental permission. I listened with interest, but we never made such plans, and I took it all in fun. Had I been a typical Cuban girl, or been raised by strict Cuban parents with grandparents around and in a traditional Cuban home, Jaime would have been my boyfriend for my entire school years. I would have married him after graduation, if not before, to be a wife for the rest of my life. But I wasn't a typical Cuban girl.

My love life began with Jaime, who at five feet three was about two inches shorter than me. He went everywhere with me, so, in 1968, like Scott and Zelda Fitzgerald, we became known as indefatigable partyers in our Little Havana social scene. Uncomfortable with the height difference, I searched the shoe racks for dressy flats to match my party dresses. During the year I spent with him, I collected an array of low-heeled shoes: silver and gold slippers with bright jewels along the straps, a slick black patent leather pair with a neat bow in the front, striped pink and white sling-backs. (By now, I had discarded my ugly brown saddle shoes, and no one could make me wear them.) With my flats and a bit of slouching, I disguised the height disparity.

Other than that Jaime was perfect: well-mannered, well-dressed, intelligent, expressive, warm, affectionate, respectful, funny. His thick hair rested sensuously across his forehead. Wide, long lashed eyes shone when he spoke. In one photograph of him in my scrapbook, the caption reads: "My muscle bound companion." Jaime wanted to be an architect and proudly showed me stacks of plans that he had created on his drafting table at school. An athlete, he played football and baseball with the school and travel teams. And he loved me.

I wish now that I had had a glimpse of the future to be able to appreciate him. I tortured him with temper tantrums, silent treatments, telephone hang-ups. I sneaked out to parties and threatened him with dating other boys. One afternoon at school, angered over something, I threw down my books on the hall floor and screamed at him. He picked each one up and carried them to my next class like he always did. Another time, I threw his watch on the ground and stomped on it. Then I jumped on my bike and rode off with my friend Ibis. I looked back and saw my mother, who witnessed the scene from the kitchen window, smile as if she were pleased. Maybe she felt I was avenging her pain from my father by inflicting suffering on men?

"No man will ever love you like Jaime," my friends said.

They were right.

I met Jaime at a party. His brother Maximo, a classmate, had brought his older brother along and Jaime, who was 16 and in the ninth grade, whispered to him: "I met the girl who will be my wife." He wanted me with the definitive feeling of a knife slicing bread. He winked at me, but I noted a sad slant in his gaze, something incomprehensible and deep. From that day on, Jaime wrote me long letters and poems expressing a type of love I could not understand. For Valentine's Day, he sculpted a ceramic heart, painted it red and drew our initials on it. He begged his mother to name his new-born sister Cecilia. He brought me piles of jewelry from his father's toy store, Los Reyes Magos, where the entire family worked. One gift was a set of yellow crystal earrings and necklace I still keep in a box along with the now shattered ceramic heart.

"*Dios mio*," my mother remarked. "He seems serious about you." But her tone was sarcastic, guarded, suspicious.

Jaime even gave me his grandmother's amethyst ring. In another rage over an insignificant matter, I threw the ring down on the sidewalk in front of my house. Jaime looked for it on his hands and knees. I want to say now that I, repentant, helped him find it. But I can't. Instead, I went back inside, got dressed in party clothes, tied a thin leather strip around my neck, and sneaked out the back door with my friend Gloria. We ran to the corner and jumped on the bus to a new disco in Little Havana. There I met Antonio. I danced for hours with him in the shadows of throbbing psychedelic purple lights to

Jimi Hendrix and Black Sabbath. A disco ball gyrated above us. At three in the morning, Antonio drove off with friends, and Gloria and I hitched a ride back home.

Jaime waited for me on the porch.

"Who were you with?" Jaime shouted when we walked up. He grabbed my purse, went through it, and found a scrap of paper with Antonio's phone number.

"*Que pasa?*" My mother walked unsteadily onto the porch. Gloria, who was staying over, asked her for some sheets to make up the couch, and they went inside.

I grabbed the paper from Jaime's hand, tore it to pieces and stomped into the living room. Jaime followed, but then he fell to the floor in a fit, thrashing from side to side. I kneeled next to him and shook him by the shoulders.

"Jaime, Jaime," I screamed. Gloria ran for a glass of water and sprinkled it into his face. But Jaime did not respond. His eyes floated back in his head. He moaned and trembled until the sun came up. Finally, he got up and drove off in his car without saying a word.

When he was gone, I called my father, "*Papi*, my boyfriend Jaime fainted last night." I described what had happened.

"That's an epileptic seizure."

"Really!"

"You have to break up with him. All you have to do is give him the cold shoulder...*dale frio, frio, frio.* He'll get the message and leave you on his own."

I ignored his advice.

I bought a pack of condoms at the corner drugstore, turning my eyes away from the cashier's surprised face, and taped it underneath my vanity table for when needed. But it wasn't all about sex at age 14. How comforting it felt for Jaime to stay with me after school until my mother arrived from work late in the evening. It was even more comforting for him to stay overnight, acting almost like a caring, attentive parent.

Everybody at Citrus Grove was talking about condoms since sex was on every teenage mind. Once, Ibis and I sat in the back of the bus reading pornographic novels: Terry Southern's *Candy*, originally banned in France only to become one of the bestselling novels in 1960s America, and John Cleland's 1748 memoir of a prostitute, *The Life and Adventures of Miss Fanny Hill.* (Just two years before, the U.S. Supreme Court ruled it did not meet the standard for obscenity and took it off the banned book list.) I felt a strange pleasurable sensation as we read the exciting passages aloud, the bus going back and forth over our route, our stop forgotten and the bus driver oblivious.

One night, Jaime came over only minutes after my mother closed her bedroom door. I switched the lights on and off as a signal that the coast was clear. Jaime walked stealthily through the back yard, opened the screen door, tip-toed through a small courtyard, slid opened glass doors, and made his way through a back room into my bedroom. When he arrived, we necked and petted but did not go all the way – not yet.

Jaime began coming over several nights a week. As a precaution against intrusion, I installed a chain on the door that led to the closet which connected to my mother's room. He nursed me through debilitating menstrual cramps, handing me tablets of Midol with a glass of water and plugging in the hot pad. When I had the flu, he eased my congestion with Vicks Vapor Rub, covering the ointment with tissues on my chest and back to keep in the warmth. How wonderful it felt to be loved.

My mother never suspected, but his parents did. Once, they knocked on the door at midnight. My mother struggled awake.

"*No esta aqui.*" She told them Jaime was not there.

"*Ay, Dios Mio*, Jesus, help me," his mother cried out. "I know my son is here."

Jaime pulled on his clothes, sprinted through the back room, climbed out the window, tore through the yard and drove off in the borrowed car he had parked a block away. When I opened the bedroom door to the demanding knocks of his mother, no one was inside but me.

12.

The Utes, a group of high school boys from the nearby city of Hialeah, organized the open house that night in 1968. The leader, Alberto San Pedro, convicted years later of drug smuggling, bribery and racketeering, smiled at the door of the Polish-American Club, tucked in a corner on the south side of the Northwest Twenty-Second Avenue Bridge. In the 1980s, when South Florida burned with drug money, race riots, and street shootings, his name appeared prominently in the news as "The Great Corruptor." The police claimed he bribed every political figure in the state: Cuban or Anglo. I handed him my money, and he looked at me with slightly crossed eyes.

Gloria poked me. "He's no good," she whispered.

I winked at him and skipped inside.

Competing Cuban youth groups calling themselves "fraternities" organized these parties throughout Little Havana almost every weekend. Enterprising precursors to gangs that later delved into criminal activity, the "fraternities" rented space in old dance halls, hired a band, charged admission at the door and sold soft drinks inside. They made a lot of money.

The fraternities appeared in the two neighborhoods where Cuban exiles took up residence, Little Havana and Hialeah. They formed partly in response to the stress of cultural conflict with the Anglos who mercilessly picked on Cuban boys unless they had gang affiliations, and partly out of loneliness from the neglect of poor immigrant parents too busy to pay attention.

The fraternity names relayed toughness: the Vulcans, Aztecs, Hawks. They were daring. One alleged fraternity member was sentenced to sixty years in prison for the attempted murder of two police officers during a car chase. Sometimes, we heard of classmates who ended up at Jackson Memorial Hospital in the pre-dawn hours, suffering from multiple knife wounds. In the sixties, poor Cuban youth, trapped in Little Havana, didn't have many alternatives.

In the mid-1970s, the fraternities disappeared; they were no longer needed for survival as the Cuban community grew economically and politically. In the 1980s, gang warfare spiked again with the arrival of 125,000 new Cubans in the Mariel boatlift. Many of the refugees had criminal records; it didn't take them long to challenge the Colombian gangs for dominance over the drug trade in Miami, an important entry point for cocaine. The 1983 film *Scarface,* in which a Cuban immigrant takes over a drug cartel, and the 1984 television series Miami Vice thrust South Florida into the national spotlight as it highlighted the era's gang violence.

While gang activity today is nowhere near as prevalent in South Florida as it is in South California, Miami-Dade has the seventh highest gang population in America, the highest in the Southeast, and the second highest on the entire East Coast, after Essex County, New Jersey. The FBI says the area is home to nearly 17,000 gang members.

At the open house, the loud, throbbing music pushed the partygoers into a frenzy of sweating, pounding bodies, releasing frustration and desire on the dance floor. My friends and I were sought after girls, and we knew it. Dressed in the latest styles and flashing the smile that kept us just out of reach, we soon had a handful of boys asking us to dance. For several hours, we jumped and swayed with everybody else.

Then, out of nowhere, chairs flew over our heads. Yells bounced up all around us. Knives flashed in the semi-darkness. Two boys jumped on tables to get out of the way. Two others charged after them, one wielding a broken Coca-Cola bottle, the other swinging a thick chain around his head, smacking it against chairs and tables before it caught another boy who dropped to the ground on impact. Ibis, Gloria and I huddled together against a wall, our arms around each other.

"It's the Crowns," someone shouted. "They got in and are fighting the Utes!"

The battling boys overturned tables. The chaperones -- mothers, grandmothers, aunts, big sisters -- sitting in rows of chairs on both sides of the dance floor, ran around screaming for their female charges. Some of them swung their purses like clubs to fight their way into the melee of arms and legs. Neither my friends nor I ever had chaperones, so we were on our own.

"Let's go to my aunt's house," Ibis said. "She lives nearby."

"I'm going to Jaime's house," I said, "He lives two blocks away." We pushed our way to the door and heard the whine of police cars in the distance.

"*Te llamo mañana,*" I called to Gloria and Ibis, who were already on the way down the street, and started a brisk walk up over the bridge. It was about ten o'clock. I looked behind me and saw three or four patrol cars squeal to a halt at the Polish-American Club. Their lights made the dark street seem festive. A dozen police officers jumped out and rushed into the dance hall, some drawing guns. Over the bridge and two more blocks and I was at Jaime's apartment just a stone's throw from the Miami River. His mother opened the door, frowning.

"*Esta Jaime?*" I asked.

"*Esta acostado.*" She said he was in bed and eyed me reproachfully. She did not invite me in. I stood there quietly.

Jaime's brother Maximo walked over.

"He's been tearing his hair out all night," he said. "He was so sick he couldn't even go with my father and me to dump the car in the canal."

"What?"

"That's the only way we can get money to buy a new car," Maximo said. "From the insurance. Get it? Jaime was tearing his hair out, crying that you had gone to a party without him, and then he fainted." He opened the door wider to let me in. He was angry, but I knew he liked me. At one party, when his brother was not there, he held me close and tight during a slow song.

"*Es tu culpa.*" His mother said it was my fault Jaime was sick, but she took a step back, her eyes following me as Maximo led me to his brother's room. Jaime lay on the bed, his face to the wall. I kneeled down and took his hand.

"Don't go out on me anymore," he whispered, gripping my arm.

"I'm too young to be tied down," I answered gently. "I want to live life."

"Don't you want a husband and a house?"

"No."

By this time, I had big dreams for my future as a writer. I worked diligently on the sample lessons the Famous Writers School had mailed me in an attempt to sell me their course. The enticing brochures offered useful writing tips. I had concluded that writing would be my ticket out of Little Havana. I figured it was the only thing I loved and the only skill I could master. I dreamed that I was going to be famous, rich and sought after by many men, just like Scarlet O'Hara in *Gone with the Wind*.

I remembered when I dictated Christmas stories to my mother in elementary school, took a creative writing class in an after school program, joined the staff of the junior high literary magazine, and tossed together words in blank verse every other day. I had just finished a series of stories based on my secret trysts with Jaime. It seemed like a logical choice of careers: I would get paid to write, and I would live an exciting life. It made so much sense.

13.

Walking home one afternoon, my friend Ibis bumped into a modeling scout. After a brief conversation with the man, Ibis ran to the phone to tell me the news. "I'm too fat but I got his number so you can call him and set up an interview," she said. "I told him about you. It will be perfect for you."

My heart beat faster. Maybe modeling could provide the money to help my mother. It could be a quick way out of Little Havana. How many things could I do and buy if I only had the money?

The modeling idea appealed to my love of fashion. Like many girls in my community, and probably everywhere else in the world, I was obsessed with makeup and new trendy clothes, thanks to the persuasive power of New York's Madison Avenue advertising mafia. From articles in *Seventeen* and *Cosmopolitan*, I put together a scrapbook of tips on hair styling, make-up application, and wardrobe coordination.

My friends and I scoured the magazine racks for new models promoting winsome styles and set out to copy them, blindly accepting their representation of the female figure. It was expensive to keep up with the latest fashions, even with the extra $30 my father sent, so we bought cheap material at the fabric stores downtown, and neighborhood seamstresses -- eking out meager livings with their needles -- created the trendy garments for a low price.

In Little Havana, a couple of entrepreneurs followed Madison Avenue's lead and launched some little newspapers and magazines – precursors of the area's lucrative Spanish language media -- to showcase products and services. They scouted around the neighborhoods and hired the locals to act as models for the ads with which they filled their publications.

I dialed the number, never considering possible danger. He answered in a flat tone and gave me his address for an "appointment" at 2 p.m. the next Saturday.

On Saturday, I applied eyeliner and pulled on a mini skirt and sweater top. I took the bus rather than my bike. I knocked on the door. He answered.

"I'm...."

"I know. Follow me," he said after giving my hand a fast shake. The house, empty and quiet, smelled of smoke and ripe mangoes.

The man walked with one leg dragging behind him. When he placed his weight on his good leg, he leaned all the way to the right, swiveled his hip around and pushed the dead leg up to the level of the other one. He wore black pants with a belt and a white shirt, sleeves rolled up to his elbow, open at the neck. He reached a recliner chair and slumped down into it, drawing up the leg rest, so he sat back in a relaxed position.

"I was hurt in a shootout against Fidel," he said, noticing the question in my eyes. "But I did a lot of damage to them too. I had a machine gun. They put my brother up against the *paredon* and killed him right before my eyes." He glanced at the immobile leg awkwardly stretched out in front of him. I didn't respond. Something about him seemed strange, and my palms began to sweat.

"Ok, I know you don't care about Fidel," he said. "So let's get down to why you're here. You need money and want to know if you have what it takes to be a famous model. Right?"

I nodded slightly. My heart thumped wildly.

"You young girls of today all want that," he laughed. "I have a modeling agency. I pick the models with talent, who have that certain something, and then I send them out to the magazines so they can be photographed for advertisements. Let's start. Walk up and down in front of me. Show off your figure."

I walked stiffly a few times, back and forth, keeping my eyes on his face, unsmiling.

"Come on, is that all you can do? You can do better than that."

I didn't answer.

"Ok, sit down over there on that chair and raise your skirt as far as it goes up on your thigh." An alarm rang in my head, but I controlled the fear and sat in the chair. "Higher, higher," he commanded. I crossed my legs and moved ever so slightly to give a view of my upper thigh.

He jerked in his recliner, trying to get the foot rest to go down so he could get up. But the recliner was stuck. He pushed harder, making a tremendous racket. The recliner trembled and shook but refused to budge. Finally, he slammed down the foot rest. He made his arms move like paddles in a canoe as he struggled up.

"Come here," he commanded. His dead leg was not cooperating so he turned around, balancing on the good leg, and grasped it with both hands. Then he twisted toward me.

Wordlessly, I jumped up from the chair and ran out of the house all the way to Ibis's some blocks away. I pounded on the door, breathing hard. She opened it. Her face twisted when she saw mine. We fell into each other's arms and cried. I was filled with shame and she with guilt.

"I'm so sorry," she said. "We'll find something else that makes money."

14.

Groovin' on a Sunday afternoon….

One day at school, right before lunch, we walked out: Gloria and her boyfriend El Chino, Ibis and her boyfriend Heri, and – forgetting our differences over the open house escapade -- Jaime and I. No one stopped us.

We walked past the football field and the basketball courts and then north on Northwest Twenty-Second Avenue to Seventh Street. We turned left and walked seven blocks to my house on Twenty-Ninth Avenue. I put on a 45 rpm record and switched the lever to repeat. I skipped to the kitchen to make lunch. My mother wasn't expected back until eight that night, so we had plenty of time. Ibis set the table with a white tablecloth from La Habana, and Gloria arranged the silverware. I filled a large pot with water and, once it boiled, threw in a box of spaghetti. I drained the pasta and put it back into the pot. I opened two cans of tomato sauce, poured them over the spaghetti and stirred. Then I sprinkled the concoction with grated cheese from a bottle. I sliced open a loaf of soft doughy Cuban bread and trickled olive oil up and down on both halves. I shook a thin layer of salt on the bread.

"*Pan como en Cuba.*" I called out that it was a special Cuban recipe.

El Chino, Heri and Jaime sat around the table. Ibis carried in the bread. I carried in the spaghetti, and Gloria brought in six plastic tumblers and a pitcher of Kool-Aid. We enjoyed this simple meal as if it were a seven course repast in a Tuscany villa. My friends and I sought attention and affection any way, anywhere we could get it, and because I was left home alone, we did whatever we wanted.

We've got a groovy kind of love…

Each couple drifted into a different part of the house. Ibis and Heri took my bedroom. Gloria and El Chino slumped into the couch in the living room. Jaime and I went into my mother's room. That afternoon, under the cool sheets, there was no stopping us. Jaime positioned himself to enter me and strained upwards; I shifted my hips to the side. One more thrust, and something gave way. In less than a second, I jumped up and ran to the bathroom.

"I want to marry you," Jaime called after me.

Several drops of blood trickled onto my hand. The condoms were still neatly taped under the table in my room. I had forgotten them. But I had known enough to stop in time.

I thought of Lena, the heroine of *The River,* a novel I found crumpled up without a cover at the bottom of a Salvation Army book bin. Lena's family ostracized her when she became pregnant. She drowned the baby. The injustice of her story had shaken me up, and I swore that I would not make the same mistake.

My father's voice sounded in my ears: "Remember that men are always out to take advantage of you." That idea supported the Cuban edict that said a girl must withhold sex to make a boy fall in love with her. Instinctively, I knew the double standard worked to empower men to discard women on a whim. Even without that sexual tug of war, my father had abandoned my mother. And didn't I have, as proof, the opposite reaction from my boyfriend Jaime? Did I feel remorse or fear for having sex with him? No.

Men would not have any power over me, sexual or otherwise. I just had to slip away from my father's control.

15.

"*Papi*," I said into the phone.

"*Dime*, Cecilita," my father sounded impatient. "I'm very busy. I have a woman with her legs open on the examining table! What is it?"

"The money didn't come this month."

"I sent it right on time."

"We didn't get it. Could you look into your checkbook? Maybe you forgot. Or maybe it was lost in the mail."

"I did not forget. And nothing gets lost in the American postal service. You just want an extra check so you can keep the money for yourself."

"No, that's not….."

The phone went dead with that awful sound of a space alien. He never sent the money, which meant my mother and I had to economize on water and electricity. My mother stopped driving and took the bus or walked, as she used to do before she bought the car.

I now had a thorough understanding of the power of money and its role in the system of class dynamics. That's how my father controlled my life. While he lived in the comfortable cocoon of a bay view condominium, my mother and I lived frugally, still fully immersed in the tumultuous life of newly arrived Cubans trying to earn a living. It was a two-tier system, and I lived in the lower one. As doctors, pharmacists, engineers, professors and lawyers revalidated licenses and dusted off academic credentials, they moved a little farther away—to Coral Gables, Coconut Grove, to the Roads—leaving behind the factory and service workers with whom they used to live. These workers, who held up the infrastructure of Little Havana, remained my neighbors.

I was an anomaly in my neighbors' eyes: a doctor's daughter living with the children of car mechanics, restaurant cooks, and housemaids. My status conferred upon me a little halo, but that was about all it offered as I struggled to survive just like everybody else. The solution: I needed to get -- not a modeling gig -- a real job. One afternoon, angry about the humiliation of asking my father for money, and walking home from school in a downpour because I didn't have money for the bus, I found one.

When it rains, as it often does in Miami, the gutters on Northwest Seventh Street overflow with brown water onto the sidewalks. But that didn't stop me from walking anywhere. I liked to get wet in the rain and never carried an umbrella. On the corner of Northwest Twenty-Second Avenue, a big two story house where my classmate Estela lived —and reputedly where Fidel had stayed on one of his visits to the United States—always caught my eye. I paused to stare. The walls were made of rough coral rock, dingy and gray. One night, Estela sneaked out through the window to meet her girl lover in the parking lot across the street. I looked up at the winding stairway and wondered how it felt to drop an entire floor down to the ground.

I continued to walk, passing businesses lining both sides of the street: Morro Castle, Miami Dance Studios, La Vida Pharmacy, El Oso Blanco Super Mercado, 7th Street Liquor, El Baturro restaurant, and a Burger King where junior high school boys threw ketchup and mustard at each other. Ducking under a ledge, I stopped to put up my drenched hair with a rubber band, and, turning, noticed a narrow, free-standing building with a neon sign in the window flashing "Diana's Bakery." Next to the neon sign, someone had artfully arranged rows of tantalizing cakes decorated with colorful meringue swirls.

Despite my wet hair, clothes and shoes, I went inside – dripping water -- and walked up to the cashier. Every Cuban pastry imaginable filled long steel pans side by side inside the counter: *tocino del cielo, pudin de pan, flan, natilla,* and *capuchinos.* I recognized the owner's son, a heavy-set boy not much older than me, who had dropped out of Citrus Grove to follow in his father's footsteps as a baker. He looked tired.

"I was up at 4 a.m.," he said when I said hi. He told me he rolled the dough into long loaves of Cuban bread and baked them in ovens in the back. He decorated the cakes himself, and mixed milk, eggs and vanilla every morning for the *natilla* and *flan.*

"It's better than school," he said. "I hate to go to class."

"Do you have a job for me?" At age fourteen, I legally could work. "My mother doesn't make a lot of money, and I …"

"One dollar and twenty five cents an hour," he said.

"Can I start this weekend?"

"Yes, but the job won't be here. We have a counter inside Zayre's."

"Ok, that's fine."

Zayre's department store was in the shopping center on Northwest Thirty Seventh Avenue and Seventh Street, the site of the Thanksgiving Day carnival. I filled out an application and some tax forms and, on Saturday, I started my first job. I served *pasteles de guayaba, churros, panatela de chocolate,* and *flan de coco* for ten hours on Saturday and Sunday and then four hours after school each day. But I lasted only two weeks. I hated the baker's son who watched every move I made with narrow beady eyes. He counted, over my shoulder, the change I gave out to customers. To thwart him, when he went to the bathroom, I sneaked pastries to the store clerks who walked by. Confident I could find another job as quickly as the first, I decided to quit.

"I can't take this job anymore," I told my friend Ibis. "Do you want it?"

"Sure."

I introduced Ibis as my cousin "newly-arrived-from-Cuba" to the owner's son and told him that she needed the job more than I did. He agreed to let her take my place. Ibis stayed for nine months. In that time, she overcharged customers, pocketed the extra money, and gave out free pastries to store clerks and friends alike. She collected an array of underclothes, toiletries, blouses, and cosmetics which she placed in boxes during her breaks and smuggled out to the parking lot where her mother was waiting in the car. She never got caught. I admired her ability to manipulate the system. Her mother, like mine, could barely cover living expenses, especially since boyfriend Lepido had moved out.

In less than a month, I had another job. My mother, now working as a clerk in a dry cleaning store in a predominantly Puerto Rican and Dominican neighborhood called Allapattah, talked to the manager, and he agreed I could work there on weekends.

I took in clothes, stapled tags on the collars and dumped them into a huge canvas bin. On Saturdays, I arrived at work fully made up and dressed to go to a party after the shift was over at 9 p.m. I liked this job a lot better: no mean supervisor, just my mother.

"Wow, you are beautiful." A young man with a camera around his neck stared at me shamelessly. He was a blond gringo, clearly not from the area.

"Thank you." I filled out an order sheet and stapled tags on his clothes as he continued to stare. My mother was in the back, so I was alone at the counter.

"I am a fashion photographer," he said. "Maybe I can take you to the beach and take pictures of you in your bathing suit. I can sell the photos and you too can make money. When are you off?"

"I don't think so," I said abruptly.

"How can you pass this up?" he insisted. His eyes were ocean blue with black streaks, his hair curly on his neck, his smile open and warm. I was tempted to accept, thinking about the money, but finally shook my head. I remembered the encounter with the so-called modeling agent. I definitely needed the extra cash, and I wanted to live an exciting life. I also wanted to avoid getting raped or murdered.

16.

Johan Strauss's *Emperor's Waltz* summoned fourteen couples onto the dance floor. They circled the hall, nodding to guests, and launched into the lively, sweeping dance of the Viennese courts of long ago. We girls wore yellow gowns with silver sequins scattered onto wide skirts, hair swept up into French twists, feet strapped into silver high heels. The boys, neatly shaven with every hair in place, wore black tuxedos with yellow carnations pinned to the lapels. I was taller than Jaime, so Cari paired me with a basketball-tall boy, while Jaime danced with a petite partner who promptly fell in love with him. All of us stepped carefully, struggling to keep the right distances and start off each time on the same foot as we had practiced in the months leading up to this night.

"Ohhhh," the guests exclaimed and burst out clapping.

Although Cari's father magical shells didn't speak for me, they delivered a stream of information for friends and neighbors who enriched Gerino with the cash to pay for an elaborate *quince* birthday party for his daughter. The celebration, a milestone in the life of a Cuban girl, marks her passage into womanhood. Would my father pay for my *quince*? Maybe I wouldn't have one! That evening in 1968, I pushed aside the unthinkable.

The dance hall, on an unlit, abandoned road running alongside the Miami River, sprawled next to a medley of rusty warehouses and junk yards, but it could have been located on the French Riviera for all the opulence inside. Gold paper clung to the walls, and Grecian arches decorated every corner. Dozens of guests—women in long gowns and men in tuxedos – sat at tables with orchid centerpieces, elegant white cloths, napkins tied up with yellow ribbons, and matchbook covers bearing Cari's name and birth date in gold-ink calligraphy.

We lined up on two sides of the hall, seven on each, to form a circle. Gerino and Cari, the fifteenth couple in the traditional Cuban ritual, waltzed in the middle. Cari's white gown gleamed, the most exquisite I had ever seen. A layer of lace covered a layer of white satin decorated with strands of pearls. Her blonde hair shimmered, make up highlighting each feature. On top of her head, she wore a pearl-and-rhinestone-encrusted tiara reflecting light from beveled glass chandeliers.

Cari's father trembled as they waltzed, nervous, until finally Esteban emerged from the shadows and took over for him. He was on loan from cousin Maria Antonia who was dancing in the circle with one of our schoolmates. Cari smiled brightly, but tensely, into Esteban's face. He enjoyed being the center of attention.

After the waltzing ritual, I skipped to the table where my mother sat by herself with strangers. She wore her New Year's dress with black lace sleeves and tiny black beads on the neckline. "Do you think I will have a *quince*?" I asked. She shrugged and handed me a pair of flat silver sandals. "I want one," I said. "How will we pay for it?" I cringed at the thought of asking my father.

"You will have to pay for it yourself," she said. I had to start saving more money from the laundry job, but even so I realized it would never be as grand as Cari's. I pushed off the high heels and slipped the sandals on before Jaime could join me. Jaime took my hand, and we walked over to the buffet table to fill our plates with mountains of *lechon* and *moros*. His infatuated dance partner watched from a corner and wiped away tears. The trumpet, flutes and conga drums of the Cuban band on the stage kept up a steady beat until four o'clock in the morning.

17.

Eight years after he had vigorously waved from the parapet of Miami International Airport as my mother and I walked toward him on the tarmac, my father repeated this action as his parents Rafael Fernandez and Amalia Rivas descended from the plane bringing them from La Habana. Eight years had made my grandparents unrecognizable. In the fall of 1968, they walked slowly through customs and down a long hallway to where we were standing.

My grandmother – fifty pounds lighter from when I last saw her -- wore a faded print dress in a grayish silky material. Nothing like the robust woman I remembered, she hunched over from a virulent case of osteoporosis. Her hair, wrapped behind her head in a gray bun, set off a prominent Spanish nose, huge in her emaciated face. My grandfather, his trousers held up by a belt too big and sporting a white worn out short sleeved shirt, slicked back his few remaining strands of hair, wispy and white. His hands, joints deformed by arthritis, shook.

"*Hijo!*" my grandfather exclaimed and hugged his son.

"*Mama,*" my father mumbled, turning to his mother.

Then he stepped aside. I was a full grown woman and no longer the six-year-old my grandparents remembered. The letters we had written back and forth had not prepared us for the physical changes. But now the stored up sorrow from so many painful years finally found an outlet when I bent down to hug my almost diminutive grandmother. Crying had no end. My grandfather, eyes submerged in tears, patted us both on the back.

My father and his wife, Beba, tossing her head arrogantly, waited without emotion. I straightened up, and my father took the opportunity to introduce his wife. He had insisted that she come along despite my outraged protestations. I did not speak to either of them on the ride to the airport. And now here stood Beba, an intruder, once a mistress, wide hips, wide nose and thick lips brightly glossed with red. Her eyebrows, neatly painted black half-moons above darting dark eyes, raised high.

"*Un placer.*" My grandmother said it was a pleasure to meet her as she shook hands, but the pursed lips and flaring nostrils told another story. My grandfather repeated the same words in a cold tone when it was his turn to shake hands. I understood that my grandparents were my allies in the struggle for my father's affection, but they had no power over their son. As we picked up the luggage, my grandmother leaned close, making sure that Beba was out of earshot. "*Y tu mama? Como esta?*" She asked about my mother. I shrugged and shook my head.

In the car, my father launched into his favorite subject. "After almost nine years of Castro, things are really bad," he said. He mentioned that Fidel had destroyed the last vestiges of private enterprise during a "revolutionary offensive" that closed 50,000 small businesses such as garages, pawn shops, music schools, laundries and even street fruit sellers. In a speech commemorating the establishment of the Committees for the Defense of the Revolution, actually neighborhood spy teams, Castro denounced long hair and fancy clothes and, soon after, the regime instituted mass shavings of long-haired men and sent mini-skirted girls and women to forced labor camps in the countryside. But while my father agreed with the hair and skirt policies, he was adamantly against the seizure of private property.

"It is the cause of all of Cuba's troubles," he cried. "It encourages people to be lazy and dependent on the government which controls them even more."

My grandparents agreed with everything, interjecting stories of family members left behind who, due to the lack of toilet paper, used leaves instead, or they sliced pieces of rubber from tires and tied them to their feet as shoes.

"The embargo has to squeeze the communists out of power," my father declared. In those days, no one admitted that the 1962 embargo the United States had placed on Cuba contributed to the island's lack of food, medicine and clothes, blaming communism instead. He particularly ridiculed Cuban doctors. My grandparents had undergone several surgeries in Cuba, including a radical mastectomy for my grandmother. "Those doctors are butchers," he said. "They know nothing."

Then he turned to the news in Little Havana: anti-Castro groups had taken responsibility for bombs exploding in a B-25 plane carrying medicines to Cuba and at two businesses which regularly shipped packages to the island. He praised Cuban pediatrician Orlando Bosch, a former CIA-backed operative, for his heroism in attacking a Polish freighter with a 57 mm recoilless rifle and in planting bombs in Cuban embassies all over South America. Later, in 1976, Bosch would be blamed for the bombing of Cubana Flight 455, killing all 73 people – including a youth fencing team -- on board.

"And I'm very happy they killed Kennedy's brother," he said, referring to the assassination of Senator Robert F. Kennedy in Los Angeles that summer. "He's another communist we had to get rid of."

Talk stopped when my father drove into a luxurious pink and white building that towered over Biscayne Bay. Plants artfully arranged filled the marble floored lobby. Plush carpet covered the hallways leading to each apartment unit.

My father swung open his front door, and the view from the bay -- spanning the length of a glass wall adjoining a balcony – rose up to greet us. My grandparents looked at the brand-new furniture in the style of the French King Louis XV. But I could not take my eyes off the aquamarine water of Biscayne Bay, splendid, a symbol of the power of money. I thought of my mother struggling to save to fix a leaky roof. The contrast between my simple house and this opulent apartment with its ostentatious wealth made my stomach ache.

My father busied himself with the luggage -- my grandparents were to have the back room -- and Beba set the table. I finally turned my back on the bay and sat on the couch between my grandparents. I gripped their hands. Their physical presence cast a net of protection over me as my father, a gourmet cook, carved the tenderloin roast, and spooned the béchamel sauce over the slices with an air of serving guests, not family.

At the table, under a massive glass and brass chandelier, my grandmother, a gourmet cook herself, turned up her nose at the blood red meat. I reached over to help myself to *croquetas de bacalao*, codfish croquettes. "Cecilita, please wait for the plate to be passed," my father said.

I reached over again, wanting to challenge my self-satisfied father.

"Your father just told you not to do that," Beba snapped.

I stared into her face and clicked my tongue against my teeth in rebellion.

We ate our first meal together without saying one more word.

18.

I listed all the reasons to break up with Jaime: too young to be tied down, missing out on life, boredom. In my head, I practiced how to tell him. During our year together, I never stopped sneaking out to parties and *quinces*. I began to drink wine every time I went out, not because I wanted to get drunk but because alcohol was readily available; back then in Little Havana, no one thought twice about handing glasses of wine or beer to minors. One night, the smell of alcohol on my breath spurred my mother into action.

"You are drunk," she yelled. She beat me with her open hand, just as she had done in Cuba when I broke a plate and in North Miami when I tripped over an electric cord and smashed up the radio. "You have shadows under your eyes. What have you been doing?"

I cowered against the wall. My mother could not be reached, the dark curtain blotting out the light. "Shadows mean you have had sex!" she screamed, pushing me to the floor. I had never heard of this; it seemed just another crazy thing my mother would say. But this time, I had had enough.

I scrambled back on my feet and fought back, fists flailing. Moving in close, I clamped my teeth over her eyebrow and bit down…hard. Pain and surprise arrested her assault. No longer weak and helpless, I beat the hell out of my mother.

She stepped backward. Then two steps, backing up all the way to her bed in the adjoining room. I went after her, tripped, and fell on my knees, remorse now knocking sense into me.

"Forgive me, forgive, forgive," I cried, kissing her feet

She pushed me away. I crawled on the floor to my room and locked the door against the madwoman outside and the one inside, me. Loneliness and frustration had found momentary relief.

The next day, feeling depressed about the fight with my mother, and oppressed by Jaime, I called him. If I were free, I'd feel better, I reasoned.

"My father's toy store burned down," he said in anguish. "We have to start all over again after everything we've gone through in this country." Burning buildings were common in Little Havana since the insurance money came in handy, just as with cars. I never found out, however, if it had been a case of arson. I paused, thinking to delay the breakup, but I couldn't let pity sway me from what I had to do.

"I don't want to be your girlfriend anymore," I said and hung up. I took the phone off its cradle. I didn't care if he fainted, went mad or jumped off a bridge.

He survived the blow.

The following week, just getting over the flu, I got ready to go to a party. I had not washed my hair in days, but neither the flu nor greasy hair kept me from going out that night. I sprinkled a powdery concoction on my scalp, designed to absorb the grease. Hair washing and bathing when one had a cold, my mother said, exacerbated fever, congestion and other symptoms. My mother and I, both always with colds, kept a good supply on hand of this product, extremely popular in Little Havana where mothers admonished their daughters not to bathe or wash their hair while menstruating. The old wives' tale came from a belief that girls would contract cancer, since the shock of the water could interfere with the menstrual flow.

So, adhering to the superstitions and with hair dry as hay, I donned flamboyant party clothes of elephant pants and a satiny blouse that crissed-crossed in the back and set out with Gloria, Ibis, Cari and Sylvia to the Polish American Club. We milled around watching the crowds, boldly looking over any newcomer for boyfriend potential.

In the week after Jaime, there had been Carlos, Alfredo, and Mario, all boys from school. They visited me at home and sat on the couch, since that's what boys were supposed to do, lapping up a few kisses and hugs on the porch. I kept them at arm's length, seeing in their dull eyes that the traditional Cuban values had taken over their power of independent thinking. They believed that any girl who went over the top with necking was *una puta*, a whore, and must be exchanged for one who held out all the way to the altar.

"He's eager to marry her so he can be with her in bed," I heard a party chaperone say proudly about a potential bridegroom. "She never gave in during their five years of courtship!" She believed the bride was a paragon of virtue. But I knew that the Cuban art of catching a husband was not for me, and boys as dull as the ones who had recently come to my door were best left for other girls.

Tonight, looking around the room, I saw that most of the boys fell into the "boring" category. They lined up along the walls, in the back, some up front near the band, checking us out with bland expressions. My gaze fell on a blond stranger dressed in a dark blue Nehru collared shirt. His light blue eyes settled on me as he danced with a move that I found interesting. I stared back, intensely. He had a serious look, but his smile promised fun. I was alone; my friends had scattered, dancing in different corners. The song ended, and the smiling stranger walked the girl back to the chaperone. I waited in the same spot.

"My name is Ovy," he said when he came back. "I go to Miami Springs High School. I live in Hialeah." Hialeah, northwest of Little Havana, a blue collar city known for its factories, seemed like another world, and this boy took on an exotic glow. He seemed different, in the margins of the Cuban taboo proponents, outside the goodie-goodie club of Little Havana.

He asked for my phone number, and committed it to memory. Then he turned to some friends and said, "Jose, remember these three numbers: 685. Watusi, remember these four numbers: 2367. That way I have back up and I won't forget."

I laughed and moved away to join my friends.

"He didn't write my number down," I said to Ibis. "He'll probably never call."

Already the cough syrup was running out of strength, and I felt feverish and weak. On the way home, in the December wind, I couldn't stop coughing. I got sicker that night and could barely speak when Ovy called the next afternoon.

"My number trick worked," he laughed. The very next day he came over, and since I still couldn't wash my hair, I dumped more dry powder on it to make it presentable. We talked on the porch before my mother scared me with getting pneumonia if I didn't go back to bed. After that, we talked on the phone every night. But it just so happened that before I went to that party, I had struck up a mild flirtation with friend Ibis's older brother Miguel. I figured I could juggle them both for a while.

19.

I didn't wear the mandatory satin and lace gown and rhinestone crown. I wore instead a wine-colored, crushed velvet skirt and vest over a pink crepe blouse a local seamstress had sewn together from a Simplicity pattern I bought at McCrory's. I did not spend the requisite hours at a beauty parlor for a stiffly teased and sprayed French twist with ringlets bouncing on both sides of my face. I arranged my own hair in loose waves past my shoulders and down my back, fluffy and voluminous from a day of being set with beer on Campbell soup cans. Unlike Cari's, my party did not take place in an echoing dance hall with a winding buffet table encircling fifteen waltzing couples that make up the "court" of the *quinceanera*.

My dining room provided the setting for this momentous birthday party – the traditional Cuban girl's debut into society. I served trays of tiny sandwiches filled with a mixture of canned deviled ham and cream cheese my mother, happy and focused that day, had made. A bowl of my grandmother's potato and apple salad, delivered earlier by my father, sat on the table. After a dozen friends sang "Happy Birthday," I blew out the candles on a cake from nearby La Gran Via Bakery that I had carried home myself. My mother and her aunt and uncle, Carmela and Manolo, sat on the couch drinking Kool-Aid with a few parents who stayed as chaperones.

"It's a waste of money," my father had said when I asked if he was going to pay for my *quince* on the scale of Cari's. Already suspecting that answer, I only felt a twinge of hurt and anger. I didn't crave a *quince* because I wanted to follow tradition. I longed for a symbol of my father's love. Instead, the party turned into an opportunity to show him my independence. I felt pleased with what I had created. If I didn't make myself feel important, no one else would.

"Then can you buy me some earrings and necklace," I asked, thinking there had to be another way for him to make up for this inexpensive gathering. To my surprise, he agreed. But the set was not the antiques I had pointed out in a downtown jewelry store window. He had a new ensemble made by a patient who was a jeweler: using 18 carat gold, garnets and emeralds, the jeweler twisted the earrings into a T shape and the pendant on the chain into the form of a bull's head with two intertwining horns. I did not like the pattern. My father even bought a matching bracelet, believing he was purchasing superior jewelry at a discount.

"Why buy something old when you can get something new," he said. Maybe he felt some affection when he asked the jeweler for an original design. To me it was just one more example of never giving me what I wanted.

Neither my father nor my grandparents attended the party. He thought it was better to stay away now that he had remarried, and that it would be a betrayal to Beba if he dropped off my grandparents at my house. The Cuban code frowns on any interaction between once-married couples and their respective families.

"Have fun," my grandmother said on the phone, voice raspy with tears. But as was customary for me during painful moments, I hurriedly buried the stab of pain and dove into the happiness of the moment.

At my simple *quince* on a cool January evening in 1969, after the sandwiches and cake and the opening of presents, my friends and I piled into several automobiles driven by boys already 16 and 17 and sped off to The Penthouse on the Seventy-Ninth Street Causeway in North Bay Village. Ovy, 16, one of the drivers, did not go as my date. I had chosen Ibis's brotherMiguel, who, quite a bit older, attracted me with a no-nonsense aura that spelled security. Still, I gazed longingly at Ovy, laughing, cracking jokes with the attitude of one who – like me -- makes the best of any situation.

In the parking lot of the club, police cars flashed their lights, and officers handcuffed some shady characters they had dragged out of the downstairs restaurant, The Place for Steak, a well-known hangout for Italian *mafioso* types. In the distance, lights from far off boats winked in the darkness.

"What kind of place is this?" several of my friends' mothers, the chaperones, asked. My mother only smiled, going with the flow. Ignoring the question, we squeezed into a mirrored elevator that took us to the top floor overlooking the bay. Smoke and loud music greeted us when we emerged.

The Penthouse – lit up with red lights visible from miles around -- was a trendy supper club for the 25 and older crowd, and I don't quite know how we managed to get in. The waitresses resembled Playboy bunnies. The chaperones, uncomfortable, sat at a table in the back, and my friends and I crowded into booths next to the dance floor where couples shared space with a three-piece band playing Frank Sinatra songs.

Ovy did not sit in the booths. He leaned against a wall and talked to a scantily clad waitress, looking up every once in a while, searching for my eyes, glaring at Miguel. Unlike the other boys, he did not wear a suit, just a long-sleeved shirt with open collar. I didn't dance with him, but I flirted from afar, keeping him in sight all night.

Miguel, who glared back at Ovy, wore a dark brown suit and tie and smelled of Brut cologne. We wrapped our arms around each other – sneaking a kiss here and then -- and only left the dance floor to eat a dinner of steak and vegetables served on steaming platters. Silverware and glass goblets sparkled next to white napkins on carefully pressed tablecloths.

At the close of the evening, Miguel reached back for his wallet and found it wasn't there. "Don't worry, I have money," I said. "I just got my allowance from my father." I whipped out some cash and paid the bill, about $10. I had already learned not to rely on boys for money, their ticket to power.

"I'll pay you back," Miguel said, and he did.

On the way out, I made a quick stop in the bathroom, marveling at the marble floors and walls and the sweet aroma. I washed my hands; an attendant handed me a cloth towel with one hand and stretched out the other for a tip. I took the towel but ignored the silent request, feeling guilty as I walked away.

20.

We sped off toward the Port of Miami, radio blaring, Cari at the wheel of her parents' slick new blue car, windows down, the November breeze tousling our hair. *He ain't heavy, he's my brother,* we shouted with the Hollies to pedestrians waiting to cross at street corners, laughing at their surprise. We headed downtown and cruised by the massive marble structure of the Dade County Library, on whose steps the homeless camped out each night, the adjacent amphitheater looming out like half an egg shell. A few blocks north, the Freedom Tower stretched up to the sky in its 1920s splendor, glowing gloriously in the sun, the bay sparkling on the other side.

The Freedom Tower, a processing site for Cuban refugees, handed out – among other things -- rations of a canned meat called Spam, a name that provoked many jokes in the community. The building is now a cultural and educational center and looks out on a string of hotels, a bayside festival marketplace and a sports arena that hug the edge of Biscayne Bay: the same place where captains of colorful fishing boats once sold fresh catch next to sailboat pilots offering midnight expeditions out at sea. Back then, the Port of Miami was in the middle of an ambitious expansion project and today, due to South Florida's unstoppable growth, Miami is the cargo gateway of the Americas and the cruise capital of the world with Carnival, Royal Caribbean and Norwegian cruise ships lined up at the harbor tendering unforgettable vacations.

But in 1969, no one I knew cared about the port or, for that matter, about the changing social fabric of America. While the Freedom Flights continued to transport Cuban refugees to Miami, and Castro instituted strict sugar rationing on the island, America exploded: students clashed with administrators on campuses, blacks battled police in the streets, gays engaged in violent demonstrations, Senator Edward Kennedy drove off a bridge that resulted in the death of a campaign aid and then left the scene, a man walked on the moon for the first time, and the Woodstock Music and Art Fair turned into three days of drugs, sex, and nudity for half a million people.

Little Havana, insulated, shut out the voices of change and went about its business of rebuilding lives and careers; however, many teens like myself enthusiastically responded to the new openness and sensed a liberation we found enticing. The counterculture spoke to me directly, a version of the voice of Elsie back in La Habana discoursing on injustice and inequality. No question that the social upheaval in my adopted country left its mark on my view of the world.

As Cari drove north on the boulevard, we spotted a gigantic Navy ship anchored in the harbor. We had never seen a ship this close before. On a whim, Cari parked, and, thinking it would be a fun place to meet boys, we joined the line for a tour. Soon, we broke loose from the group and skipped in and out of portholes and up and down steep steel stairs, causing a stir with the officers on board. We leaned over the railing as far as we could without flipping over into the water.

"Be careful with that." The blondest man with the bluest eyes looked at Cari and smiled. He wore a white officer's uniform decorated with a row of medals and a cap that shaded his face. Cari, blonde herself, a mixture of gold and silver streaks expertly created by her mother in the salon, slanted her hazel eyes in pleasure. "My name is Ben," he said. "Ben Clarke."

Right behind him stood a tall, thin, olive skinned, serious looking officer. "My name is Scott," he said and took my hand. "May I have the honor of knowing your name?" I felt no attraction, no sparks like I felt with Ovy or Miguel. Cari, already engaged in conversation with Ben, moved closer to the rail. All four of us, Scott was not unpleasant, strolled up and down the decks and kept up a quick exchange of words and laughter for at least an hour. The men, at least twenty, showed a keen interest in our teenage chatter.

The next day Ben came to pick up Cari at her house, but Cari's mother would not let her go out on a date unless I chaperoned, so I did. The day after that, he asked her to marry him.

In less than a month, I walked down the aisle on the arm of one of Cari's relatives, my bridesmaid dress a light blue gown strangely resembling the yellow one I had worn to waltz at her *quince*. Maria Antonia, the maid of honor, wore a darker blue gown, and walked behind me on Esteban's arm. Ben, dressed in a heavily decorated Navy uniform, stood tall with handsome face glowing at the altar.

It wasn't a shotgun wedding: Cari wasn't pregnant. But at sixteen, Cari —who had just dropped out of ninth grade at Citrus Grove Junior High -- didn't see a future for herself other than as a wife. Esteban, the one she loved, preferred her cousin, and Cari expressed no interest in a career. Her wedding in 1969 provided an escape from a life going nowhere, but it also served as a trap that promised a respite it couldn't deliver. I felt sad losing one of my best friends and a little frightened about Cari's sudden decision to leave her family and run off with a stranger.

The organ struck the chords of "Here Comes the Bride." Cari – beautiful -- appeared on her father's arm for the walk down to meet Ben, her wedding dress even more spectacular than her *quince* gown. Strips of pearls zig-zagged on a bodice that plunged to a point below her hips. The satin material fell in a cascade to the floor and kept right on flowing into a long train that defied the imagination. The veil, sprinkled with pearls, sat up above Cari's head like a royal crown. In a matter of weeks, Cari's mother Aurora had planned a wedding that outshone her daughter's fabulous *quince*.

"I don't care how much it costs," Aurora said. "That's why we took out a bank loan." To many in Little Havana, *quinces* and weddings were important investments, much more so than college.

As Gerino handed her over to Ben, Cari glanced at Esteban and then back to Ben. I held my breath, thinking she might turn and run. But they exchanged the lengthy vows, and I danced from one foot to another with impatience, unable to keep my attention focused on the words, distracted by Ovy, my date that night, who blew kisses to me from a pew behind me.

From the church, the wedding party drove in limousines to the reception hall for an extensive photography session and a buffet dinner. Tall candles, delicate flowers and "Cari and Ben" napkins and matchbooks decorated the tables. Ovy and I joined in the dancing with music from a live band. Then Cari threw the bouquet, but I stood in the back, making it impossible to catch, resisting the idea of marriage.

"Are you happy," I said, hugging Cari good-by, certain she still loved Esteban, who now officially dated Maria Antonia.

"Yes, there's nothing here for me." Cari had married to still the pain.

I watched her run to the car with Ben—both under a rain of rice—for the drive to Virginia Beach where they planned to live in a trailer while he worked on a tugboat.

Later at home, I looked at the map and wondered what life in Virginia was like. I had already lived in Chicago and Beaumont, but I had been a child. Would I ever leave Little Havana? It was a dangerous thought, forbidden in a community that encouraged family inter-dependence. But exciting too.

As thousands of America's youth in the 1960s turned their backs on middle class parents to live on the street or in communes, those of us in Little Havana did just the opposite. We clung to our parents, chasing elusive love from a distant father, a psychotic mother, or like Cari, demanding attention from an indifferent lover and then getting married with a stranger as the next best thing. Marriage, in our tightly knit Cuban community, symbolized the end of struggle. It solidified identities, staved off loneliness, sanctioned sex; it validated everything. To me, however, it signified betrayal, oppression and injustice as seen in my own family. But it was just a matter of time that, I, too, would succumb to the powerful pressure to become a bride.

4

ANYTHING BUT BOREDOM

Before we can go forward, we must go back.
— Lawrence Durrell

1.

The principal scowled. On his desk: two detentions written up by assistant principals. One outlined a slapping match with a student in gym class. The other detailed a screaming contest with the math teacher and included an abysmal attendance record.

"Her boyfriend is to blame," my mother said. "She never sleeps because of him. That's why she gets in trouble."

"Young lady," the principal said in a southern drawl. "If you don't calm down and tell your boyfriend you have to start coming to school, you will fail all your classes."

"This would never have happened in Cuba," my mother said.

"Do you have an explanation, Cecilia," he asked.

I stared out the window, refusing to answer questions. I didn't mention my mother's invisible strangers, or my father's meager monthly checks. I was 16, full of new strength. My involuntary coping mechanism did a good job blotting out the reality of my life, but my conscious mind demanded that I strike back at anyone who snubbed or insulted me – obviously misplaced anger against my parents. Both the student in gym class and the math teacher had been nasty, and they deserved my wrath.

Now, in high school and entering the late teens, my personal anger and sense of social injustice were tangible forces. I didn't know they were shaping me into the adult I would become. I still harbored my dream of writing, but the drama of the moment held me captive, pushing aside the nagging truth: I needed to do better in school if I wanted to leave Little Havana and become a writer.

"If anything like these incidents ever happens again," the principal warned, "you will be suspended."

We walked out of the office, and my mother stopped me in the hall. "Please, Cecilita..." Her eyes drooped, defeated. I turned away – the meeting with the principal relieving the monotony of school -- and went off to my boring biology class where teacher O'Hearn had put me in the back, so my chatting wouldn't disturb others.

It was my first year at Miami High, 1970. I loved the ornate splendor of the 1928 building on a corner of West Flagler Street, just east of Northwest Twenty-Seventh Avenue. When my mother dropped me off in her dilapidated Dodge on the first day of tenth grade, I paused to stare at the Spanish tile roof, the arched entrance way, the beauty of the architecture.

Then I noticed the cheap, muck-colored plywood covering its graceful bay windows. Thick black graffiti swirled in swaths across walls and doors, basketball gym and band room. A barbed wire fence separated the parking lot from narrow surrounding streets. Beyond the lot, stuffy pizza joints and cramped Cuban café counters huddled together to form an apron of hangouts for those who found classes too grueling. One day, pausing to look inside one particularly crowded cafeteria, Peggy Lee's hit song floated out to the street: "Is that all there is?" The question enthralled me. So much more out there, I knew. How to grasp it?

The bell rang. "Gloria. Ibis," I yelled, the visit with the principal forgotten. We waved wildly, separated by a wall of shoving students. I felt small in the wide, long, locker-lined hallways. The ceilings rose high above my head. The buffed floors felt smooth. If you looked down the hall, the shine offered a mirage of a trembling pool of water.

The students shouted back and forth in a mingled Spanish-English blur. Girls wore mini-skirts and boots, and boys sported hip-hugging bell bottom jeans and tie-dyed T-shirts. Almost everyone had long hair, girls and boys. Four thousand students slammed their lockers open and shut, desperately searching for books. The school was so crowded with the recent waves of Cuban refugees that it had instituted double sessions. (The twice-daily Freedom Flights from Cuba were in their fifth year and, under the immigration agreement, had three more to go.) I had the first session, from 7 a.m. to noon.

A group of students pushed past wearing black arm bands in protest of the Viet Nam war. Later that week, I witnessed the war's impact. On my way to the bathroom with a pass, I heard screams. I stood transfixed as a hysterical girl burst out of a classroom, clamored down the steps and burst out the front door, jumping into a waiting car which honked its way wildly out of the barbed wire parking lot. Two of her friends stood at the door crying. The teacher put her arms around them.

"It's terrible, terrible," one said. "He was so young."

That first year, screaming from grieving girlfriends and sisters echoed in the stairwells at regular intervals, signaling death on the battlefield.

Many Cubans supported the war because it was being fought against communism. But the counterculture stressed peace. Nowhere was the counter-culture message better exemplified than in the musical *Hair* that opened that year at the Coconut Grove Playhouse on Main Highway. Several of its songs became anthems of the anti-Vietnam War peace movement. One Saturday night, a classmate – not part of my little group – and I dressed up in fashionable, flowered, hippie-inspired granny dresses, and her curious and daring mother took us to see the controversial "hippie" play.

The play featured the song, "Aquarius," my astrological sign. "This is the dawning of the Age of Aquarius," the audience sang and clapped, shouting "Let the sun shine innnn!" I felt something new growing inside. I didn't know it had to do with personal emancipation. It was liberating to sway to the music in the dark theater surrounded by strangers, no Cubans except us. In the last scene, when the cast appeared in the nude, my friend's mother swiftly whipped out a pair of binoculars and zoomed in on the actors. Without a word, she passed the binoculars to her daughter who after a few minutes handed them to me.

Only English held my attention. While the teacher lectured, I raced through the text book, reading way ahead of the class but somehow managing to know what the discussion entailed. I wrote a passionate essay on the lyrics of singers James Taylor and Carole King, dissected the Beatle's "Hey Jude" and "Yellow Submarine" and developed a treatise on the good life which I entitled *Nirvana*, where no one had to get married to live together. I devoured *The Scarlet Letter* and *The Canterbury Tales*, but shied away from *Catcher in the Rye* and *Siddhartha*, turned off by the protagonists' painful alienation.

Like most teenagers, I felt different from everybody else. At Miami High, there were only a few black students, seven in the Class of '72, and I never saw them. The Anglo clique, almost invisible too, 14% of our class, ignored me, a racy Cuban girl to whom they couldn't relate. As for the Cuban majority, I might as well have been from another planet.

No question that I did not fit in with these students who went on dates with chaperones, planned weddings right after high school, and went to work as secretaries and mechanics. Nor with the ones who studied intensely and joined the Student Government Association, the National Honor Society, and the Glee Club, lining up credentials for acceptance into top national universities. These straight A students spent every moment planning futures, meeting with counselors and club sponsors who groomed them for scholarships. I walked by the open door of their meetings and always paused, looking in, envious. But I turned away, thinking "they're stupid."

I made a halfhearted effort to fit in to the world of the Cuban elite, since I rubbed shoulders with them in the honor and AP English classes. But after trying out for the Flagettes, (cheerleaders with flags), and the Yearbook – neither of which I made -- I promptly lost interest in the cream of the crop in favor of spending more time with my less ambitious friends and my boyfriend. Just as I had done in junior high, I focused on my social life.

I rarely saw my mother, who worked six days a week now at a new laundry where she stapled tickets on clothes until eight in the evening. On her days off, she lay in bed as usual, unable to think her way out of a life of manual labor, low wages, loneliness and confusion. My father and his wife Beba picked me up once a month to take me to dinner at a fancy restaurant. He sat aloof in the driver's seat of his Mercedes, or Jaguar, talking about the suits he had ordered from a Hong Kong tailor who traveled each year to Miami. The fact that he was a wealthy physician helped me as much as if he had been an illiterate farm worker.

I lived the life of the blue-collar working class, struggled alone with immigrant turmoil in a huge urban high school and did homework when I remembered. In this way, I lead a triple life: my own rebellious teenaged life, the sad and impoverished life of my mother, and the dazzling affluent life of an egotistical surgeon.

The bell rang at noon for the end of the first school session, and, in minutes, I boarded a bus to my new job which paid much more than the laundry. Family friend David, an executive now at a land development company, had helped me secure a position filing documents for his firm.

At the office, I met Ena, a twenty-two year-old secretary, and she let me borrow her driver's license so I could get into the new discos springing up all over: The Cheetah, Heaven, The World, The Place, Mix II, with their sparkling disco balls, white smoke, black lights, and throbbing music. I went with Ovy and my friends and we danced all night, drinking Singapore Slings – gin and pineapple juice.

Every day, Ena wore a new wig to work. She owned at least half a dozen in different hair styles, long, short, and in all colors: blonde, brunette, redhead. "That way I keep my husband on his toes," she laughed, smoothing down the hair at the nape of her neck. Unfortunately, the wigs did not keep her husband from straying.

Once, on a break, Ena and I cruised the streets of Little Havana to see if her husband's car was parked outside any of the houses. I sat in the car, looking on one side of the street for his blue Mustang, while Ena scoured the other, the experience similar to the one with my mother years before when we went on the same mission. But now everything seemed clearer. During my time with Jaime, I discovered that I, too, was as capable of betrayal as any man; however, what bothered me was that male philandering was accepted -- and expected -- behavior in Little Havana and in Cuba before that.

"He's unfaithful to me," Ena said. "Somewhere around here, he has a girlfriend." After our drive, Ena cried for a long time before we went back to work. The experience served to harden my resolve against becoming a victim of infidelity. If it happened to me, I vowed, I would be ready with a plan.

By 5 p.m., I had a dull pain in my shoulders and back from bending over the file cabinets, but I kept my goal in mind: a green and white 1964 Rambler – a purveyor of freedom -- that Ovy and his father had chosen at a used car lot. I needed $300 to drive it home.

"*Papi*, I need help with paying for a car," I had begged without success. I felt entitled to the money. He had recently traveled to Europe and purchased two mink coats for Beba. It was unjust.

"No, it is too dangerous for you to drive," he said. "It's not that I don't trust you driving. It's that I don't trust everybody else." He did nothing but strengthen my resolve.

If I wanted something, I needed to get it myself.

2.

What is the nature of love at 16? A lot of lust, certainly, but, undeniably, a tenderness that can only be described as pure. Love's sweetness is unimaginable the first time. So it was with us; Ovy and I were in love. I knew it then, and I believe it now. Some months after my *quince*, Ovy, charismatic, powerfully sensual, had demanded I choose him over Miguel, steady and solid; I did, his magnetism irresistible, a spirit as daring as mine.

Ovy came over every day in his 1954 Buick. He gave me his class ring, and I wore it on a chain around my neck. We went to discos and open houses. We went to drive-in movies -- Jack Nicholson in *Five Easy Pieces*, Ryan O'Neal in *Love Story* -- and porn flicks in a squalid area on Miami Beach's Twenty-First Street. None of the girls I knew went to these, but I wanted to see what they were like. After viewing a few, I concluded the films were insults to women and refused to go any more.

On the weekends, I tagged along while he delivered catered meals for a restaurant in the mornings and sold encyclopedias in the afternoons. At night, just as Jaime had done, he parked his car a block away, walked through the back yard, climbed in through the window, and spent the night. I had sex with Ovy regularly and made sure to always use condoms.

Like Jaime, Ovy provided the attention and companionship that I craved while adding an edgy dimension that excited me. He satisfied my need for adventure, introducing me to new worlds, new sensations. I liked his "bad boy" demeanor, the rebellion at its heart. One night driving around in Hialeah, he said, "I have some pot. Let's smoke." He stopped at a strange house and jimmied the lock until the door gave way.

"It's a friend's house," he said. "They're gone for the weekend." I believed him and fearlessly followed him to an empty room. He removed a small bag of marijuana from his pocket and rolled a joint, lit it, took a drag, and passed it to me. I slipped it between my thumb and forefinger and inhaled, but the smoke burned my throat and lungs. I coughed, choking, deciding I didn't like the drug. We waited, expecting something similar to a wine high. But nothing happened. "This must be some cheap stuff," Ovy said, and we laughed.

Ovy's father owned several pit bulls that he bred for fighting out in undeveloped Dade County. In his back yard, Ovy Sr. led me around the cages and described each dog's fighting record. Although I never went to a fight, I saw the dogs with missing ears and gashes on their sides. Others lay dead in their pens from internal bleeding, a shocking sight.

Both of Ovy's parents liked the excitement of gambling. While Ovy, Sr. took his son to the dog and horse races, his mother Aida took him to Jai-Alai. Ovy, a quick learner, soon turned his hard-earned cash from delivering food and selling encyclopedias into a steady gambling income. One night at the Jai-Alai fronton on Northwest Thirty-Seventh Avenue, he explained the difference between a quiniela and a trifecta and placed a $200 wager. He won $400. Then an idea took hold of him.

"I'm going to be a jai alai player," he said, excitedly digging in his pocket for more bills.

"Please stop." I worried his luck would not hold up, but felt excited at the gamble.

"No, *mi amor*, I'm just warming up."

He won again.

I didn't like the sordid atmosphere at the fronton, a microcosm of class injustice. Sunken-eyed men leaned against columns counting wads of bills. Old women pulling grocery carts, hair tied up in dirty scarves, pushed their way to the cashier and piled up nickels and dimes on the counter. On the top floor, men wearing large gold watches and chains lounged in a luxurious bar and restaurant smoking cigars, oblivious to those below. Today the old fronton is a glamorous casino, offering -- along with jai alai -- poker games, slot machines and rock concerts. It lures drop outs and kids straight out of high school with jobs promising easy cash, part of the well-oiled machine that derails teen dreamers and traps them in Little Havana.

Later that night Ovy took me to The Office, a nightclub for an older crowd near the airport. No one asked for an ID. We sat in a velvet booth near the smoke filled dance floor, and Ovy ordered Kaluah with cream from a phone strapped to the wall. Patrons used the phone to call up people in different booths, an ingenious idea that helped men pick up women, but we didn't know anyone there. Ovy was no drinker and neither was I; stirring our drinks made us feel older.

"My father wants me to sell some tape decks," he said. "He got them hot from a dealer. We're going to make a lot of money soon."

"That's dangerous," I said, remembering my shop lifting caper. "You could get caught."

"I won't."

Little by little, Ovy slipped into the maneuverings of the underground market, trying to figure out his place in the world. I loved him, but a sliver of doubt nagged at the edges. I knew, somewhere in my rational mind, that for me to get what I wanted out of life I had to go in the opposite direction from his.

The cramps began at dawn. My uterus contracted and expanded with the force of a sledgehammer. I writhed in pain, screaming to my mother to call my father and vomiting into a pail by the bed. Ovy was in the room, holding my hand. When my father arrived, he hid in the closet, his back against the wall, wedged between a row of dresses and blouses, not breathing. My mother, who knew nothing about Ovy's nocturnal visits, stood at the door, worried. My hair disheveled, my body sweaty, I moaned and thrashed my legs from side to side.

"Are you pregnant, Cecilita?" my father asked, noticing the pail. In crisis situations my father spoke in a low, soft voice. He wore a suit, hair slicked in place, trailing cologne, shoes shining. He never displayed emotion. My father felt proud of what he called his self-control, once advising that I should train myself by sitting still for at least an hour and ignoring any desire to scratch. "No one upsets me unless I allow it," he once said. However, his disapproval of me jumped out from his eyes every time I was in need, even if it wasn't my fault.

"Pregnant?" I sat up, dizzy, nauseous, confused, the cramps tearing through my abdomen. "No. Pain. It's my period."

He sighed and pulled out a round, plastic box. "This will stop the cramps in the future," he said. "Start on the Sunday after your period and take one every day for 21 days. Then stop for 7 days and start again. I have more in my office. For now, take Midol every three hours and drink hot cinnamon tea."

I slumped back on the bed, clutching the birth control pills. I knew what they were, although my father never said and I never asked. He delivered no sermon, very un-Cuban. A practical man, he pushed aside tradition when it did not serve his purposes, a philosophy I too absorbed. My father swept out of the room, ruffling the stale air. I struggled up and locked the bedroom door. Ovy stirred in the closet and peeked out.

The phone rang at 3 a.m.

"I've been stabbed."

Ovy's whisper shot me into wakefulness. "Where are you?"

"Right outside my house. I'm bleeding."

His mother's words whirred in my ears. "Take care of Ovy while I'm gone," she said before leaving for Acapulco with her boyfriend; she had divorced Ovy's dad years ago. I struggled into clothes and burst into my mother's bedroom.

"Please, drive me to Ovy's house," I begged. "He's hurt." I couldn't take the Dodge Dart because my mother hid the keys every night. She forbid me to drive although I already had my license.

My mother cowered in bed, eyes wide, shaking her head.

"I'm leaving then." I dialed the number for Yellow Cab and climbed in when the driver screeched to a stop by the front door.

"142 East 16th Street in Hialeah," I said, counting out a few dollars and thinking of the freedom my own car could offer. In less than 20 minutes I was there. I jumped from the cab and stepped into a spontaneous whirlwind that whipped up around me. The palm trees bent under the wind's force. Sand spun into a fierce funnel, pierced by the light of a street lamp. Rocks shifted under my feet as I fought the wind and struggled up the stairs to burst open the door. Ovy lay on the couch.

"They jumped me," he whispered, clutching his side.

"Who?"

I suspected Ovy was involved with one of the many gangs that roamed Hialeah and Little Havana. But when I asked, he always denied it. Alberto San Pedro, a well-known "fraternity" leader and organizer of open houses, lived just a few blocks away. I remembered Ovy never went anywhere without a switchblade.

"I don't know who."

I ran to the kitchen.

I pulled a towel from a drawer and moistened it with water from the sink. I rushed back and mopped Ovy's forehead. He had placed a bandage on the wound in his side, but blood leaked out. I held his head, and he rested between my shoulder and the pillow.

We dozed off, but, in what seemed like moments, an insistent pounding shook the door. Before I could scramble up to open it, my father turned the knob and strode in. My mother had called him to bring me back home.

"Cecilita, what is this comportment of yours? What are you doing here?"

It was such an unlikely setting for my father, dressed -- in the pre-dawn hours -- in a suit with hair neatly combed, a wannabe aristocrat with tastes for opera, classical music, zarzuelas, El Greco and Goya and gold leaf etched furniture spilling out of his living room. He stood uneasily in the simple lower middle class home of a Hialeah seamstress whose gang-fight-wounded son stretched out moaning on the couch. It was obvious what I was doing there, so I didn't answer.

"And you, young man," my father continued, turning to Ovy. "You have no right to call my daughter in the middle of the night."

Ovy moaned something that sounded like "*Sí*."

My father looked briefly at the bleeding on Ovy's side and made a clicking noise with his tongue, making no attempt to examine the wound.

"This is the type of boy you have chosen?" he asked me.

"You don't love me," I said, staring steadily into his eyes. "I don't know why you have come here to pick me up."

"Doctor," Ovy called weakly.

"You'll be all right," he said. "Just put hydrogen peroxide on that and change the bandages every eight hours. Let's go, Cecilita."

I didn't move to leave.

"Go on home," Ovy groaned, "I'll be Okay."

"No. He is a bad father." Resentment strengthened me. I stared steadily into my father's eyes. Struck speechless for once, he had no choice but to leave. I nursed Ovy for another day or two, his wound healing rapidly.

This escapade emphasized the need for my own car. I stepped up my savings plan, going without lunch for several months. Finally, clutching an envelope holding $300, I went with Ovy and his father to the car lot. I paid and signed some papers. (In those days, no one required insurance.) I turned the key in the ignition, spirits soaring. I drove home, singing loudly with the radio cranked as high as it would go. My mother came outside when I pulled up behind the Dodge Dart in the driveway, and looked sadly at the smartly painted Rambler, knowing exactly what it meant. I ignored her and called my father.

"I bought a car," I cried. "I can go anywhere I want now."

"Ahhh," he replied.

Another act of defiance, proving I was in control.

Ovy's mother Aida looked like Marilyn Monroe with wavy blond hair and thick black lines outlining her eyes. She was an outspoken woman filled with life and laughter who operated a small sewing factory in her living room, sunup to sundown. She set up several sewing machines and hired a dozen women to piece together long gowns and short dresses for a nearby factory that sold merchandise in bulk to retail outlets springing up throughout Miami and Hialeah.

At night, with the machines pushed out of the way, the house turned into a gathering place for *santeria* devotees. In the back room, a quiet place of worship, saints in full regalia presided over plates of fresh fruit, glasses filled with water, cigars, incense, candles and colorful beads. The room looked similar to the makeshift chapel at Cari's house where her father evoked spirits with cigar smoke. But after my experience with the *caracoles*, the shells, I kept my distance from the spirit world.

On a hot summer night, standing just outside the front door, I couldn't recognize the screams drifting out of the window. It sounded like an animal. I listened with Ovy, also motionless, behind me. I opened the door a crack and peeked in, stopping short at the terrifying scene.

Standing with legs astride a huge steel washing pan, Aida dissected a wriggling animal. The sound registered in my brain as the bleating of a lamb. I saw the creature lose strength, tremble slightly and succumb to the cruelty of the knife. Aida's chanting reached a crescendo and tapered off into dull mono syllables. The lamb's thick blood streamed into the pan and ran through Aida's fingers as she cut up the animal into neat pieces. A circle of strangers stood about moaning and swaying with eyes closed. I turned and pushed past Ovy, running down the street into the darkness. Ovy ran after me. *Santeria* was not new to me, but I had never seen an animal sacrifice, and it repelled me.

"Stop, it's okay," he shouted, breathless. "Stop!"

I kept running, but he overtook me.

"It's for dinner," Ovy blurted out above the rhythm of our steps. "My mother is going to cook the lamb now! Don't be afraid."

I stopped, gasping for breath. "How can she do it?!"

"Calm down. It's not a big deal. Let's go back."

I stood on the sidewalk, not moving. "Take me home."

"Come on. It will be all right."

Despite my repulsion, I felt intrigued by the exotic religion. I walked back, reluctantly. In the kitchen, Aida and her friends stirred what looked to be regular stew in big pots on the stove. It had a funny smell. I took one look at it and refused to eat the concoction.

I convinced Ovy to go to McDonald's instead.

3.

My father bought a house in the elegant Roads section of Miami, adjacent to a curling highway that led to a bridge connecting the mainland with the island of Key Biscayne. Today, the Roads is a popular neighborhood for professionals working in downtown Miami and on nearby Brickell Avenue. He and Beba furnished the house in the regency style with splashes of gold leaf everywhere, garish, pretentious stuff. Satin drapes framed picture windows. Soft carpeting stretched from wall to wall.

In stark contrast to the rest of the opulence, my grandparents' room was simply furnished: two plain square wooden night tables, twin beds covered in thin white and blue spreads, and a rocking chair. The difference in décor signaled something: my father used money to signify what he deemed important. Did his parents mean nothing to him?

The room had a sliding glass door that opened into a small inner courtyard. Sun poured in on my grandparents when they sat there alone. I visited them on Saturday when my father was at the office. Most of the time, I lay on the couch without speaking, depleted of energy, eyes closed, so, so depressed. Being at his house brought on a malaise of feeling neglected, not to mention the reminder of injustice as I compared my life with his, constantly, persistently, a feeling impossible to shed when it had me in its grip. I felt purposeless, drifting along, and surrendered to resentment.

I should have been grateful for the extravagant gifts he brought back from European vacations: a red leather coat from Spain, a woven wool purse from Greece, fine silk fabric from France, a malachite cross from Morocco that I later pawned. But I wasn't. It was chilling to hear my father rattle off the prices of each item, reminding me of his beneficence even months later. My heart hardened, steadily creeping away from him.

"Why don't you do homework?" my grandmother asked, always vigorously, still energetic. "Why don't you study?"

"I don't want to."

"You just don't like to study. That's what's wrong with you," she said. "Don't throw your life away. Your father brought you here for a better future."

My grandfather sat silently in one of the overstuffed Louis XV chairs, holding his sweater close to keep warm in the chilly air conditioned air. His irises were ringed with fading green, an expression of disconsolate sadness on his face.

"I hate my father," I said. "He's a bad man. He does nothing for me."

"Is that what your mother says?" my grandmother fired back, the same question my father often asked.

"No, it's what I say."

"You can't let him affect you. You have to make something of yourself."

I stood up and went to the dining room. I knew she spoke the truth. I had to do better in school if I wanted to have a future outside of Little Havana, but the daily round of parties and excitement sidetracked my plans.

Frustrated, I grabbed a long white-tapered, wax-smooth candle from its silver holder and smashed it to the floor. I swept up the second candle and did the same. I walked out of the house and took the bus home. I laughed, imagining my father's reaction when he got home. He never mentioned the incident.

My father drove me to the hospital. My grandfather lay in a bed surrounded by tubes. His bulbous eyes swung around the room before they focused on me. He moved forward, opened his mouth to speak, gasped and gulped down air. His body, tense, strained forward. I stood close, tears falling on the sheet. I held his hand, and he looked at me with a spark of recognition, communicating love. The grasping of hands expressed the sadness and regrets of years of separation and the tragedy of our broken family. We both knew that everything was different, including my father.

"Cecilita, you just can't cry there by the bed," Beba exclaimed. "You're upsetting him." I was too distraught to fight back, but later I wished I had. She led me away, my sobs erupting. He died that night.

My father paid for an elaborate funeral that included a slick black limousine. Dozens of friends and a few newly arrived relatives crowded to hear the mass at San Juan Bosco Catholic Church, a cavernous edifice with adobe walls on Northwest First Street in Little Havana. I will never forget the smell of the incense of death, scattered by the priest as he walked up the aisle blessing us. I had lost an ally. Now, only my grandmother remained.

I continued to visit her on Saturdays, but she now sat on her rocking chair in the simple little room, not saying much, her fire and energy crushed.

"I can't do anything in this house," she complained, the old spark of defiance busting through her apathetic stare. "They won't let me cook. They won't let me clean. They never speak to me. But you. Don't let them get away with anything. Fight back."

"I will, *abuela*."

Once, my father was home when I arrived. He motioned to me not to go into my grandmother's room. "She is a pest," he said.

From then on, I never went into her room, and she didn't come out to the living room. Why didn't I insist on going in to see her? The silence and secrecy hanging in the air in her room frightened me; her cutting remarks pushed me away. I now understand she was fighting death, unable to accept her diminished physical state. After a while, I stopped going on Saturdays all together. In another year, 1971, my father put my grandmother in a nursing home.

"I can't deal with her anymore," he told me. "I asked your mother if she would take in your grandmother, but she refused."

"Why would she take her in?" I thought of my mother's stories about the power struggle between the two, limiting my grandparents' visits to our home in La Habana.

"I was going to pay her, but she laughed in my face!"

I smiled, proud of my mother, but regretted the lost money. That same night, her first in the nursing home, my grandmother gave up trying to live. I did not have a chance to say good-by. The guilt from not insisting on seeing her threw me into depression.

My father, dry-eyed, arranged for a small funeral, this time no procession or mass, symbolic of the resentment he felt for his mother from the time he was a child. "My father was such a good man…but my mother, she was domineering and mean," he said at the cemetery. "Do you know she would wake me up in the mornings by throwing a pail of cold water on my face?"

Even on the day he laid her to rest, my father's never-resolved anger found expression. Family slights are so powerful that nothing can ever right the wrongs. Why didn't he apply his own experience to my situation?

As for me, my solitude intensified. I had lost my last family ally and the small buffer against the appalling coldness of my father. With my grandmother gone, my ties with my father weakened. I watched him as one would a film, sitting in the last row of the theater, detached in the darkness. But I still loved him. How many children adore the parent who abuses them, physically and emotionally?

4.

Withering weeds poked out from the parched soil all over the front yard. Ellen and I side-stepped broken clay pots and dodged brittle branches from craggy trees as we made our way to the wide double doors of a ramshackle house set back at least 100 yards from the street. Ellen, new in school, told me she ran away from her parents in Illinois and had just moved in to this commune on Miller Road in Coral Gables, about a mile from the University of Miami. She wore her blonde hair down to her waist, a beaded suede vest and long stained skirt, definitely a hippie. I was curious about her lifestyle and didn't refuse when she invited me home. It was 1971, and we were both 17.

After the death of my grandparents, more alone than ever, I felt wild, crazy, ready to do anything, craving sensation; they were one of the last ties to the rule and regulation ridden Cuban culture that fell on me like a heap of stones, anchored me in place. None of my friends rejected it like I did, and I didn't know anyone else who was curious about the hippie lifestyle. I pictured American culture as fluid, open; nevertheless, I felt like an outsider in both places. Not only was I a marginalized Cuban immigrant, but I also lived on the outskirts of traditional Little Havana. I wanted wholeness. Was it impossible to unify these two selves?

Inside Ellen's house, a spacious living room welcomed us with mattresses shoved up against the walls, huge pillows and blankets covering the floor. Black lights glowed from every lamp, and psychedelic posters blazed from the walls. Flowered curtains served as doors to rows of small bedrooms. Heavy incense hung in the air, forming masses of clouds in the dim light, colliding with the sharp odor of marijuana. Jimi Hendrix and Janis Joplin howled nonstop from an eight track cassette player on the floor.

Ellen disappeared down a hall, and a man walked up to me. He wore hip hugging bellbottom jeans held up with a wide leather belt and a buckle in the shape of a peace sign. His scrubby T-shirt hung limply on his thin frame.

"You want a drag?" He handed me a joint. I was here because I wanted to shed the heavy cloak of Cuban-ness, step past the barriers and experience… what? Anything but boredom.

The smoke seared my lungs just like the first time with Ovy, but now I felt a slight dizziness and floating sensation; I coughed several times.

The man, much older than me, motioned to one of the small rooms. My heart was beating, and I felt short of breath. We sat on a dirty, sheet-less, sagging mattress in silence. He handed me a water pipe. I put it to my lips and blew smoke out, not inhaling, struggling to clear my head from the effect of the joint.

Soon, we were making out and rolling around, one on top of the other.

Ellen threw herself on the mattress, too. My first experience with spontaneous sex seemed more like a wrestling match than intercourse. For a while, no one knew whose arms or legs were flailing into the air. My heart and soul retreated, but my body continued to function as the nameless man penetrated me, and I reached out to Ellen who was on her knees right next to my head. As my hips gyrated, my mouth locked with hers. Everything felt unnatural.

Another woman announced her presence by rapping on the walls with a wooden ladle. We jumped apart as she began to pour out lemonade into paper cups from a plastic pitcher and line them up on the floor. She waved her hands in the air, threw her head back and howled, already tripping on LSD. Worried the hallucinogic drug would be in the lemonade, I did not drink it. We rapidly pulled on our clothes, and I watched her run out to the common room and gallop around, boomeranging against the walls and yelling.

"Wow, she's on a bad trip," Ellen exclaimed. "But we gotta go," she told the man. "We got school tomorrow." The man walked off, taking the pipe.

I observed Ellen out of the corner of my eye as I followed her to the station wagon, dented on all sides and with one door caved in. She acted as if nothing unusual had happened. I wanted to be just as cool, so I said nothing.

She handed me a Hershey's chocolate bar, and I ate it ravenously. She dug into a bag of chips. I wasn't high anymore, and as we drove, I went over in my mind what I had just experienced. Running off to the commune with Ellen offered a possible escape from Little Havana, but, I realized, not the right path for me. I enjoyed the music, the fashion, the politics; I didn't want to be a hippie. An interesting story to tell my friends, I thought. If I dared.

"See you tomorrow," I said as she dropped me off and screeched away.

Ovy was in the living room and ran out when he heard the car door slam. I didn't expect him to be there, and I felt a bit nervous.

"Where were you?" he shouted, in a jealous frenzy.

"I was just visiting…"

"You smell of smoke!" he screamed, recognizing the pot smell. "Tell me where you were! Tell me the address. I'm going to find out what you were doing and kill them!" He grabbed me by the shoulders, eyes protruding. I shook him off.

I walked to the kitchen and picked up the telephone book. My heart contracted.

"Here," I threw the heavy volume in his direction. "Find it yourself."

Ovy jumped in his car and drove off. The next morning, he called, and we made up. But Ellen was not at school that day. She had no phone, so I couldn't find out her whereabouts, and I did not want to go back to the house.

I never saw her again.

5.

Halfway out on the pier on South Beach, summer of 1971, I climbed up on the wall and looked down into the turbulent water. Lightning ripped through the air. In a fit of fury, waves churned white froth and slammed into jagged rocks rising from the bottom of the sea like crooked teeth. The rocks scattered in clumps along the pier to the end where fishermen hauled in sharks at night. Someone said the beasts had been sighted near the shore that day. The wind whipped my hair. Several of my friends had already jumped and swam desperately against the current to the shore. I wasn't a good swimmer, and I hated salt water in my eyes. Thunder rumbled. I took a deep breath, covered my face with my hands, and leaped into the foamy mess.

Anything but boredom.

My feet banged on the sand at the bottom of the sea, and I pushed up as hard as I could. A trickle of salt water pressed its way down my throat. I spit out hard and plunged in swimming toward the shore with all my strength, eyes burning. Almost there, a powerful current intercepted and dragged me forcefully back out to sea. I kicked my legs and fought for air, screaming "Help" each time I bobbed up above the waves. I panicked, but also felt a stab of fascination with the idea of dying. Was this how it felt to die?

But I wasn't ready yet. I didn't know what I was living for, but I didn't want to stop. I fought harder against the waves. A man splashing nearby began a series of quick strokes in my direction. But before he reached me, I felt sand under my feet. A wave thrust me up and out onto the shore. Sand and shells cut into my skin. I spit out water, stretched out on my back, gasping for air, gazing at the mottled clouds above that marched undisturbed across the heavens.

South Beach, a high school hang out, shared space with retired Holocaust survivors. At the entrance of the pier on First Street, a barbed wire fence enclosed an under-the-stars dance hall. My mother and I had rented a room in a rundown hotel a block away, waiting for the termite tenting of our house to be done, and, one night, in an unusual together moment, we walked to the pier. My mother's inner light flamed, and I couldn't get enough of it. She hugged me, responded with affection and focus, commenting gaily on her surroundings. I knew it was a matter of time before she would be completely different.

Totally disconnected from relatives both in Cuba and in Miami, my mother now regularly took sleeping pills at night and something else she said was for "anxiety" in the mornings. I noticed that the silver tray was missing; then her charm bracelet disappeared. I figured she sold these items, always short on housekeeping money. Only later did I realize she pawned her valuables to buy the drugs that kept her going to work every day.

That evening on the pier, we stood at the edge of the dance floor, holding hands. Polkas, ballroom music of the thirties and forties rolled over the darkness all the way to the end where men struggled to hoist sharks out of the water. We heard elderly couples, widows and widowers who had retired here from up north, tell stories of lost family in Dachau and life in the snow. They told how they built and lost business enterprises. Men pumping accordions and women in bright dresses serenaded each other across the spaces, many dancing in circles around the pavilion as if it were the first and last time. I held tightly to my mother, willing her to stay with me longer before I lost her again to that lonely, inner space where she lived. The desire for my mother made me dizzy.

On Government Cut, a manmade shipping channel between Miami Beach and Fisher Island on the southernmost edge of our beach, another pier jutted out to sea. We called this one The Jetties. A rough path of sand with sharp rock formations rolled into an ocean deep enough for ships to cruise around the end and dock at the Port of Miami. Today, the area is called South Pointe, boasting an ocean themed playground, a dog park, observation towers, fitness course, outdoor showers and a 20-foot-wide walkway lined with Florida limestone that leads past the up-scale restaurant Smith and Wollensky all the way to Monty's bar and grill on the marina some blocks away. Residents of two towers of luxury condos, priced at a million dollars, look out on a spectacular view of the ocean.

Back then, no tall buildings cluttered the skyline. Everything spread itself out into the open, sea, sand and sun. Behind us, to the north, a vast parking lot filled to brimming with the cars of gamblers attending dog races at the track provided the only shade. Jumping from the jetties was twice as dangerous as jumping from the pier. The depth of the black water and the stronger currents were forces to be seriously considered. I knew my limits, that powerful will to survive, to live, just as I knew when to stop inhaling pot, and that day I refused to jump, watching while at least half a dozen kids dove in and struggled out bleeding, cut by the sharp rocks.

Steps away from The Jetties, Ibis, her brother Miguel – my *quince* date and brief boyfriend -- and I splashed in the transparent waters and then threw ourselves on towels spread out on hard-packed sand. In the distance, math friend Rene, dreaming of a career in marine biology and wearing snorkeling gear, emerged from the mist of the jetties. He held a spear and walked over to a cluster of rocks. I watched him unload his cargo, a dozen wriggling fish that he dropped into a bucket.

Ovy appeared behind us. Surprised, I propped myself up on one elbow and squinted into his face. At a party last Saturday, I danced with another boy and Ovy stomped off in a rage. Now, suspicious of my every move, he had left work to check up on me. My conscience was clear. I had not even been flirting with Miguel. We were just friends.

"*Oye, tu,*" Ovy, puffed up and scowling, yelled at Miguel. "Listen, you. Follow me."

Miguel jumped to his feet, and so did Ibis and I.

"There is nothing going on," Ibis cried, standing in front of Miguel.

"This is so stupid," I shouted, fully aware of the power of jealousy, provoked or not. I gripped Ovy's arm, but he pushed me away, and, with eyes narrowed, trudged behind a mound of sand.

Miguel sidestepped Ibis and, face set, valiantly followed Ovy.

"I'm calling the police," I called out, hoping to scare them into stopping.

"Go ahead," Ovy answered. Ibis paced around nervously.

Suddenly, we heard the sound of fists battering bone and muscle.

"*Hijo de puta,*" Ovy growled, calling Miguel the son of a whore.

"*Vete pa'l carajo,*" Miguel responded, telling Ovy to go to hell.

The fight lasted less than two minutes. Ibis and I ran to where Miguel lay sprawled, holding a swollen jaw. We tried to help him up, but he refused and, spread out on the sand, stared into the clouds. Ovy strode off in silence, proudly, purpose accomplished. The screams of volleyball players a few feet up the beach mingled with shouts from dog track fans.

6.

I see a red door and I want it painted black.

I slipped my Rambler up to my friend Gloria's house and leaned on the horn. Fall of 1971, still hot and humid. "Come with me," I said, when Gloria appeared in the doorway. "I'm going to find him. He's at her house."

"But you don't know where she lives." The calm, cautious one of our group, Gloria shook her head.

"Yes, I do."

"What do you want me to do?"

"Nothing. Just stand there in case we have to fight," I said. "Now, get in."

Gloria reluctantly climbed into the passenger's seat, and I sped off in the direction of where a total stranger had said the girl lived. The stranger approached me one night while dancing at The Place and told me Ovy was out on a date that very moment. I thought back to my mother's anonymous letters about my father's infidelities. In my version of the same event, the "letter" was delivered in person.

"You should know what is going on," the strange girl said, mumbling an address.

I leaned over on the dance floor and recounted the information to a surprised Gloria, rocking next to me with boyfriend Chino. Then, I walked over to the bar and asked the bartender for a pen to write down the address on a napkin. The next weekend, when Ovy said he had to go out with his father, I put my plan in gear, the one I had visualized as inevitable, since betrayal was never far from my thoughts.

"That's the house," I told Gloria, consulting the blur of writing on the napkin. "Just give me emotional support." The house, packed into a row of duplexes, needed paint, the grass uncut.

I knocked, and a woman who I guessed was the girl's mother opened the door.

"*Hola, senora.* I am Ovy's girlfriend. Can I wait for him here?"

"*Ay, Dios Mio*, we never knew he had a girlfriend," the mother exclaimed. "He never said he had a girlfriend."

"*Bueno*, I've been his girlfriend for the last three years."

Gloria and I stood at the door.

"Come inside and sit in the living room."

"Thank you." We walked in and sat on a blue velvet coach covered in thick, clear plastic to preserve its newness. I looked up on the wall. The girl in the portrait stared at me.

"That's when Marilyn was fifteen," her mother looked at the studio photograph, at least three feet by two feet. Wearing the obligatory white dress of a *quince* debutante, Marilyn – deeply tanned -- smiled. Green eyes flashed just a hint of a sparkle, black hair thick and wavy. Just a shadow of a mustache sat on her upper lip.

"She met him at Zayre's where she works."

"Oh."

"They went to the movies tonight."

"Mhm."

My mind stopped having thoughts. Gloria reached over to hold my hand, both our palms sweaty. I listened to every street sound drifting in through the open window.

An hour passed. Marilyn's mother kept up a light conversation with Gloria. I said nothing.

Another hour passed. It was close to midnight.

Then, we heard the sound of car tires squashing gravel in the driveway. I got up slowly. Gloria jumped up and wrung her hands. Marilyn's mother nervously followed me outside. Marilyn's father came out from a back bedroom.

Ovy turned off the ignition, walked around to the passenger seat and opened the door for Marilyn. He had not seen my car. He held the door while Marilyn climbed out. I stepped out of the shadows. He turned toward me. I grabbed him by the neck and squeezed hard. It was the scene at the Rascal House where my mother caught my father with the mistress; only this time, the cheating man got what he deserved. This, I thought, was what my mother should have done.

Ovy lurched sideways and tripped, toppling onto the ground on his back. My hand had become entangled on a *santeria* necklace of white beads that his mother had given to him to ward off evil. I pulled with all my strength, and the beads spilled over Ovy's shoulders and chest like flakes of snow.

"Do you know that he is my boyfriend?" I asked, not looking at Marilyn, but watching Ovy struggle up from the ground and stare aghast at the scattered beads, some of which he trampled on his way up. I felt, not saw, the quiet of Marilyn's parents, the shock in Gloria's face, the fear in Ovy's eyes, the anger in Marilyn's pursed mouth. The mustache quivered.

"He told me you had broken up." She leaned against the car, looking away into the emptiness of the sleeping neighborhood.

Ovy stood before us, anger now raging from his eyes.

"Well, who are you going to choose?" I asked.

He moved in closer to Marilyn, remorseless. I had harbored some wild hope that he would publicly denounce Marilyn. My pride demanded that he walk off with me.

"At least everyone now knows what a piece of shit you are," I said, emotionlessly. I did not shed a tear. I had mastered the technique of suspending emotion a long time ago. I marched off the battlefield to my car, holding my head high. Gloria tripped slightly behind me but regained her balance. This was one of many incidents where Helen Gurley Brown's advice came to my rescue. She had written numerous articles in *Cosmopolitan Magazine* about how to handle betrayal. I had taken her advice about confronting one's boyfriend, but the throat grabbing was my own twist on things.

"I can't believe it, Ceci," Gloria said, as I carefully backed up and drove away.

"That is how you should handle Chino," I answered. "You can't let him get away with going out on you all the time. You have to be strong. Feel pride in yourself. Show him your world doesn't revolve around him. Rely on yourself to improve your own life."

These words were almost verbatim from Brown's latest article. I felt elated. I had avenged my mother, indirectly that is, and met Ovy's betrayal with a show of force.

That night, alone in my bed, the pain of losing him crushed me, and I wept bitterly. No matter how much I loved him, I had to move on. He reminded me too much of my father.

7.

Bongos, trumpets, saxophones and flutes yelped with unrivaled passion at the Di Lido Hotel on Miami Beach on New Year's Eve, 1971. El Gran Combo and Los Jovenes del Hierro kept dancers on their feet with the most popular *danzones, guarachas and guaguancos* – different styles of Cuban music. Wine bottles clustered in the center of every table. I was a month shy of 18, the drinking age back then, but no one cared. A buffet of *lechon* and *moros* drew the sweating dancers on short breaks.

"Who is he?" I gripped Ibis's arm. He had wide shoulders, dark, curly hair in a neat, soft, longish Afro. Long lashes framed light brown eyes. "Let's meet him," I said.

"He's with a girl," Ibis said. "He goes to The Place a lot. Let's wait for when he's alone."

I fantasized about Robert every night until the following Saturday when we saw him at The Place. He was with two friends, one also named Robert -- on whom Ibis had her eye -- and another named Aurelio. Ibis, new friend Rosie and I went up to them and started a conversation. Soon, we were all laughing and making plans for next weekend.

Some months after that, Robert -- four years older than me -- left his girlfriend, and we started to date. He wrote poetry and songs, worked at a shoe factory and went to Miami Dade Junior College while he tried to figure out what to do with his life.

We went to the beach, movies, discos, malls. I met his parents, factory workers struggling to make ends meet in a small Hialeah apartment, and learned that Robert had been one of the Peter Pan kids spirited out of Cuba in 1962 in the emergency airlift sponsored by the Catholic Church. "I didn't want Fidel to take him into the military," his mother told me.

But despite my new boyfriend and the fun we were having, I hadn't forgotten Ovy. I walked around, hurting, missing him, and mourning the end of our relationship.

My mother drove me to school these days before going to work. The Rambler broke down slowly: first the brakes, then the transmission. I put a For

Sale sign on it, and a recently arrived Cuban refugee bought it for $250 after lasciviously eying my mother, who nervously watched the transaction. I was again dependent on my friends and my mother's Dodge Dart with the gaping holes in the floor.

One morning, with "Is that all there is?" blaring from the radio as my mother dropped me off at school, it struck me that life didn't have much to offer: I dragged myself to mind-numbing classes, worked at a boring job, and I had no plans for the future. All I did was escape into fun binges. I sat in the car, immobilized by the hopelessness of my situation and the loss of Ovy.

The task of walking the few yards into Miami High overwhelmed me, and I put my face in my hands. My mother pulled over and watched me without speaking, not knowing how to bridge the gap that made communication impossible.

Then she made a startling announcement.

"I'm sad too," she said. "Someone is trying to kill me."

Her words ended my bout of self-pity. Alarmed, I tried to understand. I didn't know this was a symptom of paranoia, the mental illness that caused feelings of persecution.

"You always have some problem," I said.

"It's not my fault if they want to do harm to me."

"Who are 'They?'"

She waved her hand out the window.

Bewildered, my own sorrow rushing back, I could offer my mother no comfort. I had no idea psychiatrists prescribed medicine for mental illnesses like hers. Did my father, with his psychiatric training, suspect? If he did, he took no action, allowing her to sink into an endless nightmare.

I pushed my mother's predicament out of my mind and took comfort from the next song: "If you can't be with the one you love, love the one you're with." It offered good advice; I had to forget Ovy. Strengthened, I stumbled out of the car and ran up the steps to class.

That moment of clarity in the car didn't spur me to action. I felt powerless to change my tough attitude and destructive habits and didn't know how to help my mother. I could only bury the pain, shrug off worry, and place on hold the desire for more.

For now, I could at least enjoy Robert.

8.

They called it a head shop, one of many tucked away on Miracle Mile in Coral Gables. Blouses and bell bottoms hung on racks against the wall. Soft sandals piled up on the floor. A counter on the left showcased a line-up of water pipes, the dangling hoses wrapped around the base, colorful and menacing. The one on the right displayed rows of cigarette rolling papers and little metal pinchers used to hold marijuana "roaches" without burning your fingers. A sprinkle of sawdust covered the floor. A long horizontal light bulb glared blue, lighting up the colors of the psychedelic posters on the walls: hot pink, red, green, purple and black.

Incense smoke aggressively filled every corner; it always had a strange effect on me, like that of being high. I strolled, dizzy, to a rack, and my hand lingered on a silky yellow blouse with cut outs of stars and moons in blues, pinks and greens scattered across the front. The sleeves puffed up at the shoulder and ran smoothly down to the elbow. I took it by the hanger, chose a pair of hip hugger jeans folded on a table, and bought myself a birthday outfit.

Next door, in a jewelry store, no more than a slice of counter under a cloud of dense incense smoke, I ran my fingers across the smoothness of crystal and buffed stones for sale. I chose a hand bracelet to go with the outfit. A chain fit over my middle finger, holding in place an oval yellow stone that covered the top part of my hand, and then wrapped around my wrist.

That Saturday in January 1972, at my eighteenth birthday party, my friends packed into the living room and shook their bodies to the music from 45s stacked on the tube-like contraption on my stereo. I pressed the automatic button to keep the songs coming one after the other. My mother worked in the kitchen, smiling, smearing ham paste on white bread for sandwiches. She had gone to the beauty salon, her teased hair in the shape of a bouffant.

My birthday cake stood on the dining table with its five or six layers covered with white and pink icing, waiting for the candles to be lit. My girlfriends gathered around the table singing "Happy birthday to you!!!" I blew out the candles and passed them all around as keepsakes, a common party ritual. The phone rang, and I skipped into my mother's room to answer it.

"Cecilia." It was Ovy's mother.

"*Hola,* Aida. How are you?"

"Happy birthday!"

"Thank you."

"I'm calling you because Ovy is very depressed. He wants to go back with you. He doesn't love that other girl."

Had Ovy asked her to call?

"I don't care about him anymore."

"Wouldn't you like to go to Disney World? I'll pay for the trip so you can get away and fix your problems. Maybe you two can get married. You're both very young and have made a lot of mistakes."

I wanted to be free of philanderers and not make my mother's mistakes.

"I don't think I want to go."

"He's sorry, very sorry. Remember that you went out with a lot of boys too when you were with him. You hurt him too."

"What he did was very different. He had a chance to leave her, but didn't. I don't want to see him again."

"He's a good boy. He made a mistake. He has his whole life before him."

"I have my whole life before me too."

9.

One morning right after my birthday, the Dodge Dart refused to crank up.

"I don't have any money to fix it," my mother said, eyes watering. She called a local garage, and someone came to tow the car away for free. I was stranded unless I took the bus. Then, my luck turned: during one of my visits to his house, my father offered to sell me his 1968 Volvo. He asked for $500.

"After three years, cars aren't any good anymore," he said. "I was going to trade it in but I thought you might want to buy it."

If the car wasn't any good, I thought, then why offer it to me?

"Buy it? I don't have the money," I said. "And I need a car to get to school and work. My Rambler broke down, and my mother's Dodge is gone."

"Start saving now," he answered. "You can drive it while you are saving the money."

"It's unfair," I said.

He shrugged and did not reply, standing uncertainly next to the Volvo. I opened the door and slipped into the driver's seat, red, soft cloth. I ran my hand over the gleaming black leather trim. What luxury! The keys dangled from the ignition. I placed my hands on the steering wheel. I reached over and turned on the car. I drove away.

The Volvo shone white in the sunlight as I took a curb at high speed and straightened out. It felt as if I were driving through butter. Only four cylinders, the car handled like a high-powered Rolls Royce.

I drove straight to Ibis's apartment. In her dilated pupils, I saw envy and the power of money as she gazed at the car. I never paid my father the $500. Today, I wonder why he never pushed for the money. Was it his way of giving me a gift and showing his love because it would upset Beba if he did it outright? If that were the case, why couldn't he just say so when she wasn't around?

10.

Shirley Shirley Bo Birley Banana Nana Mo Mirley…
Gyrating fans pushed hot air around in the living room where my mother and I lounged lethargically on the couch. I read. She stared off into space and talked to the air.

"I'm a citizen," my mother said, abruptly. "Since last year."

"Am I a citizen?" I put the book down. "I'm 18 now, and I want to vote."

"No, you have to apply on your own."

The law extended citizenship to children under 18 when the parents applied. I knew this because my friends' parents spoke often of including their children in the applications. I had expected my mother to do the same. By then, few people harbored hopes of ever returning to Cuba – believing Fidel too powerful to be toppled -- and applied regularly for citizenship. Not every Cuban embraced America, however. In the last four years, those desperate to go home highjacked 66 planes back to the island as a way around the travel ban.

I ran to the phone and called my father at the office.

"Are you a citizen?"

"Yes. Why?"

"Did you submit my name?"

"No. Why?"

"Why not?!"

Neither of my parents had considered me during their milestone in immigrant life. Neither thought that, with a simple stroke of the pen, they could have improved my legal status in a country to which they had brought me without my permission. Now, their inaction meant I was still a resident, but marginalized politically.

In my case, however, the citizenship process extended beyond the political into a personal naming game.

My father's name was Rafael Fernandez Rivas. When he first came to the United States, he used only my grandfather's surname: Fernandez. Then he realized Fernandez was everybody else's last name, too.

"Too many Fernandezs at the hospital," he told me. "I'm going to change my name to Rivas. From now on, I will be Dr. Rivas. So that means you too are a Rivas."

Rivas, my grandmother's maiden name, was also the name of an ancestor, an important man from the royal court of Spain, whose statue stood at the Parque del Buen Retiro in Madrid. My father told the story of this ancestor with pride. When he applied for citizenship, my father dropped the Fernandez and legally became Rivas which, to him, had something of a regal ring.

My mother's name was Cecilia Vargas Castellanos. In Cuba, a woman did not change her name to that of her husband's. But when my mother applied for citizenship in this country, she too claimed her name was Rivas.

"His name will help me here in the United States," she said. "Your father is well known. People will remember I was married to a doctor. They will help me more."

If we follow the Cuban/Spanish rules, my name is Cecilia Fernandez Vargas: one surname from my father, and one from my mother. My name was not Cecilia Rivas as my father had ordained it to be.

Days after the citizenship conversations with my parents, still upset, I took action. I went to the Federal Courthouse on Flagler Street in downtown Miami -- hot, grimy sidewalks and cold sterile building. I filled out the papers, paid about $5 -- today the cost is nearly $700 -- and attended a quick swearing in naturalization ceremony in a dingy office. As an act of rebellion, I put down my name simply as Cecilia Fernandez, the name my mother used to register me in school that first year of exile.

"My name is Cecilia Fernandez," I told my father, soon after I came home from the courthouse. "I'm a citizen now, and that is my legal name. Don't send me any more cards or letters or make any more checks to Cecilia Rivas. That is not me."

"Oh."

I could hear surprise in my father's voice, but who knew what went on in his mind?

I had seized the power of naming from him, and I had staked out my own identity. He could have felt anger, maybe even hurt. Or he could have felt relief. If my father was unsure that he wanted me, particularly after he realized he had sired a troubled teen who talked back, did as she pleased, and liked boys who gambled and sold stolen merchandise, my rejection of his choice of names could have liberated him. With different last names, my father and I were one more step removed. I was now freer to prove that I, indeed, was worthy of being my own person.

But by the same token, he was freer to shed his guilt.

11.

I want to make it with you.

A red canopy hung over the doorway, lending The Place the air of a European cabaret. A sprawling building on Northwest 119th Street and Twenty-Seventh Avenue – the main drag in a low income neighborhood of blacks and whites—the hottest disco in town sparkled purple from a coat of paint that glowed in the night, vibrating from loud music inside. Across the street from Miami Dade Junior College, the disco attracted a lot of older students. Freshly groomed, smartly dressed couples walked in, and sweat-wet, rumpled couples staggered out, laughing, shoving, arms around each other.

At The Place, four or five nights a week, I lost myself on the dance floor and in drinking Singapore Slings, a recipe for relief from the boredom that now paralyzed me at school. All of my closest friends had dropped out of high school, and I had little in common with anyone else there. I felt alone and isolated. Only at the disco did I come alive.

I leaned on my car waiting for Robert. It was midnight, when all parties started. Ibis and I had just arrived after a two hour nap and another two hours applying makeup and choosing the right outfits. Ibis popped two Quaaludes into her mouth, common for her, and offered me some, but I was afraid of pills and refused. She was dating Robert's friend Robert, who was also not there yet. Rosie walked around with Aurelio; both had taken Quaaludes. I looked to my right and saw, in another car, Gloria dropping acid with a group of people I didn't recognize. She had broken up with Chino and was on the prowl for another boyfriend.

Someone came up to me with a joint. "Try this. It's angel dust."

Erroneously thinking that it was a different kind of pot, I took a drag and in less than ten seconds, the floor began to move. Panicking, I took a step forward and floated straight up. I took another step and continued to bounce up and down in the air. Each step took me in the opposite direction of where I wanted to go. A Carol King song popped into my mind and I hummed: *I felt the earth move under my feet.* I hung on to the door handle of someone's car, trying to regain balance while the effect wore off. Later, I learned that angel dust, the street name for PCP, is a strong mind-altering drug often sprayed on pot that makes users experience being out of body, sometimes driving them to violence and suicide. I was thankful my "trip" was relatively mild by comparison.

Finally Robert and Robert arrived, and we went inside. No one mentioned the angel dust, or the 'ludes, or the acid. We felt the two Roberts would disapprove, maybe even be angry. On the dance floor, bodies collided like ping pong balls in a box. We danced; we sweated; we shouted above the music to be heard.

Sitting in a booth, Robert ordered an amaretto for me and a Long Island Ice Tea for him. I took a small sip. I didn't like alcohol. The drink burned my throat. I felt dizzy and hungry, coming down from the high of the angel dust. By now it was close to 5 a.m. Ibis had disappeared with Robert to his apartment a few blocks north of The Place. Rosie necked in the car with Aurelio. Gloria wrapped her arms around some new guy on the other side of the dance floor.

"Let's go eat," I said.

Word spread that we were going to Sambo's, a 24-hour diner that later drew lawsuits in communities that viewed its name as an insult to African-Americans. Ibis suddenly appeared with her Robert, and a car caravan started off south on Twenty-Seventh Avenue. At Sambo's, squeezing into a large booth, we ordered pancakes, ham and eggs, hot and cold chocolate and filled up with new energy for the rest of the morning. Almost everybody else from The Place began trickling in, too, and soon all the booths and tables were full. Hellos and hand waving everywhere.

"Let's go the beach," Ibis said.

We paid the bill and caravanned east to Miami Beach. We crossed the bridge and turned north to the Eden Roc Hotel, the hang out for older kids. At 8 o'clock on Sunday morning, all-night party revelers crammed the beach. No one had slept. The early morning sun caressed our faces, and a light breeze promised a sprinkle of rain. Gentle waves awakened, rolled onto shore, sand warm on bare toes.

We leaned against a rock wall separating the parking lot from the beach. Amphetamines made a round or two, but I decided to go with a natural high: adrenalin. In the distance, I saw Ovy walking with a friend. My heart stopped, but I willed myself to turn away and feel nothing. My friends and I laughed, talked, shouted, raced back and forth from the wall to the shore and through the waves, then up and down the beach until two in the afternoon.

Rosie and Aurelio went their own way, and so did Gloria and the new guy. The two Roberts, Ibis and I drove back to Miami to Ibis's studio apartment on the second floor of an old Little Havana building. She had her own place now and worked full-time. The carpets gave off a musty odor that made me sneeze, and the wood underneath creaked. The rusted door lock refused to budge without punches from the Roberts. Inside, an air conditioning wall unit rumbled weakly. Robert and I dove into one of the twin beds, exhausted. Ibis and her Robert jumped into the other.

And there we stayed until Monday morning. When I decided not to go to school.

A week later, Robert and I strolled into the ballroom of the Fontainebleau Hotel on the beach. I wore a dress of white silk stamped with a gold and silver velvet pattern, a fabric that my father had brought from England. Two slender straps crossed in the front and in the back, attached to a long flowing skirt. Robert wore a satiny smooth black tux.

We made a splendid couple, but we didn't fit in.

A sedate, orderly dance this one: my prom. Hovering on the fringes of the dance floor, we watched my fellow students shyly greet each other, most of them still going on dates with chaperones. Sheepishly grinning seniors jumped around on the dance floor as if for the first time. Robert rolled his eyes. No one said hello to me.

After an intolerably boring hour, we left to meet the other Robert and his new girlfriend at internationally renowned Les Violins Supper Club on Biscayne Boulevard. Dim lights and red velvet décor provided an atmosphere of sensual intimacy.

The waiters, after serving filet mignon with a side of rice and black beans, donned flamenco outfits and climbed on stage to perform. Sinuous arm movements, penetrating stares and guttural shouts exemplified a dance of passion and desire. Castanets clattered above their heads, and shoes -- outfitted with silver taps -- furiously pounded the floor.

After this, a female dancing troupe dressed in feathers and lace took over while singers crooned suspended from the ceiling. I had never been to Las Vegas, but a tourist at a table behind me sighed ecstatically, "It's better than Vegas!" which made us all laugh.

I drank two Singapore Slings, and everything began to spin. By then, it was nearly 2 a.m. The stage cleared of the performance. A small band set up instruments and struck up romantic tunes. Revelers swarmed onto the dance floor. I could barely stand, but I had managed to wipe out the prom experience. After a while, we drove to the other Robert's apartment for a nap, then to the beach, and then home at about four in the afternoon.

The next day, hung over, I cringed at the thought of returning to school. Could I make it through to graduation day?

ESCAPE FROM LITTLE HAVANA

*This time, like all times, is a very good one
if we but know what to do with it.*
— Ralph Waldo Emerson

1.

Someone stole my yearbook, so that broke the monotony of those two final, bleak weeks of school. Adrenalin pumping, I swept past an unattended yearbook and stuffed it in my purse. The one I have is filled with the comments of unknown people addressed to someone named "Cookie." At least it helps me with memories.

I had stopped joking and laughing in class and battling teachers, too tired from dancing until dawn. At assemblies in the auditorium, I sat impassively in a corner, watching as school monitors escorted out several boys for pitching paper balls into the air and whistling. I struggled through my afternoon job, filing like a zombie.

One day, the assistant principal called me into the office.

"You have 21 absences," he said flipping through a file. "You will not be graduating."

"Is there anything I can do?"

"You can go to summer school."

"I'm not doing that."

Outside, I leaned against a wall, dizzy, nauseous. I understood the consequences of not having a high school diploma. Drifting, without purpose, I realized I had no idea how to make my dream of becoming a writer come true.

In the hallway, I ran into Rene, now a member of Student Government. "I won't be graduating," I said. The bell rang and walls of students moved on to the next class. "I've been absent too many days. I can't even get a doctor's excuse from my father because I don't know the days I was absent."

"I have an idea," he said. "I'll find out."

"What do you mean?"

"I'll get the dates so your dad can write the excuse."

I stood in the midst of the chaos, students banging lockers, shoving and jumping around with boisterous good-bys to retreating friends.

"Isn't that illegal?"

"No one will find out."

I sensed that my father, accustomed to sidestepping oppressive systems, would not deny my request. "People everywhere always give a hard time," he said, signing the note.

In two days, I was back in the office with the medical excuse. The assistant principal stared at the note, frowning. He pulled open a drawer and put the certificate in my file. Then he walked off.

Outside that afternoon's pep rally, Rene and I huddled in a corner celebrating our victory. The assistant principal walked past, turned around, and stared Rene in the eye.

"I think I've been had," he said.

"Maybe you have, sir," Rene answered.

2.

Teresita Alvarez, Valedictorian, Radcliffe College; Hilarion Martinez, Salutatorian, Duke University; Nino Lucio, Harvard University; Isodoro Zarco, Harvard University; Emilia De Quesada, University of Virginia....

They strode across the stage with heads held high and eyes shining, one hand outstretched to shake hands with the principal, the other reaching for the diploma. They were Miami High's top seniors. We had brushed shoulders in elementary and junior high, and in high school honors and AP English classes, but they had been so far removed from me in everything else that I marveled I even knew them at all.

At our graduation ceremony in the Miami Beach Auditorium, confident, unreachable, they marched across the stage and out of Little Havana with scholarships to the Ivy League and other eminent universities. A tsunami of regret thrust my body forward in the seat, as if I had been attacked by a virulent stomach ache. Depression always made me long to dive into bed, cover my head, and stay there until the malaise ran its course. But here among 1,200 graduating seniors, I couldn't show emotion. I gripped the seat in front of me and struggled to push back a wave of nausea.

In one huge catapulting eye opener, I saw the consequences of my mistakes in the glowing faces of Teresita, Isodoro, Hilarion, Nino, and Emilia. I realized that an academic career was utterly closed to me. What if I had done my homework, studied for tests, joined clubs? Would I have been there in the front with them, on my way to college? Instead, low grades had thrust my name to the bottom of the class rankings. So here I was, wearing a cap and gown, waiting for the cream of the crop to sit before I could cross the stage to receive my diploma, resisting a horrific feeling of remorse and a strong desire to faint.

Could I have a second chance?

No. I could not undo the last three years. Top schools gave no one a second chance. From inner city schools they recruited the valedictorian, salutatorian and then the next five in class ranking, and that was it.

Not only did I have no future, I felt friendless. My closest friends had found new lives. Ibis moved to New York to earn her living serving beer and wine in a neighborhood bar. Sylvia attended night school, received her GED in between bouts of bed-bound depression and planned to apply to the police academy. Gloria got back with and married Chino. She moved into the Little Havana home he shared with his parents. Cari, still with Ben in Virginia, announced her second pregnancy and launched into an affair with an unemployed neighbor.

I didn't even have a boyfriend. Robert had broken up with me. "I'm so confused," he told me. "I need to find myself." He channeled his energy into writing songs in the style of Elton John and Paul Williams and into forgetting me. And, even if the breakup didn't spur the searing pain of lost first love, the rupture hurt. My parents existed only in bodily form, silent partners in the mess in which I found myself. Completely alone, bored, ignorant, scared, and with no way to escape Little Havana, I glimpsed the terrible abyss that waited to devour me.

Clearly, I had to change my ways to get what I wanted. And what I wanted was not in Little Havana, the scene of heartbreak, loneliness, parental abandonment and neglect, and the chaotic pit of immigrant struggle that zapped everyone's energy.

When it was my turn to walk up to the stage, I pulled on a pleasant expression. I could see the smirk on the faces of the teachers, glad to see the last of me, as I reached for the diploma. I turned and caught sight of my father and his wife far away in the distance. I was one of the few students with divorced parents, and, incredibly, I had won an extra ticket in a raffle so they could attend. My father appeared remote, unfathomable, totally uninvolved with my life, a speck in the vast auditorium.

After the ceremony, I joined my mother in the parking lot, and we climbed into the shiny Volvo. My father and his wife waved good-by from their Mercedes. I looked after them, surprised. They had not stopped to congratulate me.

"You have to do something with your life," my mother said softly on the way home.

"I know."

"Let me pay for a secretarial course for you. I saw it in a magazine. I've saved a little money." It was painful to see my mother's worried face. The stark contrast between my poverty stricken mother offering me a future and my wealthy father unconcerned about my education overwhelmed me. My mother, mentally present that afternoon and aware of my bleak prospects, realized something had to be done.

"I don't want to be a secretary!"

"You need to study so you can get a good job," she said, "and so you don't have to depend on a man."

"There's got to be something else out there."

"But what? Your father doesn't have to pay any more child support now that you are 18 and out of high school."

"I'll figure something out. Those students you saw up there on the stage, the first ones to go up," I said, "none of them are smarter than I am. I could have gotten into Radcliffe, too, if I had wanted. I'm going to get an education and a good career. Wait and see. I'm smarter than you think."

No. I was not going to be a secretary. Nor end up like my mother. I wanted that adventurous life, and I was going to employ all my willpower to get it. Leaving Little Havana to go to college would get me there. But how?

An idea tore through my mind. I remembered a talk given by a counselor the week before outlining options for those not going away to school. I sat back in the seat, shaking, hoping it wasn't too late.

3.

The line looped around one hallway and spilled into the next. Some students sat on the floor, others lay spread out over backpacks. With application in one hand and a catalogue in the other, I joined them, heart pounding.

This is what I should have done a week ago. The advice of a high school counselor in one of the boring assemblies had not made an impact then, but I had filed the information away subconsciously. Now I understood it had to be the first step in my plan.

"Go to Miami Dade Junior College," the counselor had said. "It has an open door policy."

Finally at the window, ankles aching from standing for two hours on six-inch platform shoes, I handed over the application and the class registration form. In the catalogue, I read that everyone had to take the same requirements in specific categories. I chose two humanities courses and a psychology class. I stayed away from math and science, hated subjects, figuring that I could tackle those after some practice with courses I loved.

"You have to declare a major," the person behind the counter said, pointing to some gaps in the application. "Or at least check off a program of study."

"Do I have to decide right now?" Panic and dizziness.

"You want to transfer?"

"Yes."

"Check this box. You need an Associate in Arts degree to transfer."

"Ok."

"Go see an advisor."

"I will." I peeled off some bills from a wad my mother had pressed into my hand and paid for the classes, probably the money saved for the secretarial course.

It can only be described as a miracle that I had made it in time to register for the summer session at Miami Dade Junior College – ironically just across the street from The Place disco. That morning, jumping out of bed with unusual vigor, I knew this was the only option if I wanted to get an education. The high school counselor had said that no university would accept a low GPA, but that Miami Dade, offering open enrollment, would. I could hide my shameful report card, pretend it never happened, and push regret into that black space where I dumped all pain. No one would ever know.

In addition to providing a variety of technical programs for adults, the college – like all community and junior colleges throughout the nation -- offered a second and affordable chance to low-income students like me who either slept or partied their way through high school and needed a way to prove we could be good students. Without this safety net, how many confused, abused, neglected, and abandoned teenagers trying to cope with the stressful high school years would have a shot at a decent future, avoiding dead-end jobs?

After the graduation ceremony the day before, still spinning from somber realizations, I lay in bed thinking about money, always an issue. I counted out a stack of dollars I saved from my job. I didn't know if I had enough. Setting aside the dread and gathering strength, I dialed my father's number. The conviction that he owed me an education drove me.

"*Papi*, I'm going to take a few classes at Miami Dade," I said. "Could you help me pay for them?"

"I'm going to do better than that," he said. "I will continue to give you child support and the thirty a month as long as you are in college."

So how was that better? Did it mean I had to get the money from my mother? Or pay for college myself? Looking on the bright side, at least my mother and I wouldn't be forced into the welfare lines to survive. I told my mother, who sighed with relief, as if we had just received a reprieve from a firing squad.

It did not occur to me to apply for financial aid, so I paid for the classes and found the career services office. I took a number and pulled out my astoundingly high scores on the CLEP test (College Level Equivalency Placement) I had taken during one of the assemblies. They proved I hadn't been totally brain-dead.

When it was my turn, I handed the scores to the advisor.

"This means," she said, "you'll be getting credit for four classes: two English and two Social Studies." She took out a grid and plugged in a full year of courses; she penciled in all the requirements, including the four classes I had received credit for, and drew lines for the electives.

She calculated I could graduate after the summer session of 1973 and then transfer to a four year institution. Two years of college in one! And with a row of As on my transcripts, I figured, I could apply, not to the coveted Ivy League, but to a leading university.

"Come back when we're not so busy," she said. "You can take tests to find out your interests and aptitudes so you can choose a major that will get you a job. After that, you go over those catalogues over there to choose a school to transfer to."

Everything felt different. Even the humiliation of graduation day seemed like a distant nightmare. I had purpose. No more drifting, my goal only a year away.

"Ok, thank you." Gone was my tough demeanor. In its place: compliance with rules to get what I wanted.

Loaded with pamphlets, catalogues and dreams, I stepped out into the hall. Out of the corner of my eye, I spied Robert leaning against a wall, studying his class schedule. I turned away, glancing down at the floor to avoid an encounter. Then, from the other direction, Ovy approached. He hadn't seen me yet, so I ducked back into career services, not wanting to talk to him, either.

I was done with boyfriends for a while. I couldn't let anything, not even romance, the only love I could grasp, interfere with my plans.

4.

I gunned the Volvo eight miles north on Twenty Seventh Avenue, squeezed into a parking space in a field a block away, and ran clumsily on platform shoes the distance to the first class of the summer term. I was late, over-sleeping as usual. I opened the door quietly and tried to slide unnoticed into a seat, but my ankle twisted; I fell off the platforms and spilled onto the floor.

My instinct to laugh out loud and deliver off-color jokes rose up to overpower me, but I successfully fought back the temptation. I couldn't repeat my destructive high school behavior now that I had a clear goal. I knew I had to get attention from success, not from failure, so I jumped up, suppressed all merriment and tip-toed quietly to the back. The professor did not pause in his lecture, and the students ignored me.

At my seat in psych class, I copied notes from the board: "What I believe is true becomes true." The professor said, "Answers come into your mind from the flow of the unconscious." None of it made sense. If I couldn't understand what went on in class, I thought, I'd just rely on my memory then spit back information on tests. The professor picked up a stack of handouts and counted ten for each row. I looked at the title: "Behavior Modification." I missed the rest of the lecture, absorbed in reading the article, just as in high school.

The words penetrated my wall of ignorance. Suggestology, I read, "leads to changes in individual awareness and behavior. Suggestion is the source of our highest aspirations and our best achievement." Something was happening; it felt as if I had dived into a pool of silver light, swimming endlessly to the bottom to retrieve a speck of shining gold, the key to knowledge.

Drama was next, forever changing my passive approach to watching plays and films. "Stop being a popcorn eater," shouted the professor, striding back and forth between desks. "Resist the immediate pleasure of the theater. Consider why what's being viewed is not working!"

Finally, art history. The professor presented slides of paintings from the Renaissance. The assignment: pick an artist and write a paper. I zeroed in on Botticelli's *The Birth of Venus,* different from the religious works of the period.

The poetic, mystical aura of the painting attracted me, and I identified with Venus balanced on a clam shell floating on the sea.

Why did everything resonate so deeply?

The summer session, much shorter than either fall or winter semesters, didn't leave me much time to do anything else but read, write, study for tests and go to work. Disco outings had stopped. My friends, involved in complicated lives of their own, didn't seem to mind. We sometimes got together on a special day, but no more 48-hour marathon partying.

To survive the grueling schedule, I set up a study corner at home, spreading out textbooks and notebooks on a long table in the back room where both Jaime and Ovy had climbed in through the window. I wrote up a calendar for upcoming tests and assignments and taped it to the wall. I read each chapter carefully and outlined it in my notebook. I reviewed the lecture notes, aware I needed to grasp what went on in class so I wouldn't look stupid to the professor and classmates. I had to participate in the discussion and not just sit there reading.

I had been a good student. Once. I struggled to recapture what that felt like. How had I made the honor roll in elementary school? It was so very long ago. I battled the loneliness that threatened to swallow me in my new scholar's isolation. I was friendless, loveless, depressed. But the high of learning, the rush of mind expansion, like drugs spurring ecstasy, propelled me, kept me on track.

One day after class, I stopped at career services to take the tests the advisor had mentioned would help figure out a major and a job that went with it.

"I just started school," I said, "and I don't know what to study."

"That's why we are here," the advisor said.

She set me up to take the California Occupational Preference Survey, the College Interest Profile, and the Educational and Vocational Exploration for Women questionnaire. She put the tests through a machine, and the results popped out: literature and journalism topped the list, then teaching and social science.

How could I get a job in literature and journalism? Maybe teaching the subjects would be a good choice. After all, my mother, grandfather and several other relatives had been college professors in La Habana. I had even been a member of Future Teachers of America in sixth grade. But I remembered a high school counselor saying there wasn't much money in it. I couldn't continue to be poor. How about owning a bookstore? I loved books. What would I need to do for that? Get a loan from a bank? Impossible. How about writing? I wrote poems, but I knew that would not pay the bills.

"The next step," the advisor said, "is to go through the career files."

"Ok, thank you."

In the back of the room, I flipped through a pamphlet listing careers for those who scored high in literature and journalism. I copied them in a notebook: Lexicographer, Proofreader, Playwright, News Reporter, Magazine Editor, Advertising Copywriter, Public Relations Specialist. Dizzy from all the choices, I rushed home to write two papers, both due the next morning; despite my attempts at organization and scheduling, I had procrastinated as usual.

In my room, I pulled out the old, rickety Olivetti, a banged up typewriter I had bought at the flea market to do my high school English papers, and rolled in a fresh white sheet. I stared at it. What if I made mistakes? I dug up an old grammar book and kept it open beside me for reference. Nothing popped into my mind. I rolled the paper back and forth. What happened to my writing skills? Why didn't my subconscious work? Finally, I pecked out the title: "A Look at Sandro Botticelli." Then, words began to form on the page; I described my reaction to *The Birth of Venus* and its colors and lines; quoting from two library books, I discussed how Botticelli and the painting fit into a historical context. Very slow going.

Four am. An all-nighter. I started the psych paper, the title: "Where I'm At Now." This one went much faster. It wasn't difficult to narrate my disappointing high school track record, the painful disintegration of my group of friends, and the hopes I had for the future. I ended with: "I have so many more things to discover. I never want to stop experiencing." Exhausted, I collapsed into bed for two hours of sleep, knowing I didn't have the option of ignoring the alarm.

The following week, I got the papers back: As on both.

The psychology professor wrote at the bottom: "Far Out! Best Wishes."

5.

The land corporation where I worked closed its doors one day, offering no explanations. Desperately, I scanned the classifieds and found an ad for a job as a clerk in a bookstore.

"Do you like to read?" asked the owner, a dark skinned man with deep scars that cut across his face as testimony to youth's hormones. He looked me up and down. His son sitting at the desk stared with lash-less eyes.

"Yes."

"Then you have the job."

The next day, I parked the Volvo in the lot next to the Downtown Book Center.

"Cecilia has entered society," the owner's son sarcastically exclaimed when I walked in to the bookstore. "I saw you driving that Volvo. Woo, hoo!"

An obese, pimply faced teenager about my age, he continuously pushed aside greasy hair hanging in his eyes. As the owner's son, he had an inflated sense of self. He shuffled his wide frame onto the swivel chair at the desk and swung around to stare at me.

"My father is not here today, so I am the boss," he said. "You can start by filling up the shelves. The books are in the back."

I walked to where he pointed and entered a small, cramped storage room. I breathed in the exhilarating smell of new books, passing my hand over the shiny new covers. I loaded up my left arm with books, and held the stack with my right. Then, I went up and down the narrow aisles, filling all the empty spaces on the shelves.

The cashier, a young woman about 22, had been working there for a few years while she went to college, but now she was leaving to get married to a police officer. "I can't wait to get out of this place," she whispered. I wondered why as I went to the storage room and picked up a pile of magazines from Spain. I filled the racks with newspapers and periodicals from France, Germany and every country in Latin America, reading the headlines and loving the knowledge at my fingertips.

I soon understood the cashier's comment. The job proved so boring and the owner's son such an irritant that I quit after a few months. I never forgot the intoxicating smell of new books, the way they felt in my hands. I hoped I would publish a book of my own one day.

In no time, I had another job, this one as an assistant to an ear, nose and throat specialist. I gingerly held a small tray underneath a patient's ear, out of which grew a bush of hair.

"Hold it steady," the doctor said. I closed my eyes and tried to balance the tray without moving it. He pushed the syringe into the patient's ear, and a stream of water washed out huge brownish yellow chunks of wax.

"Three, two one," the doctor counted and squeezed the syringe for the second time. Another wad of wax broke loose and erupted as if from a volcano. "I'm finished."

I carried the tray to a sink and disposed of the contents, turning on the faucet full force. The patient and the doctor walked out of the examining room, and I stayed behind to take off the paper covering the table and tidy up the instruments. I went to the front desk and took up yet another file, walked to the door, opened it and called out, "Mr. Hirsch?" It was awful and I hated it, but I needed the money, determined to earn my way through school. Unemployment was not an option, not matter the type of job I had to do.

Then, walking out of class at Miami Dade, I bumped into my future.

6.

"Student reporters! Get paid to cover news!" I read the yellow flyer taped to the wall at Miami Dade. Reporting had been on my careers list. This might be an opportunity to try it out, not to mention to leave the hated medical assistant job and make some money.

I hurried down the hall on wobbly platform shoes, past a long corridor and a huge lake filled with ducks to the other side of the campus. Stacks of newspapers lined every wall in the *Falcon Times* office. Old desks holding typewriters, dictionaries, atlases, pens, pencils and paper filled up every available space. I smiled, absorbing the seductive atmosphere of a newsroom, both a place of action and of intellectual inquiry, the site of engagement with the world.

But no one sat writing; the office was deserted. The advisor, Jose Garcia, a stocky man wearing bottle-thick glasses, came out of his cubicle when I stumbled in, the strap on the platform shoes digging into my ankle.

"I'd like to apply to be a reporter," I said.

"Any experience?"

"I worked for my high school newspaper," I lied, "and the year book."

"Here," he said, handing me a press release. "Just go cover this rock concert out on the football field right now. I have no reporters, so you're it."

I grabbed a narrow pad from a desk and wobbled out to the sunbaked field. The singers, Lawrence, Acker and Williamson from Youngstown, Ohio, performed a blues-based hard driving rock, stomping around on a makeshift stage, with fans stretched out on blankets and dancing to screeching guitars. The lead, Williamson, mounted his instrument and yelped like a dog, prancing from one end to the other with the guitar between his legs. The press release said he had performed with Crosby, Stills, Nash and Young in California.

I wandered around the field, exhilarated, but with no idea of what to do. Finally, I scribbled in my pad the few lyrics that I could make out from the screaming singers, interviewed some students -- writing as fast as I could to keep up with their words -- jotted down what they were wearing and took notes on the ambiance.

Purely by instinct, back at the *Falcon Times* office, I wrote an informational lead with the five Ws taught in journalism classes: who, what, when, where and why, but adding color and emotion by describing the field and the fans. I quoted students and ended with the date of the band's next concert. I didn't know I had learned this style by reading countless newspaper and magazine articles.

The stiff keys on the manual typewriter barely moved at my touch, and I had to bang down hard. I ripped out two double-spaced pages from the rubber roller and proudly handed them to Advisor Garcia, who pushed up his protruding glasses and, with a worried look, threw himself on a chair in the middle of the newsroom. He took a broad tipped charcoal pencil and drew bold marks all over the page. When he finished, he threw the story into a box marked TAKE TO PRINTER. I peeked in. He had rearranged the paragraphs and slashed the colorful descriptions and quotes.

"Should I come back tomorrow?" I asked as he retreated into his cubicle.

"Sure. You're hired." I had no idea this was a work-study job, which eliminated my tuition. Garcia came back out with some forms for me to fill out; I must have qualified since I began to receive checks through the mail: $52.80 every two weeks, less than the medical job, but worth it, since I was saving on tuition.

At home, I called the medical office, gave notice and told my mother – now working the early shift at the laundry -- of my good fortune. "*Que bueno*, Cecilita," she said. When the concert story appeared in the newspaper, it was much reduced and didn't have a byline. But I didn't care. I cut it out carefully and taped it into a huge artist's sketchbook.

Not all stories were as easy as that first one. I struggled with hard news leads.

"You have to be succinct," yelled Myron, the editor. "No adjectives, no adverbs. Just subjects and verbs."

"Write faster," Coralee, managing editor, shouted. "We're on deadline!"

I shut out the noise of a convulsing newsroom, editors and reporters running every which way, and kept pounding on the keys of the dilapidated typewriter, trying over and over to get it right: "Broward County Sheriff Edward Stack wants to shut down the Hollywood Sportatorium, saying it is unsafe and a public nuisance. Today, he filed a lawsuit against the company that runs it." I flipped the two sentences around, and then flipped them back. No computers, so this took a while. There was so much information about the lawsuit; I didn't know what to add next.

"Your trouble is with the first few paragraphs. Then it flows," Coralee said, looking over my shoulder. "A feature is your natural voice, not straight news. Just bang it out."

I hated the dry, brittle style of daily news. But I could do it with practice. I had to force the words out quickly and simply and forget artistry, style, and the color and mood I saw in every story. Just the facts.

Finally, I ripped out the page from the roller and handed it to Coralee, who began to mark up the copy with her big, black pencil. I didn't have time to stand around and watch the painful process; I had to cover a student sit-in that started in ten minutes.

Despite the struggles, I loved reporting. Out on assignment, I felt at home taking notes, marginalized from the action, an outcast as I had always been. I felt privileged to watch life's dramas unfold, and then encapsulate them in words so that others could experience them, too. A reporting job would pay, not an exorbitant salary, as I found out from a career booklet, but one that would allow me the freedom to live as I wished. I had to find a way to write more feature articles and avoid straight news.

7.

Killing me softly with his song....

"I want to marry you," Ovy said, staring into my eyes and clutching my hands.

We sat at our favorite restaurant, La Hacienda, a block from my house, eating steaks with mushroom sauce and yellow rice, like we had done so many times before. I had not spoken to him since the evening of our breakup months earlier.

"What happened to your girlfriend?" I sneered, taking back my hands.

"I told you I never loved her."

"I don't want to marry you," I answered. "I'm going away...to a university."

"You! Hm. I don't think you're college material. You couldn't even get past those math classes if it hadn't been for me."

"High school is over now. I have thought about it, and I want to be a writer."

"Who put that stupid idea into your head?"

"I'm going to be a newspaper reporter first." After reading a magazine article about starving writers and artists, I concluded that working for a newspaper was the closest job to daily writing and would provide a steady paycheck. I needed to be practical. After all, Hemingway had been a reporter for years until he wrote his first bestseller, *The Sun Also Rises.*

"Sure! I can just see you being a slave to that job. Reporters are on call night and day. Don't you know that?"

"I won't mind. I'm saving money to get my degree in journalism."

"You're crazy!"

"A lot of people I know are going away to school: Teresita Alvarez, Nino Lucio. Yes, they have families that support them; that's why they're so successful. But I can do it by myself. Watch."

"You have no idea how hard it's going to be. First of all, it's going to take a long time to save enough money. Second of all, no college will take you. Your grades stink."

"I'm going to get straight As at Miami-Dade. I'm writing stories and building a portfolio. I'm good at writing. I wrote a lot of your essays! Some journalism school out there will accept me. I know it."

"But what about us? It would be so much easier for you if you married me."

"You were unfaithful to me."

"I made a mistake. I have loved only you since I met you."

"That was so long ago. Things are different now…"

"I can make it up to you. Don't you want to have a husband, a house, children?"

"Not me. I want to live an adventurous life."

"Look, we can set up a clothes factory, make a lot of money, buy one of those new townhouses out in Kendall. Then I can go play Jai Alai professionally and you can go with me, traveling to different cities, while my mother runs the factory. That will be adventurous. Don't you think you might want to do something like that?"

"No. I don't want to do any of that. That is not my dream."

I wanted Ovy, but I didn't like the life he offered. I realized that he would never accept a woman with an independent life. He, like many young men of the time, wanted a traveling companion – a surrogate mom, so to speak – to tag along while he followed his dreams. I decided, for the second time, to give him up. If Ovy wasn't going to believe in me or let me live the life I wanted, then he clearly wasn't the man to marry, no matter how much I cared.

"I thought you loved me."

My eyes said I do, but I remained silent. I placed his hand gently on the side of my face and closed my eyes.

Killing my life with his words…..

8.

Lovejoy's College Guide held my dream as lightly as a sea flower floating on a wave. I just had to reach out and pluck it from the turbulent water. The book listed all the universities in the world. Sitting in career services at Miami Dade with the heavy tome on my lap, I lingered on the sections about Oxford, Cambridge, the Sorbonne, visualizing myself at those exotic campuses. I read the listings on the Ivy League, enviously eying the ancient buildings that meant access to the elite, inner sanctum of America, the dream that drove so many.

Reluctantly, I pushed away the tantalizing reveries, and moved on to more practical places. I came across a section that enumerated the universities with high-ranking journalism schools, accredited by the American Council for Education in Journalism. Focused now, I picked five randomly from all four corners of the United States, copied down the addresses, and used my old Olivetti typewriter at home to request applications and catalogues: Syracuse University, University of Maryland, University of Southern California, University of California at Berkeley, Northeastern University.

When the booklets arrived in the mail, I slumped on the couch in a near faint, shocked by the price tag of the private colleges and the out-of-state tuition at the public institutions. How could I save all that money? I added up the figures: tuition, room and board, books. Insurmountable.

I considered my mother's savings for secretarial school. Not enough. Then I grudgingly thought about my father. I closed my eyes with phone in hand, forcing myself to dial the number. What other alternative? I had to do whatever it took. Maybe he would see the logic in my thinking and help me out. I decided to test the waters.

"*Papi*, I want to go away to a university!" I said on the phone. "There's nothing here that fits me. The University of Miami is too expensive, and Florida International University doesn't offer a lot of choices yet."

After a long silence, my father gathered his habitual energy into his voice. "Come over tonight," he said. "I'll sit down and help you decide something."

I packed up my catalogues and Career Outlook pamphlets and drove to my father's new home in Miami Lakes: a roomy, three-bedroom, ranch style house on a lake in a brand-new, tree-lined subdivision just north of Hialeah. The back yard stretched out on both sides in a wide expanse of freshly mowed grass.

I walked into the air conditioned living room and marveled at the new furniture: a beveled glass dining table, secured on a solid wood base in the shape of an exotic sea creature, showcased the silver candle holders I had dashed to the floor in a fit of anger. The elegant table triggered images of my own house. My mother and I still lived without air conditioning, and we set out buckets to catch the rain from a leaky roof.

"The table is from France," my father said, leading me to the family room and leaning back into an overstuffed maroon leather chair. Dark wood beams and wrought iron decorations gave it the look of a Spanish *taberna*. Fighting disgust, I forced myself to proceed with my mission.

"Here are some of the universities I have been looking at," I said and sat on the floor, spreading out the pamphlets, all of which he ignored.

"Every university," my father's voice hit the low tones, as if dragging his words through a muddy tunnel, "is the same. After you finish Miami Dade, you can go to FIU and live at home. It is the least expensive and just as good as anywhere else. All the out of town universities are dens of drugs and prostitution!"

I sighed, not surprised.

"I am telling you what is best for you," he continued, his tone taking an authoritative edge just like when he bashed Fidel and the evils of communism. "You have a car to get there. Tuition is cheap. And you will be a lot safer living at home. All colleges are the same, Cecilita. Believe me." Shouting, he sprayed spit from his mouth.

Why did I ever have the hope that he would understand why I had to get away? Maybe he needed more time to get used to the idea?

"Why don't you study to be a pharmacist?" my father kept going. "You could set up a pharmacy right next to my office, and I could send you my patients. Isn't that a good idea? Or how about being an antiques dealer? That's a great job for a woman. You could travel to Europe and import fine pieces. Many of my friends would buy them. Or you could be an interior designer. They have those programs at Miami Dade. You don't even have to go to FIU."

"*Papi*, I want to be a writer. I want to be a journalist."

There. I said it out loud to my father.

"Cecilita, you must be confused," my father's voice went lower. "All the young people these days are confused. You don't know what you are saying. Don't you know that *periodistas* are crooks? Just look at those two *estupidos* reporting on Nixon, who is a great president. Someone must be paying them to write those stories!"

He was referring to Carl Bernstein and Bob Woodward, Washington Post reporters who set the stage for Nixon's impeachment in 1974. In Little Havana, the Watergate burglary scandal had captured everyone's imagination. While I admired the media for exposing a corrupt president, my community rallied behind four of the five Watergate burglars, anti-Castro Cubans involved in the 1962 Bay of Pigs invasion. These men became heroes for installing electronic listening devices in the national Democratic Party campaign offices, hoping to obtain information about Nixon's political opponent, George McGovern, believed by many in the Cuban community to be a Castro sympathizer.

"*Periodistas* are all corrupt, just like lawyers!" my father said. "*Esta niña esta loca*! All your problems are based on your mother who has not known how to raise you."

"Stop insulting her. She's my mother."

This outburst shocked my father into silence. Without waiting for a response, I picked up my pamphlets and rushed out the door.

I remembered what I had learned in psych class: answers flow from the subconscious.

They flowed: I could save the money for the first semester and apply for grants and scholarships. After a year, if I chose a public school, I could qualify to become a resident of the state, allowing me to pay a much lower tuition. I'd get a roommate. Work part time or full time, whatever had to be done. I didn't need transportation. I planned to drive there in the Volvo, sleep in the car if I had to. I felt alive, driven.

My father would not deter my dreams. I was leaving with or without his help.

9.

How wonderful life is when you're in the world….
Robert stood on my doorstep.
"Can you forgive me?" he asked. "I was confused."
"You left me." My hands shook.
"My parents are getting a divorce, and I was going crazy."
"I'm sorry. I know just how you feel."
"And I didn't have anything to offer you, just a factory job and no savings. I felt I was nothing. Then, I realized I loved you."
"I love you, too."
So we started dating again. He was everything Ovy was not. Solid, dependable, focused, and he stayed clear of the law.

Why is love such a splendored thing? Twists and turns on the road to romance, with both partners resisting, or maybe one and then later the other, means suffering. Does the eternal chase bring rewards?

One Sunday, Ovy came to visit; Robert decided to swing by as well. The confrontation took on the aspect of a head of state summit; each measured up the opponent. This time, Ovy didn't punch out the competition. He knew he had no claim on me.

Refusing to get involved, I stormed into my room, too stressed with trying to stretch my money and studying for finals. Almost finished with the fall semester and in the lull at the *Falcon Times* just before winter break, I realized the pay at the paper was not enough to get me through college. Although the experience had been invaluable, I needed to find another job. Frustrated, after Ovy left, I broke up with Robert, saying I didn't have time for any more conflict. I had to get on with my goals.

But the next day he called. "I think we have a lot more to give to each other," he said.

"I'm going away to school."

"I don't want you to go," Robert said.

"I'm going, and no one will stop me."

"Why don't we take a drive up the coast and see a few universities."

What a great idea.

We drove in his Volkswagen Beetle to the University of Florida in Gainesville and Florida State University in Tallahassee. They were different from Miami Dade, a commuter school founded in 1959. Students actually lived here in dorms, the buildings more than a hundred years old and filled with tradition. The college ambiance held me captive; it stirred such longing I stopped breathing. I stared at the campus covered with fall-colored foliage, narrow hallways, red-brick buildings. Students walked around as if on air, holding tightly to books, purpose in their eyes, worried about nothing but building their futures.

"It's where I need to be," I said. "There's nothing in Miami for me."

"I want to go away to school too," he said. "I don't want to work in a factory all my life."

"Maybe we can go together? Let's get married and leave."

Why did I have to add the marriage part? Wasn't I liberated enough to go without the legality? No. I wanted it all. The illusion that those vows would make all the difference in my chaotic life ensnared me. I knew that there were no guarantees, but marriage would make me feel protected, sheltered, safe, with a person of my very own under the lock and key of a contract! Security. Is that all there is?

Looking back, I realize that, by embracing marriage, I followed the social construct that said life would be easier with a man. But I used it conveniently for my own ends. Why not? I loved him. Marrying Robert would make my departure from Little Havana a lot less difficult. I craved freedom, excitement, new experiences. I didn't know if marriage would be compatible with those goals. Could I be free and secure at the same time?

I didn't have time to find out just then. I had to move forward. Robert, unlike Ovy, believed in me and supported my plans. He didn't offer me a life of subservience to his dream. We could both grow in our chosen fields.

Our love felt different from the one I had experienced with Ovy: less passionate, more companionable; our decision to marry was romantic but practical as well. I was beginning to understand that few people had it all.

10.

The building, marked breathtakingly with the words *Miami Beach Sun Reporter*, spread out over several blocks. A year ago, publisher Paul M. Bruun merged his small *Reporter*, which he started back in 1962, with the *Sun*, a paper that had covered the city since the days of the Great Depression, giving the new publication the highest circulation on the beach.

I gripped my portfolio, now filled with dozens of stories. Was I ready? I could barely save money with the job at the school paper. So in the middle of the winter semester, 1973, when *Falcon Times* Advisor Garcia announced the *Sun Reporter* had a job opening, I called to ask for an interview.

My heart sank when the stiff-faced editor waved me over to his cubicle. A crusty man with a head sprouting patches of gray hair and wearing a scruffy beard, he did not stop frowning. I gingerly opened the portfolio: "Nearly 400 classes closed," "Like a joyful rhapsody, Godspell comes on strong," "Consumer movement activity unprecedented," "The two year degree: desirable job opportunities," "Latin Fire spellbinds audience," "Miami Dade to join UM in workshop," "Travel open to all walks of life," "Suit brings tighter drug security for Sportatorium."

The stories did not impress the editor. Was it disdain I saw in his face? Was it because I was a woman, a Cuban woman? Or because I didn't have a degree? Were my stories badly written? I had no way of telling.

"We have no reporter openings at the moment," he said.

Then why look at my clips? I closed the portfolio and sat there wondering what to do.

"But there is a job in proofreading and paste up if you want it."

"When do I start?" I didn't hesitate, knowing that the proofing job was still an opportunity to move up into a bigger and better paper. My days of challenging authority figures were over -- for now; the job fit in with my greater goal of saving money for the move out of Little Havana. I had to save enough for the first semester's tuition by the end of the year, my deadline for leaving. Maybe I could learn other aspects of the newspaper business in the meantime.

Who knew if I would have an opportunity to cover a story for simply being in the right place at the right time? Just like at the *Falcon Times*.

"Tomorrow at 3 pm."

The presses buzzed like angry bees, churning out pages of news, obituaries, theater reviews, and four-color advertisements. I breathed in the odor of raw moist wood pulp mixed with ink, hooked on the energy of publishing. That first afternoon, as I made my way over to the paste up department, I gazed longingly at the newsroom; white-haired men swiveled in chairs at a horseshoe-shaped copy desk, passing stories back and forth, holding thick pencils in the air before slamming them down on the page to correct grammar, style, and sentence structure.

A few energetic twenty-somethings rushed out at regular intervals to cover society news, the police beat and city hall meetings. I ran into one young reporter in the hall.

"I know you!" she said.

"Weren't you in the *Falcon Times* the other day?"

"Yes, but I graduated already, and I just lucked out here," she brushed past me, heading for the door at a jog. "Going to City Hall."

Going to City Hall. I repeated the words several times. Maybe one day I, too, would be rushing out on a story at a city paper. *Going to City Hall.* I couldn't get her words out of my mind. I paused once more to look at the typewriters, desks piled with books, tall shelves jammed with dictionaries and old encyclopedias. My heart beat fast. Everyone here worked with words. Not just reading words, but writing them and getting paid to do it. I wanted to be like them. I turned away and walked to the paste-up department on the other side of the building, willing myself to stay focused.

At the paste-up desk, I looked around uncertainly. Almost immediately, a curly haired man briskly approached with a long strip of proof copy. "Hi, I'm Bill. I run this department." He delivered quick instructions and walked off.

I took up a wax pencil and a strip of copy and started reading. No mistakes. Then I took the perfect story to the galley room and brandished a short cutting knife like a surgeon's scalpel to make sure it fit into the news hole. With a gooey substance, I pasted the copy neatly in its place. I excised a line that didn't fit in the column and placed it, very carefully, at the top of a new column. A blank page and I was filling it with words that would be read by thousands! It was the most fascinating work I had ever done.

I went back to the desk and tackled a fresh pile of copy. Looking up, I saw a man who appeared to be Paul M. Bruun. It *was* Mr. Bruun! I recognized him from his picture on the front page where he prominently displayed a daily editorial. He walked by with two others, waving his hands around. His face was lined and droopy, but his hair was carbon brick black with red glints glowing in the light. A small, chiseled mustache sat on his upper lip, as carefully shaped as my straight lines of copy in the galleys of the *Sun Reporter.* I saw him as a hero.

At about 7 p.m., on my dinner break, I went out to the car to eat a sandwich and do homework for an hour. This was a full-time job, 3 to 11 pm, and I carried a full load at Miami Dade. I had to make everything work, so I convinced a few professors into allowing me to take their classes without actually attending, a precursor to distance learning. They agreed, so I completed the assignments at home and went in for the tests.

Reclining in the car seat, I opened the sociology book: "Women have been advancing steadily in the labor force of American society through education since World War II." I sat up straight and read the entire chapter.

I thought of my friends, leading busy lives. Sylvia, after recuperating from an abortion, pursued an affair with a married police officer. Ibis, back in Miami, worked full time for Florida Lumber and conducted *santeria* rituals in the evenings and on the weekends. Gloria worked at a small restaurant close to home and only went out with husband Chino. Cari, in town from Virginia for a weekend, consulted the magical *caracoles,* hoping to get answers about the fate of her crumbling marriage.

Was this all there was to life for them? I knew that without educations, it was. So I could not fail, or that's all there'd be to life for me too. Education was, no doubt, the key.

11.

The keys of my Olivetti refused to bounce back into the carriage. I shoved them into place, unraveling a few locked together; my fingers came away smeared with ink. I didn't have much time left. The deadline for college applications was rapidly approaching for the winter term of 1974, and I still had not written the college essay. I couldn't wait around to have the old typewriter repaired, so I gathered my papers, sped to Miami Dade's library and found an electric typewriter.

Luckily, all five universities asked similar questions, so I could write one essay and make copies. The question asked about overcoming obstacles and planning a future. I had a lot to say on both counts, but I sat in front of the blank page, typewriter whirring, nothing popping into my mind. Then I remembered my psych paper, "Where I'm At Now." It answered the question perfectly. Maybe I could revamp it? Would I be able to convince the admission committee to accept me? I had to make them see I had talent and determination.

Pushing down anxiety and fear, I took out the psych paper from my notebook and started typing. I added and deleted paragraphs. I even described how the article on behavior modification changed my life. Then I proofread for typing errors and made five copies.

After that ordeal, the applications were easy, and I typed them out in no time. I placed a large manila envelope in the typewriter and typed the address of one of the universities, then carefully slipped an application and essay inside and licked it sealed. From a list, I checked off each school as I assembled five packets. I stacked the envelopes on top of each other and held them close to my heart.

"Soon," I thought, "Robert and I will be starting a new life."

With the stack under my arm, I skipped down the stairs and ran into Rene. I smiled, remembering how he had helped me at Miami High, allowing me to graduate. He had not gone away to college, and I was surprised to see him.

"My plans changed," he said.

"I thought you wanted to be a marine biologist or a lawyer."

"Maybe someday."

For him, it was a dream deferred. But nothing and no one would stand in my way.

I had succeeded in breaking a lot of bad habits, earning an Associate of Arts in one year instead of two. No fancy graduation ceremony, just a transcript with my GPA. Not a 4.0, but a 3.58. I was on my way to a top journalism school; it would only be a matter of time before I worked for a newspaper or magazine, writing the feature stories that I loved.

Although I liked *Washington Post* reporters Woodward and Bernstein, and we closely followed the Watergate scandal in school, I didn't see myself as a political or hard news reporter. The experience at the *Falcon Times* helped me realize that I wanted to write more than just the facts of a story. I didn't know it yet, but my style had a name, creative nonfiction, much closer to those of the New Journalists of the 1960s, Joan Didion, Gay Talese and Tom Wolf – authors that would become my role models.

12.

One by one, envelopes stuffed with papers arrived in my mailbox. I tore them open and yelled for joy each time I read an acceptance letter. Five times I yelled: all the universities to which I had applied accepted me for the winter term of 1974. I went through piles of information on enrollment, room and board, extracurricular activities. Maps of the campuses, cities and states were stapled to lists of restaurants and local attractions.

Clutching the letters, I ran to the world globe on my bookshelf and measured the distances from each city to Miami. Syracuse, Baltimore, Boston, Los Angeles. Berkeley. Which was the farthest away from home? The University of California beat out the University of Southern California by a few miles.

"*Mami*," I shouted. I grabbed the globe and ran with it into the kitchen. "This is where I'm going to the university!" I pointed to Berkeley.

"*Ay, mi hija*," she exclaimed. "*Que bueno*. Do you have enough money?"

"I do for the first semester." I figured my grades were good enough to qualify for grants, and, in the second year, as a resident of the state, the tuition would drop from $700 to $225 a quarter. I would only have to pay for books.

I couldn't wait to tell Robert the news. Our relationship had not derailed us from our dreams. When we weren't working or studying, we went to the beach or the movies, the discos a rare destination. But my mother's face stopped me from rushing to the phone.

Hair flat and limp, she looked pale with dark circles under her eyes. A finger width of white stood out prominently next to her scalp, separating itself from the dark brown hair she colored in the bathroom.

"I don't want you to be alone," I said, watching her wash dishes.

I knew she was sick; I noted a slight tremor in her hand as she picked up a dish towel to dry a bowl. My mother's mental illness had progressed from hearing voices outside the door, to feelings of persecution, and then to carrying around her food everywhere she went. She claimed a co-worker at the laundry wanted to poison her, adamant about not leaving food in the refrigerator. I thought that was odd, but I didn't know what to make of it; the question of mental illness never entered my mind and neither did I think of mentioning it to my father, who had made it clear he didn't want to talk about my mother.

She struggled with the bills, but I occasionally helped with a repair here and there and bought groceries. She gave me some money from the child support payments, but I paid for all car repairs and maintenance and school expenses.

"You have to get an education," she said, passing her forearm across her brow to push back her hair. "I will be all right until you come back." Unlike many Little Havana mothers, she never discouraged me from pursuing my dream or pressured me to stay.

I paused, worried. She dried her hands and walked to her room, and, in an instant, I sprinted to mine and picked up the phone. "Robert," I breathed into the receiver. "They all accepted me, but I think Berkeley has the best journalism program. Do you think you'll like California?"

"It's the best place for the television industry," he said. "I'm thinking of becoming a producer. But…my mother is having a nervous breakdown about the divorce, and she doesn't want me to leave Miami. She's going crazy!"

"You told her already?"

"I had to tell her. My father left the house last night to live with his mistress."

13.

"What about school?" my mother asked when I told her that Robert and I were getting married. In moments of lucidity, knew the priorities. She sat up in bed, eying me coldly as I stood by her door, Robert hovering close behind.

"I'm still going. We're both going. Right after the wedding."

"*Que bueno.* So good, so good," she mumbled, drawing up the sheet around her, bottles of pills lined up on the night table.

I felt guilty about leaving home, and saw it as "abandoning" my mother. Robert felt the same way about his, who had been hit with two abandonments at once -- her husband's and her son's.

We didn't feel the same about our fathers, though.

For me, nothing but joy and relief as I drove to Miami Lakes. In my father's living room, I threw myself on the floor to wrestle with Joaquin, the black German Shepherd. My father sat on a Louis XV chair with gold leaf arm rests and read a book.

"*Papi*, I'm getting married."

He hiccupped. Got up. The book fell on the floor. Sat down.

"And right after the wedding," I continued, "Robert and I are going to California. I'm going to a university in Berkeley, and he's applying to the Ron Bailey School of Broadcasting in San Francisco."

"Now you'll be safe. You'll have someone to go with."

"What?" I asked. "Was that the problem, or was it the money?"

Beba came in from the kitchen and interrupted the conversation. "We don't have to worry about you," she said. "You won't be alone in a strange city."

I narrowed my eyes and looked from one to the other. I didn't believe them. Had this been the case, wouldn't my father have underscored his fears when I first brought up the subject? Let's say he had been concerned about safety but just couldn't bring himself to reveal his emotions, wouldn't he offer to pay the out-of-state tuition right now that I was out of danger?

Could I have been so cynical at age 19? Yes. Under my father's tutelage, I learned to doubt everything, keep one step ahead of everyone, and rely only on myself: the perfect preparation for life. *Gracias, Papi!* Whereever you are.

While he didn't offer one extra penny -- and I didn't ask -- he had an alternate plan.

"I'm going to transfer $100 a month from the child support to you in California," he said. "That should help with living expenses."

I frowned, but kept quiet at this new miserly trick.

My mother would be strapped for cash, but she wouldn't have to pay my utilities, lowering household expenses. And if I didn't need the money in Berkeley, I would just secretly mail it back to her. Both Robert and I were going to work while going to school.

I believe today that, while my father harbored affection for me, his jealousy and resentment blocked him from being generous with love or money, or from being the father he should have been. He felt jealous because I loved my mother, and he resented me because he couldn't control me.

At least he offered no objection to picking up the tab for the wedding. In my community, only marriage could validate self-hood, especially for a woman, and nuptials were what he could wholeheartedly support.

Robert's parents, on the other hand, thought the world was coming to an end. They never considered as important the issues of personal growth, academic advantage or career advancement. Family first, they said. In our community, the strong interdependence between family members caused many to renounce individual dreams.

"If you stay in Miami," Robert's mother said, "I'll buy you a bedroom suite."

"And I," his father added, "will give you the down payment for a new townhouse in Hialeah. You know. The new ones they're building over by the canal?"

I marveled at the stark contrast between their generosity and my father's stinginess. The disparity pained me. I hesitated, tempted to accept the offers and bury myself in the warmth that Robert's family offered. How easy it would all be to stay and be part of their family!

Wasn't that what I always wanted?

"Should we?" I asked.

"Let's go take a look at the townhouses," Robert said.

We walked all around the small yard, peered out the balcony and gazed into the adjoining canal; the smell of fresh paint and plaster made me giddy.

"A place of our own!"

"Centrally located," Robert said.

"A lot of space."

We considered it, but, in the end, we refused the offer, the bedroom suite and down payment only momentary temptations. We could save for all that ourselves, we figured, when we both had degrees.

"I'm ready for adventure," Robert said.

Mentally, I was already more than three thousand miles away.

14.

My father hired a Little Havana butcher to help him plan a delectable menu, purchase the finest in meats, poultry and vegetables and concoct tantalizing dishes for a food extravaganza the likes of which his friends and family had not seen before. He took control of my wedding buffet not only because he paid for it, but because he was an epicurean whose taste buds only came alive when stimulated by the very best ingredients, refusing to eat anything but freshly made meals, proud of his knowledge of fine cuisine.

"Doctor, I think this is too much food for the number of guests!" Ernesto, the butcher, complained as my father scribbled down lists of dishes and crossed out others that did not meet his approval.

"No, it all has to be perfect, Ernesto. Remember it is also Thanksgiving Day. No margarine, only butter. No Mazola or Wesson, only pure olive oil."

"Will we have turkey?"

"Of course! Turkey, gravy, cranberry sauce, pork, frijoles, roast beef, mashed potatoes, salads. Everything!"

Now a solid member of an emerging Cuban upper-middle class that, in less than a decade of hard work, drove Mercedes Benzes and enjoyed annual European vacations, my father liked to flaunt his wealth. The buffet provided another opportunity for him to do so.

Dressed in a long-sleeved shirt and tie, he looked out of place in Ernesto's modest home on Southwest Seventeenth Avenue, close to Eighth Street. He sat in the cramped living room, after long hours at his Hialeah office, poring over recipes with Ernesto. Together, they examined the pages of a gourmet food encyclopedia and flipped through my grandmother's Cuban and Spanish handwritten recipes bound in notebooks.

My father's attention on the food would make anyone think he doted on his daughter. Quite the contrary. He hugged me only when his wife wasn't looking. And his wife never left his side.

"*Papi*, take me to lunch," I begged once.

"I can't go if Beba doesn't go."

Why couldn't I get him to love me?

"Your father loves you," his friends and coworkers told me. "He just can't show it because his wife is jealous." I didn't believe it, even when I looked at pictures of him holding me close as a child. He wanted a boy, my mother had said to someone. Maybe that was the reason.

"Children are cute when they're little," he said to a friend once. "But when they grow up, they are nothing but trouble."

That was it. I was nothing but trouble.

While my father focused on food planning, I concentrated on getting a good price from the seamstress for my dress and the bridesmaids' dresses, the flowers, the table decorations, the tablecloths. I jotted down the details on a pad and ran the event like a business. I wanted to show my father I wasn't wasteful of his money, but I secretly set aside a few dollars for a new dress for my mother.

I looked at my wedding reception as a farewell party. I was leaving my old life behind: the good -- lazy beach outings, disco dancing, aimless wanderings through shopping centers -- as well as the bad – poverty, hunger, heated fights with my mother, the hurtful absence of my father. I couldn't wait to escape all that and begin my life as a writer as far away from Little Havana as possible. All was falling into place: Robert had just received his acceptance envelope from the school of broadcasting and was just as excited as I was.

Finally, it was November 22, 1973, Thanksgiving Day and The Feast Day of Saint Cecilia. We celebrated with a traditional mass at The Church of the Little Flower in Coral Gables, with one of David's sons as ringboy. Then, a limousine drove us to the reception at the nearby Sons of Lebanon Banquet Hall on Coral Way.

As the band struck up lively salsa music, Ernesto and his wife Margarita beamed from the top of a buffet table that curved around the far end of the hall. Ernesto wore a tall chef's hat and white jacket and Margarita a blue, floor-length gown. Three servers wearing smaller white hats stood at attention along the length of the table. An open bar with cases of champagne stacked up on the floor beckoned from the other side.

"She's a *mulata*," a friend whispered to me about Beba as Robert and I walked toward the buffet; the beat of the music already had guests swinging on the dance floor.

Beba's features revealed African ancestry. I had considered this before, but disregarded it as another of my father's contradictions. He did what he wanted, regardless of social prejudices and customs.

"Your father isn't such a refined man as he'd have you think!"

I nodded, giving all my attention to the food spread out in magnificent abundance.

There it was, all that my father had been planning for months: a gigantic turkey carved up in thick slices and assembled back to its original shape, chestnut and sausage stuffing, pureed cranberries with cinnamon and powdered sugar on top, a slab of roast beef oozing aromatic juices, crisp *lechon* in spicy garlic and onion *mojo*, prawns arranged in half-moons, chicken salad with slices of apple and decorated with green peas and red peppers, dainty triangle sandwiches filled with chopped ham in a béchamel sauce, mounds of *moros*, mashed potatoes, asparagus spears, yucca steeped in garlic chunks, marinated tomatoes with chopped basil, butter lettuce in dizzying circles, moist white biscuits with tubs of *La Vaquita* butter, and, at the end, a white wedding cake. Tall Greek towers covered with icing held a second layer high above the first. In the center of the first layer and under the second, a fountain of purple water rapidly gurgled, forming little waves at the base.

What if my father's love was wrapped in these painstakingly prepared dishes? What if the buffet was a symbolic gesture of love to me, a gastronomical manifestation of emotion? Crippled love, if love at all. Answers elusive.

From the old group, only Sylvia came to my wedding. She sat quietly with her date, smiling shyly, detached. Rene, helpful math friend, came in on a break from his job. Both congratulated me on getting accepted to Berkeley, such a far off place in their minds, it lost a sense of reality. The breakup of our group of friends hurt, but it receded into a distant regret as I focused on my future. I functioned now in another dimension, severed from what had gone on before, as unreachable as my Ivy League schoolmates had seemed to me on graduation day.

Robert's parents, in the middle of a chaotic divorce, stayed away from each other, greeting us one at a time and then sitting at tables at opposite ends with their own relatives. My father avoided my mother, who came up to pose with me for a picture. After the photography session, she walked from table to table greeting guests, hair stylishly coiffed, gray sequined gown fitting snugly over a slim figure.

My father strutted around in a tuxedo, his two-carat diamond ring sending out a spear of light from his left hand. His eyes met mine for an instant, expressionless, before he turned away with his wife, who wore a shiny black gown splashed with brilliant red tulips. They moved as far away as they could from my mother to a table on the other side of the room.

At least there wasn't a scene from either my parents or from Robert's.

15.

On the morning of departure, mid-December, the temperature dipped into the low fifties, a cold front dimming the sun, portending snow on the road once we cleared Florida. I hugged my mother good-by. Her body felt thin and fragile against mine, and we rocked back and forth, locked in an embrace, unspoken anguish from the past still binding our hearts. A sob pushed out of my throat, but I fought it down.

"I will call and write to you very often," I said. She smiled, tearless, not totally present, her eyes swinging back and forth.

"I will write every day," she said.

Robert's mother wept uncontrollably, while his father stood around awkwardly.

Today, I was leaving Little Havana, my family and my culture. I couldn't say good-by fast enough and begin the three thousand mile drive to California, a journey into a mysterious world that promised the elusive adventure I had always wanted. But this wasn't just any adventure. The journey westward, into the endless expanses of America, where anything and everything was possible, meant getting the long-awaited education that would transform me into a writer.

So after waves of the hand, Robert drove north on I-95, the car heavy with a steel U-Haul container strapped onto the roof, holding all our possessions, including the newly-repaired Olivetti typewriter. I flipped through a Triple A "triptik," a spiral bound map highlighting the main roads and highways of our journey, studying the route. Today, the triptik sits on my bookshelf, a reminder that dreams are just a systematic planning session away.

We sat in silence, hands clasped, on that never-ending stretch of highway through Florida. Excited, apprehensive, scared, we stared out the window at the flat fields filled with grazing cows and orchards of oranges and grapefruit.

I thought of Ovy, married now I heard, and wondered if he had gone off to play Jai-Alai. I thought of Cari in Virginia, and Ibis, Gloria and Sylvia in Little Havana, the cruel but comforting place that had sheltered me while I healed a frequently broken heart. I thought of David, who gave my father a boost into America.

I conjured up images of my homeland, its rolling landscapes and ancient colonial buildings, and its people – particularly those who had sustained me with their loyal letters for nearly fourteen years. I thought of my dear grandparents, traveling to America only to die a few years later. I thought of those still on the island: nanny Ana Maria on her Matanzas farm, housekeeper Amparo in the black ghetto of La Habana, Tio Cesar and his son Cesarito in their villa by the sea, step-grandmother, Elsie, whose views had transformed my thinking, in her small Vedado apartment teaching English. I took out my writing pad.

Querida Elsie,
I'm having so much fun driving to California! I wish you could see everything I'm seeing on the road. I always think of you and will never forget the comic strip of the dog Scamp and all the books and stories we read together, especially The Little Match Girl.
Because of you I love reading. It was you who helped me decide to be a writer. All those stories made me want to write some of my own.
Reading and writing are the only things I do well. So, that's what I thought I would do with my life. Write to me soon.
Te quiero, Cecilita.

I slipped the letter into one of many envelopes I had brought for corresponding with my parents and friends, setting it on the dashboard to mail later.

That evening we reached Lakeland, and the cold set in, stubbornly. The meteorologists on the news had forecast a particularly frigid winter that year, so we planned to avoid the snow by driving up through Florida, west across the Panhandle and southern portions of Louisiana, Texas, Colorado, and Arizona to Bakersfield, California where we would turn north to Berkeley. We could only drive from Monday through Friday during daylight hours. Every gas station in America was closed at night and on the weekends because of the oil crisis. A few months before, the Arab members of OPEC (Organization of Petroleum Exporting Countries) slammed down an embargo, hoping to discourage U.S. support for Israel by withholding their oil.

On the fifth day, we drove along the edge of the Grand Canyon. We parked and gazed into its depths, a red-orange color I had never seen before, transfixed by the sight. "How beautiful," I said, as if in church. Bundled up in knit caps, turtlenecks, flannel shirts and heavy wool overcoats, we still shivered; the cold burned our exposed faces. To a Cuban girl saturated by sea, sand and sun, these landscapes appeared as if they had popped out of books or movies.

That night, in our cabin, the wind blowing in through the cracks, we saw a deer nonchalantly grazing a few feet away from the window. The next day, December 24, *Noche Buena*, I thought of the roasted pork feasts everyone in Little Havana was enjoying. We drove as much as we could and stopped in a nondescript town where we rented a room at a Motel Six next to a smelly, rundown gas station. At a Seven-Eleven, we bought two cans of spaghetti and a box of plastic spoons. In the room, I ran hot water over the cans in the bathroom sink for five minutes. Then, I snapped off the lids and handed one to Robert. Our first married *Noche Buena* feast was one of the best.

On Monday, we started out with renewed vigor, making it all the way to California. It was siesta time in Bakersfield, everything quiet. Billboards and neon signs advertised a variety of Mexican beers everywhere we looked. Mexican restaurants on every corner touted *tostadas, chile rellenos, menudo,* dishes I would grow to love.

"This is why Cubans don't like Mexican food," Robert exclaimed after he bit into a hot pepper. I took a bite and regretted it. I wiped my tearing eyes and running nose. Back on the road, in the early afternoon, we slipped into Oakland. The greenery rose up on swollen hills on both sides of the highway, lush and verdant like in Cuba, but the air dry, light and cool. The Berkeley hills blazed in the distance, coming closer, the Florida flatness forgotten.

In minutes, we cruised past the University of California, spilling out at the foot of Telegraph Avenue. Vendors hawked their wares -- beaded jewelry, pipes and colorful blankets -- from the sidewalk in front of business establishments such as Moe's Bookstore and the Renaissance Café, soon to become hangouts.

Robert parked, and we walked on campus to Sproul Plaza, its spacious rotunda the scene of numerous student demonstrations in the sixties. "Boycott Gallo" signs clung to every wall. We strolled to the Student Center and ordered alfalfa and cucumber sandwiches on wheat bread, marveling at the unfamiliar medley of tastes. We walked some more, clear to the other side. I stared, awestruck, at the bell tower casting a light shadow over the School of Journalism.

I belonged here, the center of infinite promises. This is where I would succeed and thrive, the place where I finally touched the hard-won dream.

ACKNOWLEDGMENTS

My deepest gratitude goes to my professor and role model Dan Wakefield, the first to believe an essay I wrote for his class could grow into a master's thesis and book. Without him, there would be no *Leaving Little Havana*, whose title he so generously offered. *Mucho cariño,* Dan!

Dan retired just before my defense of the MFA thesis — which was this book — but Les Standiford, chair of the FIU creative writing program, stepped into his place, and, together with professor Lynne Barrett, offered advice I couldn't have done without. Thanks Les and Lynne!

Special thanks go to Beating Windward Press publisher and editor Matt Peters, who immediately connected with the book -- becoming an honorary Cuban -- and offered insightful comments that deepened and expanded my ideas. Matt, you are the best editor ever! Thanks to Melanie Neale, nonfiction editor, who offered support and suggestions in the last freak-out weeks of editing. Her book, *Boat Girl*, is a model of the figurative language I love.

Warm thanks to all my friends who encouraged me during the grueling editing process: Maria Karatzas, who first heard me dream about this book decades ago; Judy Swerlick, who read every word of my self-published stories; Isabel Bahamonde, who helped with the research on Little Havana; and David Delgado and Griselle Nogueira, who offered numerous marketing tips. Thanks also to Mayra Martinez and Olga Cancio, who listened patiently as I shaped the book's narrative out loud.

Endless gratitude goes to my step-grandmother Elsie Lopez, a resident of Heaven, who first instilled in me the passion for reading and to my mother, Cecilia Rivas, who – with a flash of foresight -- signed me up for my first creative writing class. *Gracias, mami y Elsie. Las quiero mucho.*

ABOUT THE COVER ARTIST

Victor Bokas grew up on Florida's Gulf Coast against a backdrop of sunbathing tourists, palm trees, fish and other tropical images. A graduate of The University of Florida, Victor is Senior Designer for Tupperware and full-time painter. His work appears in several Permanent Collections, including Tupperware, Darden, Maitland Art Center, Orlando City Hall, Walt Disney Production and the Orlando International Airport. "Florida Vacation" became part of Orlando International Airport Public Art Project in 2000. Victor's painting was turned into an 88' x 15' mosaic masterpiece welcoming visitors to Orlando.

ABOUT THE AUTHOR

Cecilia M. Fernandez is an independent journalist and college instructor with a passion for literature. Her work has appeared in *Latina Magazine*, *Accent Miami*, *Upstairs at the Duroc: the Paris Workshop Journal*, *Vista Magazine*, and *Le Siecle de George Sand*.

A former reporter for *The Stockton Record*, *The San Francisco Chronicle*, and the Miami television stations WPBT, WSVN, WSCV, and WLTV, Cecilia covered the state legislature, the National Democratic Convention, local and presidential elections, Operation Desert Storm, Hurricane Andrew, the drug trafficking trial of Panamanian dictator Manuel Noriega, the rape trial of William Kennedy Smith, the Mariel boatlift, and the Miami riots among many other stories. She believes her best reporting – and writing – happened while covering the lives of the simple folk living in the ethnic neighborhoods of California and Florida.

An Emmy nominee from the National Academy of Television Arts and Sciences, Cecilia received Dartmouth University's Champion Tuck Award (Honorable Mention for Television), the Scripps-Howard Award: News Writer of the Month and a Fellowship for Independent Summer Study from the National Endowment for the Humanities.

Cecilia earned an MFA in Creative Writing from Florida International University, an MA in English Literature from the University of Miami, and a BA in Journalism and Social Science from the University of California, Berkeley.

Her debut memoir, *Leaving Little Havana*, was selected as a finalist in the 2011 Bread Loaf Writers' Conference Book Contest.

She lives in Weston, Florida and teaches writing and literature at Broward College and Miami International University of Art and Design. She is working on a collection of short stories, among four other projects.

Website: www.ceciliamfernandez.com
Blog: www.ceciliamfernandez.wordpress.com
Email: fernandezcm@bellsouth.net